IRVINE

IRVINE
POLITICALLY CORRECT?

Dominic Egan

MAINSTREAM
PUBLISHING PROJECTS

"know thine enemy"!
Have a Happy Christmas
Daddy. lots of love
Allan (1999)
xxx

First published in Great Britain in 1999 by
MAINSTREAM PUBLISHING PROJECTS LTD
7 Albany Street
Edinburgh EH1 3UG

ISBN 1 84018 193 1

A catalogue record for this book is available from the British Library

Typeset in Bembo
Printed and bound in Great Britain by Butler & Tanner Ltd

For Karen,
who gave a sucker a break

Contents

Acknowledgements

Many, many thanks to John-Paul Flintoff for not letting me be a coward and to Catrin Griffiths for giving me faith. Thank you both for your excellent editing.

I am grateful to the numerous journalists upon whose work I have relied. The cliché is true: the British press *is* the best in the world. I would particularly like to thank Ian Hargreaves and Tim Rayment who were both so generous in their help and encouragement. I hope I can return the favour some day.

I owe a huge debt to all the people who found the time to speak to me despite their busy schedules. Meeting you and talking with you was one of the principal pleasures of writing this book.

Thanks as well to the staff at the British Library Newspaper Library at Colindale, Guildhall Library, Lewisham Library, Marylebone Library and Westminster Reference Library.

I would also like to thank a few people who have helped me along the way: my parents for a lifetime of kindness and support; Nigel Rawding for making me raise my sights; James Barnes for his excellent introduction service; Jim White for sound advice and encouragement when I most needed it; Philip Coggan for support and a good reference; Karen Dillon for being the best editor a rookie journalist ever had; Catrin for always making me do the right thing; John-Paul for reminding me of simplicity's virtues; James McLean for fixing my computer (but not me); Mark Brandon for making me swallow a bitter pill; Penny Cooper for calming me down; and numerous other friends for their many kindnesses.

Saving the best till last, I have to thank the wonderful Bree for her love and understanding. Well, was it worth it?

CHAPTER ONE

A Storm in a Teacup

David Ruffley was obviously up to no good. The select committee had summoned Lord Irvine to talk about privacy and freedom of information, not his £300-a-roll wallpaper or any other part of the £650,000 refurbishment of the Lord Chancellor's residence. So, when Ruffley, the Conservative MP for Bury St Edmunds, brought up the subject of the £650,000, everyone could tell there would be trouble.

Everyone except Irvine. Still smarting from the criticism he had received in the press, the Lord Chancellor simply could not resist the opportunity to justify himself and launched into a lengthy explanation of why the £650,000 was money well spent. The Palace of Westminster, he stated, is 'the mother of parliaments, it is a Grade I listed building. It is clearly right that when it is refurbished, it should be refurbished to the highest possible standard.'[1] Redecorating the Lord Chancellor's residence was a noble cause and future generations would be grateful.

Warming to his subject, Irvine rambled on and on, blind to all danger. The materials used in the redecoration were expensive, he explained, because, 'We are talking about quality materials which are capable of lasting for 60 or 70 years. We are not talking about something from a DIY store which may collapse after a year or two.'[2] The entire affair was nothing but 'a storm in a teacup'.[3]

But the storm had only just begun. The next day's newspapers tore into Irvine. *The Sun*, for instance, described Irvine's performance as a 'VIRTUOSO SHOW BY MAN WITH NO SHAME', declaring:

> Labour MPs found the unelected Lord Chancellor 'pompous, abrupt and disdainful'. The Tory verdict was unprintable. The roof tiler's son with delusions of grandeur saw no reason to apologise or explain why £650,000 of taxpayers' cash is being spent refurnishing his flat.

Remarkably, the wallpaper fiasco was Irvine's third high-profile gaffe in just three months. In December 1997 *The Times* had revealed that Irvine saw himself as a modern day Cardinal Wolsey. In February 1998 the *New Statesman* carried an interview in which the Lord Chancellor, while calling for tighter controls on the media, had cited recent press coverage of Foreign Secretary Robin Cook's adulterous affair as proof of the need for greater regulation.

The Prime Minister decided enough was enough. After Irvine's performance before the select committee, he banned the Lord Chancellor from speaking to the press. It was the only thing Tony Blair could do. Irvine was not a safe pair of hands.

The problem was not simply that Irvine had been saying the wrong things. It went deeper than that. Irvine had been displaying childlike naïvety and a total lack of judgement. Comparing himself to Wolsey in a private speech was not wise, but handing a copy of the speech to a journalist was plain stupid. Calling for stricter control of the press was asking for trouble, but using the example of Robin Cook's affair was particularly reckless. Spending £650,000 of public money was bad enough, but failing to spot David Ruffley's none-too-subtle attempts to entrap him into making indiscreet comments about DIY stores was the real crime.

Irvine was out of his depth. Apologists blamed Irvine's sudden elevation from the Bar to the Cabinet and pleaded that he needed time to come to terms with his new role, and political life.

But all the time in the world was never going to make a difference. The problem was not the complexity of the job. Nor was it Irvine's lack of political experience. The problem was Irvine.

Tony's crony

In May 1997, nobody cared about Irvine. One or two newspapers mentioned that the new Lord Chancellor was an old friend of Tony Blair and his wife; indeed, had been their pupil master when they began their careers at the Bar. Irvine, it was said, was Tony Blair's mentor and still exerted considerable influence over the new Prime Minister. But few journalists delved deeper than that.

Why would they? Irvine was going to be the Lord Chancellor and no one outside the legal profession had given a damn about the Lord Chancellor in many, many years. Irvine's immediate predecessor, Lord Mackay of Clashfern, had rarely troubled the front pages during his ten years in office and there was nothing at first sight to suggest that the new Lord Chancellor would be any different.

But Irvine *was* different. The humble but quietly effective Mackay had been happy to maintain a low profile. Irvine, on the other hand, had come to office determined to make his mark. Moreover, Irvine had a much wider brief. Mackay had concentrated on legal issues and endeavoured, so far as possible, to steer clear of politics. Blair had charged Irvine with overall responsibility for the new government's ambitious programme of constitutional reform, made him chairman of a string of Cabinet subcommittees and given him a seat on several others.

It was not very long before newspapers discovered that they had misjudged Irvine. He was not dull after all. Political correspondents began to pick up rumours of stand-up rows between Irvine and some of his Cabinet colleagues, while legal correspondents discovered that all was not well at the Lord Chancellor's Department. Irvine was proving a most demanding boss, working his staff extremely long hours and behaving as if he was still at his old chambers in the Temple.

Stories began to circulate that Irvine was spending a great deal of taxpayers' money on a lavish redecoration of his residence in the House of Lords. Some of the figures bandied about were so high it seemed impossible they could be true. With all the scandals of the Major government still fresh in the mind, could a Labour Lord Chancellor possibly be so extravagant?

The media became even more confused in July 1997, when Irvine launched an attack in the House of Lords, on 'fat-cat' lawyers, complaining that high legal fees prevented people from going to court. Wasn't Irvine a barrister? Hadn't he made a pile during his time at the Bar? How did he now have the nerve to be pointing the finger at others?

Irvine delivered another surprise in October. He announced the virtual dismantling of civil legal aid. Incredibly, the Labour government was advocating the kind of policy it had bitterly resisted when in opposition. Once again, Irvine never blushed.

By this time, the newspapers' confusion was mixed with concern. The Lord Chancellor had been making comments about privacy and the need for tighter regulation of the press – a sure way to attract editors' attention and, for that matter, their enmity. The Prime Minister stepped in to make soothing noises, stating that the Government was still committed to self-regulation of the press. But Irvine continued to arouse journalists' suspicions with a series of comments clearly showing that, in the battle between privacy and freedom of the press, his sympathies did not lie with the media.

Thus, when Irvine began to stumble, the newspapers did nothing to break his fall. They humiliated him over the Wolsey speech and were scathing about his views on press regulation. With Irvine now established as a hate figure, journalists began to probe for fresh embarrassments, focusing their attentions on the refurbishment of the Lord Chancellor's residence.

Irvine had been claiming that he played only an insignificant role, and that all decisions made had been taken by a House of Lords committee. However, a letter leaked to *The Times* at the end of February 1998 showed that Irvine had persuaded the committee to carry out the redecoration on a much more lavish scale than originally intended. In a leading article, *The Times* accused both Irvine and Downing Street of a lack of candour.

Days later, Irvine made his fateful appearance before the House of Commons Select Committee on Public Administration. That appearance, plus the subsequent media coverage, sealed Irvine's fame. A man who had barely been known outside the legal profession less than a year before was now a household name. Even more remarkably, a Lord Chancellor, for the first time in living memory, was hot news.

Irvine was a celebrity, but for all the wrong reasons. He was not applauded for his contributions to the Human Rights Bill or the devolution process. He was jeered for being 'Tony's crony' and a walking disaster zone. For much of his life, Irvine had been desperate to go down in history. But not like this.

Upwardly mobile

Irvine is not used to failure. As a boy, he rose from humble beginnings to win a scholarship to one of the finest private schools in Scotland, before moving on to Glasgow University. There he met future Labour Party leader John Smith. The two became firm friends, not least because they shared a love of serious drinking.

Irvine did not have much time for socialising, however. He was absolutely determined to achieve his boyhood dream of becoming a lawyer and was not prepared to let anything come between him and his studies. All the long hours of revision paid off when he won a scholarship from Glasgow to Cambridge, where still more hard work obtained him a further two degrees, both first-class.

While completing his legal studies, Irvine lectured at the London School of Economics, briefly becoming embroiled in volatile student politics. He then did his pupillage (the equivalent of an apprenticeship) at one of the best sets of chambers in the country. Here, however, he suffered a rare setback. On completing his pupillage, Irvine was not offered a tenancy (a permanent place) at the set: not for the last time, Irvine's arrogance had made him enemies and he was forced to move on to alternative chambers.

In 1970 he stood in the general election as the Labour Party candidate for Hendon North. It was a promising seat, but Irvine performed poorly after failing to capture the working-class vote. Chastened perhaps by his experience in Hendon North, he would never make another attempt to enter Parliament.

Shortly after the general election, Irvine's private life fell apart. In 1971 his wife, Margaret, whom he had married upon leaving Glasgow University, walked out on him because he had started an affair with the wife of an old friend, Donald Dewar. Irvine and Alison Dewar eventually set up home together, marrying in 1974 and having two sons.

By now, Irvine's legal career had taken off and he was establishing himself as a force in the field of employment law. In 1978 he 'took silk', becoming the youngest Queen's Counsel in the country. Two years before that, Irvine had taken on two pupils: Tony Blair and Cherie Booth. Although Booth clearly had greater potential as a lawyer, Irvine recommended that Blair, not Booth, should get a tenancy. He continued to assist Blair in every way possible, introducing him to John Smith and advising him throughout his political career.

In 1981 Irvine turned his back on the set where he had made his name. Desperate to be in charge, Irvine created his own chambers by tearing his old set in half. Having got what he wanted, Irvine ruled as a benevolent despot, making 11 King's Bench Walk into one of the finest – and most expensive – chambers in the country.

Irvine's legal career was also highly successful. Now focusing on commercial work, Irvine was renowned for earning big fees. As a result, he was able to enjoy the good life – fine wines, expensive meals, beautifully appointed homes and an extensive and valuable art collection. He liked to be pampered. Irvine's clerk at 11 King's Bench Walk not only won him big fees, he also acted at times as his butler.

In 1987 Irvine was made a life peer. This was in part a reward from Labour Party leader Neil Kinnock for Irvine's work in several legal actions against the Militant tendency. If not for Irvine's efforts, Labour might easily have lost one or more of the cases. But Irvine carried the day, sometimes through nothing more than force of personality. By giving him a peerage, Kinnock was also lining up Irvine as a potential Lord Chancellor. Thus, Irvine was now close to achieving a long-held dream.

It appeared at times that nothing could stop Irvine from fulfilling his dreams. When Labour lost the 1992 election, Kinnock's replacement as party leader was Irvine's best friend, John Smith. And when Smith died in 1994, the new leader was none other than Irvine's former pupil and protégé, Tony Blair.

On 3 May 1997, two days after Labour's landslide general election victory, Irvine attended Buckingham Palace to receive the Great Seal from the Queen. At that moment, he entered history as the 258th Lord Chancellor.

Saints and sinners

Four of Irvine's predecessors have been canonised, the two most famous being Thomas à Becket (Chancellor from 1154 to 1162) and Sir Thomas More (1529–32). Becket's Canterbury tomb became a place of pilgrimage after he was murdered in 1170 by knights during a feud with Henry II. Like Becket, More fell foul of his sovereign, and was executed at the block in 1535 for refusing to condone Henry VIII's break with Rome.

Other Chancellors who have met a violent end include Simon Sudbury (1380–1), who was hacked to death on Tower Hill during the Peasants' Revolt of 1381. His head was then carried in procession through the City of London and displayed on London Bridge. Sudbury had incurred the wrath of Wat Tyler and his men by suggesting that the war with France be financed by means of a poll-tax.

But Sudbury is not necessarily the most unpopular man to hold the office – he faces healthy competition for that title.

William Longchamp (1189–97) had to flee the country in 1191 after coming close to provoking a civil war through his autocratic running of the country in Richard I's absence. Lord Jeffreys (1685–8) is better known to posterity as Judge Jeffreys, the man whose Bloody Assize of 1685 dealt so mercilessly with supporters of the Monmouth rebellion. Jeffreys later narrowly avoided being lynched by the London mob before ending his days in the Tower.

Sir Thomas Wolsey (1515–29) was resented for his fabulous wealth. His home, Hampton Court, was the finest palace in the country, inciting envy even from Henry VIII. Despite handing over Hampton Court, Wolsey lost the king's favour when he failed to persuade the Pope to grant Henry a divorce from Catherine of Aragon.

If not the most hated Chancellor, Wolsey was certainly the most powerful. With Henry little interested in affairs of state, the cardinal enjoyed a virtually free hand in the running of the country. After Wolsey's dramatic fall from grace, Henry and his successors were far more careful about granting power to their Chancellors.

Another major change occurred at this time. Before the Reformation, Chancellors had tended to be clergymen. After Wolsey, they tended to be laymen. (The last clergyman to hold the office was John Williams, Archbishop of York, whose four-year term ended in 1625.)

In the reign of Elizabeth I (1558–1603), the Chancellor, now known as Lord Chancellor or Lord High Chancellor, was supplanted by the Secretary as the most important officer of state. As a result, Lord Chancellors began to focus on their judicial functions and on their role as the monarch's representative in the House of Lords.

The decline of the chancellorship is not nearly as remarkable as its rise. The most historic office under the Crown has the most humble of origins. In the late Roman period the *cancellarius* was no more than a court clerk named after a screen, the *cancelli*, that separated the court from the public. At some stage, and by an unknown route, the court clerk became the king's secretary and keeper of his seal.

The first reference to a *cancellarius* in English records is to be found in a document from 1068, though the office may have been established before then. In his eight-volume *Lives of the Lord Chancellors*, published in the 1840s, John Campbell went as far back as the seventh century and named St Swithin among early holders of the office. But Campbell, himself Lord Chancellor from 1859 to 1861, may have been on a Victorian flight of fancy. Modern historians look no further back than the reign of Edward the Confessor (1042–66) and suggest that Edward took his lead from the Holy Roman Empire.

With education firmly in the control of the Church, the early Chancellors were inevitably clerics who served both as the king's secretary and his chaplain. However, laymen soon came to covet the office, for it offered the opportunity to gain prestige, power and wealth.

The vital factor in the rise of the Chancellor was his responsibility for the king's seal, later known as the Great Seal. Writs – commands from the king transcribed on to parchment – were one of the main tools of medieval administration. Since writs were authenticated by means of a large wax seal, possession of the king's seal put the Chancellor at the heart of government.

As early as 1180 the role of Chancellor was considered good enough for a king's son. Geoffrey, Henry II's illegitimate son, was made Chancellor to compensate him for the Pope's refusal to confirm him as bishop of Lincoln. (Not unreasonably, the Pope had asked Geoffrey become a priest first.)

The Chancellor soon came to rank only behind the king in importance. Thomas Langley, who was twice Chancellor (1405–7 and 1417–24), ran the country in Henry V's absence on campaign in France. Cardinal Beaufort (1403–5, 1413–17 and 1424–6) was the most powerful man in the country during the minority and early reign of Henry VI.

He was also the richest. Indeed, any Chancellor who survived in the post for a decent spell could expect to amass a fortune from the fees charged for the issue of writs. In 1189 William Longchamp considered it a good investment to pay Richard I £3,000 (worth millions today) for his appointment as Chancellor.

With writs playing a central role in the legal process, it was inevitable that the Chancellor would become involved in legal matters. Once again, however, the Chancellor's responsibilities quickly became more than just secretarial. The reign of Edward I (1272–1307) saw a huge increase in the number of petitions from subjects seeking redress from injustices suffered at the hands of the slow, inflexible and harsh courts of the day – the Court of King's Bench and the Court of Common Pleas. Unable to cope with the burden, the King chose to delegate judicial powers to the Chancellor.

At first, the Court of Chancery developed along very different lines from its rivals. There were no paper pleadings and no rules of procedure. Chancery was a court of conscience where justice and fairness counted for more than rules and regulations and it developed its own system of law – equity – which to this day operates alongside common law and statute.

With time, however, the court became bogged down by procedure, developing a notorious reputation for delay, expense and corruption. In 1725 the then Lord Chancellor, Sir Thomas Parker, Earl of Macclesfield, was impeached after someone discovered that huge amounts of litigants' money had gone missing. Chancery staff had invested the money for their own gain in the South Sea Bubble, which had burst in 1720.

Parker was not the first nor the last Lord Chancellor to be impeached for corruption. That misfortune even befell the most illustrious figure ever to hold the office – the poet, philosopher and scientist Sir Francis Bacon (1617–21). If he was corrupt, he did nothing out of the ordinary for the times. It was Bacon's misfortune to get caught in the crossfire of the fight between Parliament and the Duke of Buckingham, the King's favourite and Bacon's patron.

Chancery's reputation for corruption was still strong more than 200 years later. In 1852 *Bleak House* was published, in which Charles Dickens savaged Chancery for its delay and expense, creating the world's most famous fictional law suit, *Jarndyce v Jarndyce*, in which all the parties eventually lost out – except the lawyers.

In 1873 the Lord Chancellor lost direct control over Chancery when it was merged with other courts into the High Court. This did not mean that the Lord Chancellor was short of work. Over the years successive Lord Chancellors had proved as acquisitive as magpies, picking up powers here, there and everywhere. Having previously sat in the Star Chamber, the Lord Chancellor was now a member of its successor, the Privy Council; he (it has always been a 'he') had been drafted into the Cabinet; he had become recognised as head of the judiciary; and he had evolved from the monarch's agent in the House of Lords into Speaker of the House.

Frozen in time

The office changed little during the twentieth century. When Irvine became Lord Chancellor, he would have found certain aspects of the job quaint, some risible and at least one plain offensive.

For some reason, the Lord Chancellor's dress has not changed since the seventeenth century, obliging all Lord Chancellors since that date to wear a full-bottomed wig, court gown, breeches, tights and buckled shoes in the chamber of the House of Lords.

Irvine, who is self-conscious about his large frame and does not wear clothes well, took exception to this. In November 1998 he asked peers for the right to dispense with the breeches, tights and buckled shoes on all but state occasions. This was granted only against considerable opposition from traditionalists, who claimed Irvine was diminishing the stature of the office. The vote went 145–115 in Irvine's favour only after the Government unofficially encouraged Labour peers to support Irvine in his hour of need.

Although he has never officially complained, Irvine must find his duties as Speaker of the House of Lords a chore. Unlike his counterpart in the House of Commons, the Speaker of the House of Lords does not play a significant part in the business of the upper house. He is not addressed in debate, nor does he decide points of order (peers do that themselves). Instead, he merely plays a part in formal proceedings and puts the question at the end of a debate whether the 'contents' or the 'non-contents' have it. Unlike the Speaker of the House of Commons, he may take part in debates. When doing so, he performs the slightly ludicrous tradition of stepping away from the woolsack (the cushion on which the Lord Chancellor traditionally sits) in order to distance himself from his office and take his place in the house as a peer. He takes part in divisions and votes, but has no casting vote.

Again, Irvine has sought, and achieved, a modification here. When he was granted permission to abandon his breeches, he was also given the right to spend more time behind the dispatch box when steering his own legislation. It would make much more sense if the Lord Chancellor were relieved of his duties as Speaker altogether. Sitting on the woolsack, in a ridiculous uniform, doing next to nothing is hardly good use of a Lord Chancellor's time. As a result, Irvine regularly takes reading material into the chamber, so that he can do a little work during the debates in which he has no interest.

Irvine does seem to enjoy sitting as a judge, however. As head of the judiciary, he is entitled to adjudicate in the House of Lords and the Privy Council. Pressure of work has severely limited Irvine's judicial opportunities, but he has nonetheless found time to hear several cases.

Some believe this whole concept is wrong. For one thing, Irvine, like some of his predecessors, is not qualified to sit in the two highest courts in the land. Prior to becoming Lord Chancellor, his only judicial experience was as a deputy High Court judge. This means he helped out at the High Court on a part-time basis. All the other Law Lords have worked their way up through the High Court and the Court of Appeal. Even judicial superstars like Lord Hoffmann and Lord Steyn took ten years to get from the High Court to the House of Lords. In an echo of his political career, Irvine went straight in at the top from nowhere.

It might seem inappropriate that a member of the executive and legislature is also a member of the judiciary – the potential for conflict is unlimited. But the office of Lord Chancellor has always defied logic, and continues to do so.

Irvine is almost the loftiest of all, taking precedence to all the Queen's subjects except the Archbishop of Canterbury. To slay him would be to commit high treason. He is the formal medium of communication between the Queen and Parliament. If the Queen is not available, it is his duty to read the Queen's Speech from the throne, as well as deliver any other messages from the Queen to Parliament. It is also his duty to report the Royal Assent to Bills.

Most remarkable of all, perhaps, is that there are religious restrictions on the office. Historically, the Lord Chancellor was 'Keeper of the King's Conscience' and enjoyed certain powers of ecclesiastical patronage. As a result, Catholics were barred from becoming Lord Chancellor until as recently as 1974.

In that year, legislation was passed lifting the restriction. However, thanks to some sloppy drafting, non-Christians were accidentally barred. In 1998 Lord Alderdice sponsored a private member's Bill to correct the situation, but the Bill failed for technical reasons. With Lord Irvine's support, Lord Alderdice is now in the course of putting together a new Bill. This will not only remove the restriction on non-Christians, but also allow non-believers to be Lord Chancellor for the first time. Until then, the office of Lord Chancellor will remain the only political office in England still restricted on a religious basis. (Irvine, who is a member of the Church of Scotland, only attends church when staying at his second home in the Kintyre peninsula, Argyll.)

Politically correct?

The office has remained unscathed in modern times mainly because recent Lord Chancellors have kept a low profile, concentrating their efforts on legal administration and law reform. Before May 1997, the chancellorship was a half-forgotten, 1,000-year-old constitutional relic.

But Tony Blair reversed history, making the Lord Chancellor once again one of the most powerful figures in the Government. Blair justified the decision by claiming that Irvine was a towering intellect, the right man to take charge of constitutional reform. But the Prime Minister had another reason for turning back the clock – insecurity.

Blair has, for some years, relied extremely heavily on a small inner circle of advisers. With no previous experience of government, the Prime Minister wanted his old friend, mentor and adviser close to him. Indeed, Blair wanted Irvine so badly that he was prepared to put up with the inevitable claims of cronyism. He was also prepared to ignore the fact that giving a peer authority over elected ministers was undemocratic. Indeed, it went against Labour's manifesto agenda of delivering greater democracy through such measures as House of Lords reform, devolution and stronger local government. Most remarkable of all, the Prime Minister was prepared to turn a blind eye to Irvine's many faults.

Blair cannot plead innocence. As Irvine's former pupil and junior, Blair knew that Irvine's character was unsuited to politics. No one who dealt with Irvine during his professional career is surprised that he has struggled since entering the political arena. They could see that Irvine was always going to make enemies in the Cabinet. His arrogance, pomposity and excessive aggression had made him enough enemies when he was at the Bar. They could see that Irvine's demanding ways were always going to upset staff at the Lord Chancellor's Department. He had upset enough of his pupils and juniors over the years. They could see that Irvine was always going to be a liability to the Government and the Labour Party when questioned by journalists or a select committee. He had never excelled at thinking on his feet in court.

At the Bar, Irvine was usually able to cover up his limitations. There, he could spend days preparing for his court appearances. He could call upon the assistance of brilliant young barristers. And he could make up for what he lacked in intuition and subtlety with naked aggression. But reading from a script and playing the bully were never going to get him by as a politician. The moment Irvine entered government, the Wolsey, Robin Cook and wallpaper fiascos became virtually inevitable.

CHAPTER TWO

Constant Craving

Derry Irvine is his mother's son. 'My mother was an unusually clever woman and was frustrated to be held back,' he told *The Sun* in 1998. 'I took the view that it was a gross injustice.' [4]

Christina Macmillan's hopes were thwarted when her father's bridge-building business collapsed. Following that disaster, the family moved from Lairg, Sutherland, to a council house in Inverness, where her father became clerk of works with the town council. Irvine has said: 'My mother had a powerful intellect and her headmaster had begged my grandfather to allow her to go to university. But, in those days, women weren't given the same chances as men.' [5]

Instead, Christina took work as a waitress and ended up marrying a roof tiler. Of his father, Alexander, Irvine has stated: 'My father was a bright man too, very creative. He wrote poetry and loved reading, but he was a product of his generation.' [6]

The couple's only child was born on 23 June 1940. They named him Alexander Andrew Mackay, but everyone called him 'Derry'. Irvine has explained:

> I remember my mother telling me how she had wanted to give me a different name to Alexander, which took after my father and her father. But women didn't have much say in those days and, of course, I was named Alexander. My mother got her own back by calling me Derry. And the name stuck. [7]

With her husband away at the war — Irvine has said his father served as a sniper in the commandos — Christina Irvine was free to mould the boy as she saw fit. Irvine still shows signs of having been doted upon by his mother — his constant desire for approval being but one example.

Irvine is a dreadful boaster, as the Wolsey speech and other events have proved. Christina Irvine also instilled in her son the acute ambition that has driven him throughout his life. 'My mother's frustrated ambition impinged on me,' he has acknowledged. 'She was determined I should have the education she never had.'[8] This desire to get ahead and achieve great things still burns. Irvine told *The Sun*, 'I still push myself to this day. I have an enormous commitment to giving of my best.'[9] So enormous, indeed, that Irvine's entire life has been tainted by an insatiable need to prove himself.

Jenny Rowe, Irvine's private secretary at the Lord Chancellor's Department, has stated:

> I wouldn't say he was happy in the sense of being content, because he's the sort of person who will always be seeing something else he can do or achieve ... I think he is happy to have achieved what he has achieved, but there is still more to do. He has the sort of restless intellect that will always find a challenge waiting for him, so he will never achieve the happiness some people achieve, because there's always something else there.[10]

Beyond his mother's influence, little is known about the factors that moulded Irvine — there is a serious dearth of information about his distant past. Irvine rarely talks about childhood and is never expansive. The shroud over Irvine's early life has been maintained by his relatives, who are few in number and uniformly reluctant to speak to the media. One cousin, Margaret Sutherland, has said, 'He was very clever from quite an early age. I remember all the rest of us would think he was an obnoxious little character because he knew all the answers! As a boy, he was also very cheerful and made friends easily.'[11]

Irvine's primary school record was good rather than outstanding. In one year at Inverness Royal Academy he came fifth in his form. In another, he came equal third. Nevertheless, Irvine won a scholarship to a private school. At the end of the 1940s, the family left their rented flat in Inverness for a tenement flat in Gorbal Street in the heart of the infamous Gorbals district of Glasgow and the nine-year-old Derry began to attend the nearby Hutchesons Boys' Grammar School. Hutchesons was one of the best schools of its kind in Scotland, enjoying a particularly strong reputation for classics.

Shortly after the move to Glasgow, the family's financial position improved. After just a few months in Gorbal Street, the Irvines moved to a far superior flat in a much better location, overlooking the park in Queen's Drive, one of the smarter parts of south Glasgow. Since Irvine has on occasion described his father as a union official, it may be that his father found better-paid employment at this time. But times were still hard, according to Irvine: 'My family were very short of money and there was always the problem of buying the school uniform. Mine was usually second-hand.'

Hutchesons, or 'Hutchie' as it was commonly known, was a grant-aided school with around 600 pupils. Like direct grant schools in England, it received government funding. However, unlike its English equivalents, it was not obliged to set aside free places for deserving cases. Nor had Hutchesons adopted the policy taken up by some other granted-aided schools of voluntarily making such places available.

'It was a very conservative school in both senses of the word,' remembers one of Irvine's former classmates, Jack Geekie, now a politics lecturer at Bell College, Hamilton. In fact, Irvine's arrival at Hutchesons was good news for Geekie, who had, until then, been the only boy in the class who lived in the Gorbals. 'I think we were the only two from Labour families in maybe the whole school,' he says. 'I wouldn't swear to that, but I wouldn't be surprised.'

Not that Irvine showed many signs of his working-class roots. He described his father as a builder rather than as a roof slater; his refined Inverness accent immediately set him apart from the Glaswegians around him; and he gravitated towards the high-fliers of the class. Geekie remembers: 'He was confident, very gregarious. I was actually quite surprised when I learned how modest his family background was, because he came across as being the child of very solid, middle-class, professional parents who had imbued him with this self-confidence.'

The future Labour politician was an assured and articulate debater – but no idealist. Even as a youth, Irvine never voiced any strong opinion about inequality or the like, says Geekie, he simply enjoyed debate for its own sake.

Irvine was much more interested in his own career. 'The one thing I will always remember about him is his single-mindedness and ambition to become a barrister from such an early age,' says Geekie. 'It's quite incredible for a boy of nine to have that ambition.' Where the desire to be a lawyer came from is not clear. As Geekie points out, Irvine 'didn't seem to have anything of that in his family background. It's just he'd set his mind on being a barrister and his articulateness and his skill with language, I suppose, complemented that.'

As at primary school, Irvine did not dazzle anyone with his academic ability. Geekie recalls: 'Academically speaking, he was in the top third or so of the class. He wasn't right at the top, but he was in the top third.' Nor did Irvine's sporting skills leave a big impression. Rugby, for example, he played without distinction. Irvine was big for his age, says Geekie, and got selected as a lock forward, but 'wasn't really a sporty person'.

It was Irvine's attitude, rather than his ability, that set him apart. Geekie declares that Irvine was 'sui generis. He was a unique individual in many respects. There may well have been some teachers who had slightly more influence on him than others, but

Derry was his own man, a man who knew where he was going and had his whole life carved out for him.'

Neither Geekie nor Irvine completed the full six-year stint in Hutchesons' senior school, both leaving in June 1957 when 17 years of age. Geekie explains:

> Hutchesons boys usually had university entrance qualifications by the time they were in the fifth year and for many of them – I suppose Derry was in a hurry to go wherever he was planning to go – there didn't seem much point in staying for another year. If you had the university entrance qualifications, why not go then?

Irvine won a minor scholarship to Glasgow University. A former Glasgow student explains:

> There was a Glasgow University bursary competition in which all the schools in Glasgow competed. If you got in the first hundred you got some sort of bursary; if you got in the first ten you got quite a substantial bursary. Hutchesons, they used to get eight or nine of the first ten. They practically went into mourning if they didn't win it each year.

A driven man

At Glasgow University, Derry Irvine met a kindred spirit. John Smith was another young man determined to make his mark. Mutual friend and fellow Glasgow University student Menzies Campbell MP recalls that Irvine and Smith were 'both grown-ups even as students. It's not that they were dour. They were mature, they had weight, they were heavyweights. They gave the impression of clear objectives, very considerable determination to achieve those objectives and the capacity to do the work.'

Before studying law, the two men took arts degrees. (At that time, the Scottish education system stipulated that no one could study law unless they already had a degree.) Smith took an honours history degree, while Irvine chose to do an ordinary degree. This was a shorter course, which involved taking a range of subjects, such as English, Greek and philosophy.

Irvine was devoted to his studies, working long hours night after night. 'He had the most prodigious appetite for work,' states Campbell. 'He was just extraordinarily good at work. Tremendous energy. He never flagged.' Irvine was a driven man, suggests Campbell: 'I think he was a man who would not allow anything to divert him or deflect himself away from the principal purpose, which was to achieve the best possible qualification and then to make his way in the legal profession.'

'He's always been first and foremost deeply serious about his work,' confirms another fellow student, Iain Macphail, now a judge. 'I first met him in the law library . . . we started talking about this problem and he was very tenacious about getting to the bottom of it and wanting to know all the cases and what they said and what did I think and really getting his teeth into it.'

The legal profession was the right career for Irvine, suggests Macphail:

> Being a barrister, or an advocate as we say up here, does suit his robust, rather combative style of arguing . . . When it comes to discussing something, he can be very trenchant and robust. But it's not in the sense of wanting to dominate. I think that's the impression people sometimes get, but, knowing him as I do, what he's really interested in is getting to the bottom of whatever it is and wanting to be convinced.

As at Hutchesons, Irvine had to get by with only limited funds. This was a regular source of embarrassment, he has claimed: 'My friends would have parties for their 18th and 21st birthdays and they would invite me, but there was never any money for us to have a party. I felt that I was taking hospitality which I could not give in return.'

Irvine's fellow students, however, remember him as someone who was good at coming up with money-making schemes. He set up a tutoring agency that hired out friends to school students. He also produced notes on the conveyancing course, which he sold to fellow students. Unfortunately for Irvine, someone proved even more enterprising. One of the students photocopied Irvine's notes and started selling bootlegs at a price that undercut him. Still, Irvine made enough money out of his various projects to run a Messerschmitt bubble car. It may have been a bit basic, but at least Irvine had his own means of transport – a rare luxury for a student at that time.

Irvine's time at Glasgow University was not all work and no play, recalls Campbell:

> When they [Irvine and Smith] decided to have a night out – and it was true all the way through their lives together – they could have a night out like very few of us. An extraordinary capacity for taking huge quantities of alcohol and apparently being unaffected either at the time or the following day.

Fuelled by drink, Irvine and Smith sometimes reverted to their childhoods, indulging in a game they called 'horses and chargers'. With Smith on his shoulders, Irvine would gallop up and down the debating hall in the university union. Late one night, the future head of the judiciary tried to break into the college bar to get a drink. Suddenly, there was a crash. Irvine came running out, crying, 'Quick! Give me an alibi!' [12]

But Irvine was never long away from his books. He had the remarkable ability to switch almost immediately from beer-swilling hedonist to candle-burning student. Former Glasgow University student John Hart has stated that Irvine would 'go home after a long night's drinking, and, next morning, he'd obviously been up all night reading law. He was a wee bit unusual.'[13]

Irvine was so focused on his studies that he only rarely found time to participate in the debates that formed the centrepiece of student life at Glasgow University. While future politicians such as Menzies Campbell, John Smith and Donald Dewar each took a full part in the debates, Irvine spoke only infrequently. John Hart has explained that Irvine 'wasn't interested in politics as such. John Smith was a very political person, even at that stage, but Derry wasn't.'[14] This has been confirmed by Smith's widow, Baroness Smith, who was also at Glasgow University. She has stated: 'Derry wasn't involved with the in-crowd. He wasn't a political animal at all. He loved the law.'[15]

Nevertheless, it is curious that someone who had his eye set so firmly on a career at the Bar should not seize the opportunity to test his advocacy skills in the heat of university debate. It was not as if Irvine was some shrinking violet. As Menzies Campbell points out: 'Intellectually, he's extremely hard, very robust. He takes no prisoners in argument. That was always the case.'

It could be that Irvine avoided debates because he knew he was out of his depth. His great friend John Smith was a natural communicator who could stand up and speak at a moment's notice, but Irvine was not comfortable thinking on his feet. He always wanted time to prepare.

Irvine certainly did not enjoy coming off second best in verbal jousts. John Hart has commented that 'Glasgow humour is like Liverpool humour – very quick and cutting. And his [Irvine's] way of dealing with that was to become very pompous.'[16] Hart has attempted to justify Irvine's behaviour by claiming that Irvine's pomposity is not serious and that 'people don't always see the humorous concept behind it'.[17] However, this excuse just does not wash.

Irvine is pompous because it is in his nature to be pompous. He takes himself too seriously and is always desperate to impress. So desperate, indeed, that he sometimes says things he should not say.

In October 1998 the *Sunday Times* revealed a claim by Irvine that he had for a time written John Smith's university essays. According to Irvine, when Smith was selected to stand as the Labour Party candidate in a parliamentary by-election, one of his teachers took umbrage. Professor David Walker felt that Smith was not devoting sufficient time to his studies and decided to set him a series of additional essays. To the professor's surprise, Smith not only did the extra work, he did it extremely well. What Walker did not know of course was that the real author of the essays was Irvine.

The *Sunday Times* stated that Irvine was not embarrassed by his role in the deception. It declared that, when asked about the essays, Irvine 'saw no reason to feel uncomfortable and even boasted about his role. Smith, he said, had never managed to match the marks he was awarded for the work he [Irvine] had written for him.'[18]

Menzies Campbell, however, finds the story a little hard to swallow. Smith, he says, is unlikely to have taken the risk of getting caught and being sent down by the university. In particular, Smith would not have risked crossing Professor Walker, who had a reputation for being something of a martinet, as Donald Dewar found out to his cost.

Walker noticed that Dewar was 'a bit slack' about attending his classes, reveals Campbell. Rather than issue a warning, Walker waited until Dewar had failed to attend 10 per cent of the classes and then wrote Dewar a letter informing him that he would not be entitled to a class ticket. Without such a ticket, no student could sit the final exam and Dewar was forced to do a further year. Given Walker's austere disciplinary approach, Campbell believes the story about Irvine writing Smith's essays 'may be a tale whose enchantment has grown with the passage of time'.

Certainly, the *Sunday Times* story displays a remarkable lack of judgement on Irvine's part. On a private level, he offended his old friend Baroness Smith, who was naturally none too pleased that Irvine should denigrate her late husband's reputation. On a public level, it does not seem to have crossed Irvine's mind that it is inappropriate for a lawyer, a senior Cabinet minister and, most important of all, the head of the judiciary, to boast about cheating at university. But Irvine was too busy showing off to take such considerations into account.

Union and separation

If Irvine had stayed in Scotland, 'He'd have been a star,' suggests Menzies Campbell. 'He'd have dominated the Scottish Bar. He'd have been head and shoulders above people.'

But Irvine's life was to take a different course. He passed his law degree with a distinction (Glasgow University did not, at the time, grant honours for the LLB), and also won a scholarship to study law at Christ's College, Cambridge. It was a fateful moment, suggests Campbell:

> I think he was slightly diverted by winning the scholarship to Cambridge. I always had the impression he was going to the Scottish Bar, but he got the scholarship to Cambridge and then I think he realised there was a bigger, wider world . . . Clearly, when he got to England he realised, by comparison with others, that he was as good as we all know he is, and he thought that he could be much bigger on a bigger stage.

Irvine did not head south alone. On 5 September 1962 he married Margaret Veitch in a white wedding at the Old Church, Cumnock, Ayrshire. The daughter of a master butcher, Veitch was 23, a year older than her husband, whom she had met while at teacher training college in Glasgow.

Veitch's sister-in-law, Kay, has said of Margaret: 'She did everything a young wife could to help him get on. She really loved him and encouraged him and looked after him.'[19] It seems, however, that Kay Veitch did not totally approve of her brother-in-law. She has declared:

I was scared of him, to be honest. He's a most intimidating man. He'd sort of interrogate you. Maybe it was tongue in cheek, but I was terrified. He could know nothing about a subject and you a lot and he could make you believe you knew nothing and he a lot. And he always had the lawyer's air of a man who knew where he was going. [20]

As Irvine's married life was beginning, so his parents' marriage was foundering. Irvine is extremely reluctant to talk about this episode. When, in 1998, the *Sunday Times* asked him about his parents' separation, he replied: 'It's not quite as simple as that. They never really separated: they just ceased to live together. But this is all very painful and I think I'll not go any further.' [21] Later the same year, he was slightly more forthcoming, telling *The Sun*:

My parents ceased to live together permanently in the early '60s, but they still went on holiday together and met at weekends.

When I became successful as a barrister, I bought my father a small flat in Hampstead, North London, and my mother a cottage in Cambridgeshire and remained very close to them. But it was difficult. [22]

Both Irvine's parents are now dead, his mother dying as recently as 1997. She had been suffering from Alzheimer's disease and was no longer able to recognise her son. It is a source of huge regret to Irvine that his mother was not able to share in his proudest moment. He has revealed:

When I became a peer in 1987 she was absolutely fine but, by the time I became Lord Chancellor, my mother was very ill. It was very depressing, sad and painful. She had sat in front of the television screen when I delivered the Queen's Speech to Her Majesty, but she didn't recognise me and that was a deep tragedy.

The man does have his softer side. In March 1998, during a speech by Dame Helena Kennedy, Irvine was moved to tears by a reference to his mother's influence. He is also said to have cried when, as Lord Chancellor, he returned to Hutchesons to deliver a lecture and receive an award.

A great worrier

At Cambridge, Irvine showed the same steely-eyed determination he had shown at Glasgow University. He obtained a further two degrees – a BA and an LLB – achieving firsts in both and winning a prize for his jurisprudence paper. As an affiliated student (one who already holds a degree from another university), Irvine did not have to study for three years before obtaining his Cambridge BA. However, he did have to satisfy a two-year residency requirement. So Irvine chose to sit the final examination of the BA after just one year and then follow that up with an LLB, a postgraduate qualification that was the equivalent of a masters degree.

Professor Paul O'Higgins, a fellow of Christ's College since 1959, became friends with Irvine and his wife during their stay and retains fond memories of both. Irvine, he says, was 'a very convivial person. We tended to have coffee in the local Kenco at least weekly, in fact, in mid-morning or mid-afternoon. And occasionally he'd come to my house and I'd go to his and Margaret's flat.' Margaret Irvine, he declares with considerable warmth, 'was a very good human being and very devoted to him . . . She was working as a teacher in Cambridge. I think she taught either in a special school or was herself a teacher for children with disabilities.'

O'Higgins admits that his recollections of the Irvines' home may be a little imperfect after all these years, but believes the couple lived in a second- or third-floor flat over what may have been a doctor's surgery close to Sidney Sussex College. It was, he suggests, a happy home: 'She looked after him very well. She was a good cook and he is very much a man for good wine and good food.'

There was a price to be paid for this good living. 'He was very much concerned with his weight, that was another thing that bugged him,' reveals O'Higgins. 'He went on slimming regimes, but I think it was the good food that Margaret cooked him and the drinking. He kept tight control of himself.'

Irvine had his fun, but never lost sight of his reason for going to Cambridge. O'Higgins recalls:

> He did his drinking but I don't remember his participating in any outside activities such as the union or politics or anything of that kind. As far as I know, he concentrated on two things at Cambridge: firstly, very hard work and, secondly, teaching.

Irvine did a lot of what is known as supervision – tutoring undergraduates in small groups. Such was Irvine's commitment to his studies and teaching, he had little time to waste on the other parts of university life.

One of Irvine's former supervision students remembers him as an excellent teacher who took a genuine interest in his students: 'He was extremely good, very thorough and made it all very interesting . . . He took everybody very seriously. He knew the law thoroughly. It wasn't a dry subject, it was a very living subject. His enthusiasm was infectious.'

During his own studies, Irvine grew close to Professor Glanville Williams, one of the most distinguished – if not the most distinguished – academic lawyers of his generation. 'I know that Glanville Williams was a great admirer of Derry Irvine,' states O'Higgins, 'a great admirer in the sense that he regarded Derry Irvine as an academic high-flier.'

Irvine's great qualities, muses O'Higgins, were that he was 'an enormously hard worker and a very intelligent student'. However, he fights shy of rating Irvine among the best to have passed through the university's law faculty. He says:

There are those people who do brilliantly at Cambridge as a result of very creative thinking and some hard work and those, in fact, who do well with intelligence and a great deal of hard work. I'd put Derry, myself, in the second category . . . He would have got his first essentially on the basis of great hard work and intellectual ability, but he was not one of those who got their very good firsts on the basis of real insight.

Irvine himself harboured major doubts about his own ability. It was standard to sit the LLB examinations after two years' study. Irvine, however, elected to study for three years in order to improve the odds of his getting a first. O'Higgins recalls that Irvine was 'a great worrier' about his exam results. This is why Irvine adopted such a cautious approach:

He was entitled to make that choice, but it was concern that he would be certain of getting a first that led him to taking three years over the LLB . . . It was very important to him to be successful and he sweated with fear at the thought of not getting a first in each of his exams here.

O'Higgins says he is not entirely certain why Irvine was so desperate to get a first:

I never discussed it with him, but if you come to Cambridge from outside you may have an image that these are all wonderfully clever people, as it were, and you're damned if you're going to let yourself down. You've got to show that you're at least as good if not better than they are. I'm conjecturing, but that's what a lot of people feel who come from the outside.

However, he acknowledges that Irvine was 'dedicated to getting on' and 'very ambitious' and that he was very keen for others to see that he was successful. 'I remember,' says O'Higgins, 'at quite an early stage of his career [at the Bar] when he had a Porsche. Whether it was on hire or bought I don't know. But, clearly, that kind of thing was important to him.'

Thus, O'Higgins believes that it is unlikely that Irvine ever seriously considered an academic career. While at Cambridge, Irvine's ambitions were 'essentially material', he recalls: 'I think he wanted to be a success at the Bar and have the money that goes with a successful career at the Bar.'

Irvine has told friends and acquaintances, including the former deputy Labour Party leader Lord Hattersley, that he turned down a Cambridge fellowship. A friend of Irvine's who knew him at Cambridge goes even further: he suggests that Irvine turned down the chance to replace none other than Glanville Williams when the professor chose to call it a day.

However, Professor O'Higgins finds it hard to believe that Irvine turned down a fellowship and is totally dismissive of the suggestion that Irvine was given the opportunity to fill Glanville Williams's very considerable boots. On the question of the fellowship, he says:

> Whether he was actually offered a fellowship I would be very unsure about that. That's really not the way the system works, quite honestly. The only way you could be offered a fellowship is if you'd entered for it and they then said, 'You've won the competition, are you willing to accept a fellowship?' as it were. But I don't know of any college where one could go to somebody and say, 'We'd like to offer you a fellowship' – I don't think it happens that way. There are annual competitions for junior fellows and one enters. Maybe he turned it down. But the story is just odd, quite honestly, because it doesn't fit in with the way the system works. But it could be that Glanville Williams said to him, 'Look, there's a fellowship coming up at Jesus, why don't you apply for it? I will support you.' I doubt if it went beyond that.

What makes O'Higgins have doubts is that, during his time at Cambridge, Irvine never mentioned anything about turning down a fellowship. He remembers:

> I never knew that at the time and I'm surprised I didn't know it, because we were fairly intimate and I'd have thought he would have told me that. I don't remember him telling me that. It may well be that what really happened was that somebody suggested that he apply for a fellowship and he decided not to. Because he was clear it was the Bar that he really wanted and I don't think he'd have thought that being a junior fellow would have given the rewards which he wanted.

The idea of Irvine replacing Glanville Williams is simply not realistic, says O'Higgins: 'Glanville Williams was a professor. You don't become a professor in Cambridge until you've been at it 10, 20 or 30 years. And Derry had only recently graduated. So, there is no question of him standing in for Glanville Williams.'

The student sympathiser

Irvine did go on to teach, but at the London School of Economics, not Cambridge, and only as a means to an end. Working at the LSE provided vital income while he took his Bar exams, did his pupillage and established himself in practice.

Irvine's time at the LSE proved significant. He made important contacts and, for the first time, allowed himself to be sucked into university life. He even took a stand on principle against the university authorities, getting involved in a dispute that might be described as farcical had it not ended in tragedy.

In 1966 the LSE was a tinderbox. A reactionary board of governors was badly out of touch with the increasingly disgruntled student body. All that was lacking was an issue to spark the inevitable conflict.

That issue duly arrived in the summer with the announcement that the governors had chosen to appoint Dr Walter Adams as the school's director in succession to Sir Sydney Caine. Adams seemed well qualified to be the LSE's main administrator, having previously been First Principal at University College, a multiracial university in Salisbury, Rhodesia.

However, in October a student pamphlet appeared, criticising Adams's appointment. It had been written by a group of students who produced a magazine called *The Agitator*, linked to the school's Socialist Society. This body had been formed in 1965 with the heady goals of overthrowing capitalism and generating greater militancy in the 'corrupt, effete and bureaucratic' student union.[23]

The pamphlet argued that Adams had been supportive of Ian Smith's government after it unilaterally declared Rhodesia's independence in 1965. Adams's supporters claimed this accusation was totally unfair. Adams, they said, had been in a difficult situation after UDI and had taken a non-political stance, opting to keep the school running as best he could. Whatever the truth of the matter, it had little bearing on what followed. The real issue was the way in which the students' concerns over Adams were dismissed by the governors.

With the dispute attracting considerable public attention, the chairman of the board of governors, Lord Bridges, wrote to *The Times*, declaring that the appointment of a new director was a matter that did not concern the students. Lord Grabiner, an LSE student at the time and currently chairman of the LSE governors, says that, in his view, the board's paternalistic response was a major catalyst for the later troubles: 'The school administration took the decision that they simply wouldn't debate this with the students. It was an authoritarian decision and they were going to stick to it. And there was terrible strife in the LSE.'

Naturally enough, many students wanted to respond to Bridges' letter. In particular, the student union wanted its president, David Adelstein, to write on its behalf. However, the school's regulations stated that students could not write to the press in their capacity as students of the LSE without the director's permission, and Sir Sydney Caine was not prepared to give his consent.

It was at this stage that Irvine first intervened. He and another lecturer, Lee Albert, told a meeting of the student union that its president was not bound by the restriction on writing to the press. This advice was based on their interpretation of a somewhat opaque section of the regulations. However, after Adelstein's letter was published, he was served with notice of disciplinary proceedings.

Even though Irvine and Albert had both only recently joined the LSE teaching staff, they did not back down from confronting the board of governors. At the end of October, a letter from the two lecturers appeared in *The Guardian*. It accused the governors of adopting an authoritarian approach: 'We hope our academic colleagues at the LSE recognise that the vital issue now at stake is preservation of the freedom of teacher and student alike to think and speak without fear of reprisal.'[24]

Caine, the retiring director, also sent a letter to *The Guardian*. He reiterated that 'Under the constitutional procedures of the LSE, the students' union has no part in the appointment of the Director of the school.'[25] He said he was perfectly happy for Adelstein to write to the press as an individual, but not as president of the student union.

Far from lying down, Irvine and Albert responded with another strongly worded letter to *The Guardian*. They wrote:

> The director invokes a student regulation . . . We speak of the more significant right of the student representative association, the union, to speak in its own name . . . If the LSE students are so inhibited, they are unique among students at British universities . . . It would be ironic for a controversy which began with denials of academic freedom at the University in Rhodesia to end with violations of those freedoms at the LSE.[26]

To his eternal credit, Irvine appears to have been the one person to have recognised that the affair had now escalated out of all proportion. In mid-November he contacted the LSE secretary, Harry Kidd, in the hope of finding a solution satisfactory to both sides.

He warned Kidd that Adelstein was considering legal action to halt the disciplinary proceedings on the basis that the rules of natural justice were being contravened. Kidd explained that there had been misunderstandings and the two agreed that the only real point outstanding was Adelstein's objection to Sir Sidney Caine's participation in the upcoming hearing. Irvine suggested the eminently sensible compromise that Caine should withdraw because, in his letter to *The Guardian*, he had expressed a view on matters to be discussed at the disciplinary proceedings.

Caine agreed, but his withdrawal came too late to prevent a student boycott of lectures that had been called to protest about the way the hearing was being handled. When the student union president was let off with nothing more than a warning as to his future behaviour, some of the more strident students claimed the day as a victory for militant action – also known as 'direct action'. Further conflict was now inevitable.

In January 1967 the students were due to hold a meeting in the Old Theatre, the LSE's main lecture hall. This was originally billed as a discussion about Dr Adams's appointment. But a student leaflet suggested that the meeting was also being convened to prepare for direct action. When Caine discovered this, he withdrew permission to use the Old Theatre. Because this only happened at the eleventh hour, a large number of students gathered expecting the meeting to take place. When the students tried to enter the Old Theatre, the porters were called to block the entrance. In the ensuing squeeze, Edward Poole, a 64-year-old porter with a history of heart trouble, had a heart attack and died. Two of the student leaders, including David Adelstein, were later suspended.

It was a tragedy waiting to happen, suggests Lord Grabiner. 'It was an age of student revolution – big time!' he recalls. 'All the troubles from America had been imported into the UK, principally from UCLA and such establishments.' Many of the worst troublemakers had no right to be at the LSE, he claims:

> The LSE was just full of students, many of whom weren't even LSE students. There were all sorts of characters who'd arrived from Paris . . . There were German students, there were American students. There were people who had nothing to do with the LSE at all. Professional troublemakers. Everyone piled into the LSE.

Nevertheless, he believes Irvine was right to take the students' side: 'Derry took the view that the administration handled it all quite badly. And, I must say, looking back, I think it was handled quite badly.' Irvine, points out Grabiner, went about his tussle with the governors in the right way: 'He never got himself into a direct confrontational position with the authorities. There was certainly never any suggestion of Derry having broken his contract or anything like that. But he did take a clear position.'

The LSE's students' union rewarded Irvine's efforts by making him an honorary vice-president for life. Also recognised at that date was the Chinese leader Mao Tse-tung.

Mr Modesty

After sitting his Bar finals, Irvine did his pupillage with Denis Henry, a member of one of the chambers at 2 Crown Office Row in the Temple. The set, which has since moved premises and is now known as Fountain Court Chambers, was and is one of the very best commercial sets in the country.

According to a reliable source, Henry, who is now a Court of Appeal judge, is no fan of his former pupil, who made himself extremely unpopular during his time at 2 Crown Office Row. So unpopular, indeed, that when he completed his pupillage and was called to the Bar in 1967, he was not offered a tenancy at the set.

Failing to get the tenancy of one's choice is not necessarily a black mark against a barrister. Competition for tenancies is always stiff, and luck and timing can also play a part. As a result, there are numerous examples of good barristers who have been turned down by their first set, only to go on to illustrious careers at other chambers. That said, being turned down by his first chambers must have been quite a blow to Irvine's considerable ego, unaccustomed as he was to failure.

He only had himself to blame. It was not bad luck or bad timing that proved Irvine's downfall; it was his own arrogance. When describing Irvine, 'modesty isn't the first word you would think of', says a tenant at Fountain Court Chambers. The reason Irvine was refused a tenancy, this barrister explains with considerable tact, was that 'it wasn't thought that he was likely to be a very good team player'.

Fortunately for Irvine, a solution was very close at hand: 2 Crown Office Row was home to another chambers, headed by Morris Finer QC, and this set was prepared to offer Irvine a tenancy. It may be that Finer, who was friendly with a number of the barristers at Irvine's first set, got to know Irvine simply because they worked in the same building. However, it seems more likely that Finer met Irvine at the LSE, where Finer was a member of the board of governors.

Joining Finer's set was a great move for Irvine. Finer was an outstanding barrister with an excellent practice in both commercial and employment work. A leading silk recalls:

> Morris Finer was an exceptional talent, truly exceptional. He was a very brilliant lawyer. He was also a fabulous advocate. He was one of the greatest lawyers I've ever seen. He was also extremely nice: he had a heart of gold ... I don't think Derry's nearly as clever as Morris was, but then I don't think many people were as clever. I think Derry would agree with that.

Finer had a high regard for Irvine, says the silk, and used him regularly as his junior, kick-starting Irvine's career. Finer and another senior member of the set, Peter Pain QC, both did a lot of cases involving trade union legislation, the field in which Irvine first established a reputation.

The way Irvine tells the story, however, he only became an employment specialist through chance. He has claimed:

> I happened to be the only one in chambers that day at lunchtime – hadn't gone out to lunch – and literally this case came in the door ... And overnight a labour law expert was born. I knew nothing about labour law before that! That was the fashionable, big case in labour law. [27]

Irvine's story is not as far-fetched as it may seem. There have been occasions when a barrister's career has been made simply through the barrister being in the right place at the right time. However, if the case was such a big one, was there really anything so vital that it could not wait an hour or so until a more senior barrister was available?

There are echoes here of the tale of John Smith's essays. Both stories are probably founded on fact, but over the years the part played by other participants has steadily diminished and Irvine has ended up claiming much of the credit.

North poll

In 1970 Irvine considered a complete change of direction, when he chose to stand as the Labour Party candidate for Hendon North in that year's general election. The decision appears a trifle odd. At Glasgow University Irvine had shown no interest in politics, making it perfectly clear that his only ambition was to succeed in the law.

If Irvine had won the seat he could, of course, have continued to work as a barrister. Indeed, there were plenty of practising lawyers in Parliament at that time. However, Irvine must have known that entering the Commons would have meant sacrificing his grander legal ambitions. Reaching the top of the Bar requires absolute dedication: there is little enough time for sleep, let alone political distractions.

Perhaps Irvine was persuaded to give it a go by his friend John Smith, who fought – and won – North Lanarkshire that year. Whatever the reason for this sudden change of heart, Irvine was, by the end of May 1970, telling the local party in Hendon North that he desperately wanted to get into Parliament. According to one person present at the selection meeting, Irvine was a raw candidate, but showed considerable promise, not least through his oratory.

Irvine's cause was helped by the fact that the local party was keen to make its selection as quickly as possible. Labour Party HQ had not been impressed by the names the constituency had put forward and had put forward several recommendations of its own, one of whom was Irvine. With time before polling day running out, the decision was made to go with the Scottish barrister whose charming wife would surely prove a considerable asset.

Hendon North was anything but a bad opportunity for a young Labour candidate fighting his first general election. Irvine, who would turn 30 just after polling day, faced the challenge of taking a traditionally Conservative seat. (Hendon North had gone to Labour only once since the Second World War – in 1945.) However, there were several reasons for Labour to be optimistic.

At the 1966 election, the Tories had held the seat with a majority over Labour of just 600, with the Liberals coming in a poor third. Plus, the recent omens were in Irvine's favour. A council by-election in the constituency's Colindale ward had been won by the Labour Party in early May with an 8 per cent swing. Best of all, the long-serving MP, Sir Ian Orr-Ewing, had chosen to retire. So, the Conservative candidate would, like Irvine, be new to the constituency.

The Tories' replacement for Orr-Ewing was going to be no pushover, however. Unlike Irvine, John Gorst was a campaign veteran, having fought Chester-le-Street in 1964 and Bodmin in 1966. Although he lost both seats, Gorst had on each occasion substantially reduced the sitting candidate's majority. Furthermore, Gorst, who ran his own PR company, was an excellent self-publicist.

Certainly, it was Gorst who made all the early running. This was partly because the Hendon North Labour Party had been so slow to adopt its candidate. Indeed, even though the election had been called for 18 June, Irvine was not formally adopted until 26 May. Gorst took the opportunity to set the agenda, promptly seizing the high moral ground by warning that the general election would the dirtiest campaign in history. If it was, nobody in Hendon North noticed. The fight between Gorst, Irvine and the Liberal candidate, Gerald Cass, proved a tame affair, even by the standards of 1970.

It was Gorst himself who was to pull the slickest trick of the Hendon North campaign. The recent Representation of the People Act had included a provision allowing voting papers to carry a fuller description of candidates' political affiliation and activities. Gorst chose to make the most of his predecessor's reputation in the constituency by describing himself as 'Conservative; successor to Ian Orr-Ewing'. Irvine did his best to appear outraged, describing Gorst's conduct as 'distasteful . . . surprising and highly question-able'[28] and argued that the Tory candidate should fight the election on his own merits.

Gorst also outmanoeuvred his opponent when Irvine played his trump card. With Hendon North targeted by Labour as one of 13 key marginal seats, Irvine received the support of a visit from none other than the Prime Minister, Harold Wilson. Using his PR expertise, Gorst managed to attract some of the media attention away from Irvine. He sent a cheeky letter asking Irvine whether he would like Gorst to attend upon the Prime Minister during his visit and declared that he was flattered that so important a member of the Labour Party should feel it necessary to oppose him in person.

Gorst was not obliged to fight the campaign alone, however. In an attempt to attract the younger voter to the Conservatives' cause, the actress Hayley Mills was employed as the question master at one of Gorst's public meetings. Irvine countered with his own celebrity, Harry H. Corbett, star of BBC comedy series *Steptoe & Son*. The intellectual Scot and the cockney actor must have made an interesting combination.

Towards the end of the campaign, the three candidates appeared together at a public meeting to face their electorate. Questions were asked touching on such issues as council rents, capital punishment and immigration. Irvine declared himself against the reintroduction of hanging on moral grounds. He was also against the introduction of tighter immigration controls, as proposed by right-wing Conservative MP Enoch Powell. 'We in the Labour Party,' said Irvine, 'are united in our detestation of everything Powell stands for.'[29]

As polling day approached, local pundits were putting their money on a Labour victory. However, the result, when it came, was a devastating blow to Irvine. Gorst not only held the seat for the Conservatives, he increased the majority from 600 to 3,179. To make matters worse, the Labour vote declined by almost 2,800. Although the Liberal candidate lost his deposit, he did at least get more votes than his predecessor had received in 1966.

The victor thanked his opponents for a clean and fair fight, and an amusing one. Irvine put a brave face on things by assuring everyone that Gorst's victory was 'purely temporary'.[30] This was not one of Irvine's better political judgements. Gorst went on to hold Hendon North for 27 years, defending the seat successfully on no fewer than six occasions. In 1984 he was knighted for services to politics and retired just before the 1997 election, when Hendon North finally went Labour again.

The suspicion remains that Irvine missed a real opportunity in 1970. True, there were factors beyond his control: he was not given much time in which to mount his campaign; to some extent, Hendon North simply followed a national trend that saw the Conservatives return to power under Ted Heath; and Irvine was up against a very able candidate. But Irvine also contributed to his own downfall. He ran a lacklustre campaign – so lacklustre that Sir John Gorst finds it difficult to remember much about his former opponent. 'I didn't really see anything of him except at the count and at one meeting where I don't really recall anything about him,' he says. 'He didn't have a personality that makes an impact.'

Gorst suggests that Irvine's style had only limited appeal. The Labour Party candidate, he says, did well enough with middle-class Labour voters:

> But he didn't seem to have the common touch to maximise the vote in what you'd call the traditional Labour areas . . . [The] feedback from my own supporters talking to Labour [was that] he was all very well in Edgware and Mill Hill, but he didn't really make any impact in Burnt Oak and Colindale. He didn't seem to know how to talk to people in their own terms.

It is the most remarkable irony that the son of a roof tiler and waitress could not communicate effectively with working-class people. Irvine had not merely escaped his roots, his manner gave the impression that he had turned his back on them.

Alison

Irvine never made another attempt to enter Parliament. Perhaps defeat at Hendon North proved too painful. A more likely explanation, however, is that Irvine had never been that serious about the idea in the first place and always intended to pursue a legal career.

There was a further factor. In 1974 – the year of the next general election – Irvine was busy getting divorced and remarried. His marital difficulties would not have helped Irvine's chances of being selected for another seat at a time when the public was less tolerant of politicians' infidelities. And Irvine's was a particularly messy divorce. Not only had he run off with a married woman, he had taken the wife of his old friend from Glasgow University, Donald Dewar.

Alison McNair had married Dewar in 1964, two years after Irvine married Margaret Veitch. The Dewars made a slightly improbable couple, says a friend: 'They weren't an obvious combination when they got married. They were rather different people. Donald was quite reserved about relationships – still is – and Alison is very outgoing and warm.'

There was little time for the marriage to settle before Donald Dewar was swept away by politics, states the friend:

> Poor Donald Dewar won a seat he wasn't expected to have won. He won in '66 in South Aberdeen. He wasn't expected to win it at all and it destroyed his life in one sense. It was wonderful to win, but he'd very recently got married. There was one child and there might even have been another one on the way.

The couple's move to London only put further pressure on the marriage, suggests the friend. Whereas Dewar was and is most comfortable at home in Scotland, Alison Dewar was attracted by the capital and all it had to offer. Even after Dewar lost his seat at Aberdeen South in 1970, Alison Dewar continued to visit London.

Just how long the affair between Irvine and Alison Dewar lasted is not public knowledge. What is known is that Margaret Irvine walked out on her unfaithful husband at some time in 1971. She did not obtain a divorce until 1974, however, when she cited Alison Dewar as the co-respondent. Dewar had already divorced his wife on the grounds of adultery the previous year. Alison Dewar, who retained custody of her first two children, married Derry Irvine in

1974. In the same year, she gave birth to their first son, David. A second child, Alistair, would follow in 1976.

Irvine's second marriage has not merely endured, it is remarkably strong. Irvine dotes on his wife and is simply a different person when she is around. So much so, the Lord Chancellor's Department has an unofficial policy of encouraging Lady Irvine to accompany her husband to as many events as possible. 'He loves it when she's around and he's better when she's around,' says one observer. 'Not in the sense, "Alison is here, so I've got to behave well," but, "Alison is here, therefore I'm a better person." He softens, he mellows.'

This is no comfort to Donald Dewar and Margaret Veitch, neither of whom has remarried. Dewar has since 'found emotional issues difficult', suggests a friend. 'I don't think he's ever really recovered from that . . . He is quite reticent and I think he still carries the wound. He likes his own company and he's adjusted.'

It is part of Labour Party legend that Dewar and Irvine did not speak to each other again until 1994, when both were pallbearers at John Smith's funeral. Irvine has denied this, stating that the two maintained a relationship for the sake of Dewar's children. Mutual friends suggest that, if they spoke at all, Irvine and Dewar never spoke more than was necessary.

Irvine has proved an extremely generous step-parent, suggests someone who knows the family well:

> There has been absolutely no question of treating one lot [of children] differently from the other and, in that sense, I've never ever heard a single word of criticism from Donald Dewar . . . Indeed, I could put it more positively than that. I've heard him actively say how generous Irvine has been to his children.

As regards his first wife, however, Irvine's conscience still troubles him. He told *The Sun* in 1998:

> My first wife was a wonderful woman, an admirable person.

> She was completely without fault and I felt extremely guilty
> at the time, but the fact is that Alison and I fell in love. I did
> feel guilty, but what happened to us is not all that unusual.
> I think it has happened before . . . But, of course, if a
> marriage breaks down with someone who is not at fault,
> you would be a very unthinking person if you didn't feel a
> strong sense of guilt.

The way Irvine has dealt with that guilt is to pretend that his first
marriage never happened. His *Who's Who* entry makes no reference
to his first marriage – poor reward for a wife who was so devoted
to him, supported him financially in the first years of their marriage
and helped him fight the campaign at Hendon North in 1970.

Irvine has made the excuse that he was invited to contribute an
entry to *Who's Who*: 'My *Who's Who* was six years after my divorce
and I was looking forward, not backwards.' Irvine has not
explained, however, why he never took the trouble to correct his
entry since then.

Margaret Veitch has commented:

> If it were up to him, nobody would know he'd ever been
> married before. Our break-up was very unpleasant, but I
> cannot talk about it because, even after all these years, I
> know the details would upset Donald Dewar.
>
> We were married for a very long time. I still think about
> him and our life and I am still bitter about what happened.
> It hurts that he doesn't even acknowledge my existence. I
> wish I knew why. [31]

After leaving Irvine, Veitch returned to Edinburgh. In 1976 she
moved to Canada, where she now lives alone near Toronto and
teaches children with special needs. Fortunately for Irvine, Veitch
has generally refused to discuss her marriage and its break-up in
any detail, preferring to maintain a dignified silence. But, in 1997,
she did reveal:

I haven't spoken to my ex-husband since I left Britain. I've cut all that out of my life. I had to put him behind me. After the way he behaved, I wouldn't want to stay in touch with him. It still upsets me . . . I have a new life here in Canada. I'm very proud of my work.[32]

CHAPTER THREE

All the King's Men

In 1976 – almost 20 years after he had met John Smith – Derry Irvine began the other most important friendship of his life. It started shortly after Irvine received a rather hopeful application from a young man looking for a pupillage, Tony Blair.

Irvine has since confessed, 'I remember being not overly impressed. His qualifications were perfectly respectable, but there was nothing that stood out on paper.'[33] In fact, the only thing special about Tony Blair's application for a pupillage was that it was late – so late, indeed, that the position had already been filled. Irvine had agreed to take on Cherie Booth, a former LSE student with a stunning CV. Booth not only had a first-class law degree, she had come top in her class at the LSE and top in the 1976 Bar finals as well, a truly fantastic achievement. Blair, by comparison, had a second-class degree from St John's College, Oxford, and scraped through the Bar finals with a third.

Irvine's decision to give Blair an interview was slightly odd. He usually did not consider candidates for a pupillage unless, like him, they had first-class degrees. (Irvine has since justified his actions by claiming that Blair would have got a first if he had applied himself to his studies.) Plus, Irvine tended to discriminate in favour of applicants who had come up through the state education system. Blair, on the other hand, had attended Fettes, a public school in Edinburgh. Indeed, Blair later told his old school's magazine, *The Fettesian*, that in one of their first meetings, Irvine had challenged him, 'So, your parents were rich enough to send you to a public school then.' When Blair replied rather hesitantly, 'Well, of course you can criticise my public school education . . .' Irvine spat, 'I bloody well will!' [34] (At the time of this incident, Blair was not in a position to know that Irvine had himself been to a private school and that he would send both his sons to the fee-paying City of London School.)

It may simply be that Irvine saw Blair out of respect for Colin Fawcett QC, the barrister who had advised Blair to apply to Irvine after Blair bumped into Fawcett at a friend's birthday party. Whatever the reason, Blair saw his chance and, at the interview, grabbed it with both hands. Indeed, Irvine has since said that Blair 'bowled me over with his enthusiasm'. [35]

Irvine has always claimed that Blair's Labour leanings played no part in his getting a pupillage. Shortly before the 1997 election he declared, 'When Tony Blair became my pupil, I didn't have the least idea what his politics were. I never asked him and he never told me. The truth is I only learned subsequently, and several years subsequently.' [36]

Although that may seem somewhat improbable, it could be that politics was not an important factor in bringing the two men together. Like many other people since then, Irvine was no doubt charmed by Blair. Irvine is particularly susceptible to charm: he does not find forming new relationships a simple matter and is attracted to people with a relaxed style who can put him at his ease.

Perhaps Irvine also recognised a kindred spirit. Despite an age gap of some 13 years and a considerable difference between the two men's personalities, they most definitely share one characteristic: acute ambition. 'They're both pretty determined,' acknowledges someone who knows them well. 'Having decided on their objectives, they then work out how they're going to achieve them. They have that very much in common.'

Irvine took such a liking to Blair that when Blair and Booth's year of pupillage was up, it was Blair, not Booth, who got a tenancy at 2 Crown Office Row. James Goudie QC, who was one of the tenants at 2 Crown Office Row at the time, suggests that the main obstacle to Booth getting a tenancy was none other than her future husband:

If Tony hadn't been there, then Cherie might well have been taken on. But I think it was looked upon as an 'either or' because they were both obviously commanding candidates. There was also an element that Derry tended to attract the best pupils and therefore quite a lot of his pupils were taken on as compared with [the] pupils of other [barristers]. And I think that rather militated against taking two of Derry's pupils in one year.

Irvine himself has said that Booth was offered, and accepted, a tenancy elsewhere 'before the time arose for chambers to consider whether she should be offered a tenancy'.[37] This seems to be a whitewash. If Booth did choose to move on before a vote was taken, it was in all probability because Irvine had told her she did not have a future at the set.

The chambers' decision to choose Blair rather than Booth was made on Irvine's recommendation, says another former 2 Crown Office Row tenant, Michael Burton. Now a High Court judge, Burton states, 'We always did what he [Irvine] suggested in relation to his pupils and he did not recommend taking them both, he only recommended Tony. So we voted accordingly at the chambers meeting.'

Irvine dominated proceedings each year when the time came to discuss the award of tenancies. 'I didn't have a pupil taken on for some time, because it was always Derry's pupils and he was the big personality,' remembers Burton. When other people's pupils were under discussion, 'We used to have bitterly contested meetings with half going one way and half going the other,' he confesses. Irvine's pupils were another matter. 'Derry normally got his way.'

Booth moved on to 5 Essex Court, which is now New Court Chambers, the set headed by the well-known libel expert George Carman QC. However, her career failed to take off and she turned back to Irvine for help. In 1989 he approached Michael Beloff QC, now head of chambers at 4–5 Gray's Inn Square, one of the best sets in London.

Beloff recalls: 'Derry rang me up on a personal basis and said, "Look, there is this very able lady who is marooned in a set where she oughtn't to be, would you see her?" And, having great respect for Derry, I said, "Of course I'll see her."'

Although nothing came of the interview at the time, Booth made a strong impression on Beloff. A couple of years later, a vacancy opened up at Beloff's set and Booth was offered a tenancy. Since then, Booth has gone from strength to strength, taking silk in 1995 and emerging as one of the country's leading barristers in the fields of employment and public law.

After Booth quit 2 Crown Office Row, Blair continued to work closely with Irvine, who frequently selected him as his junior. According to Irvine, Blair was:

> A brilliant lawyer. A complete natural. He had a tremendous talent for assimilating, very quickly, complex factual material and I have no doubt at all that he would be a QC by now if he'd stuck with the law. He was a fantastically fast gun on paper, producing high quality legal opinion with remarkable fluency and speed. [38]

Just as Irvine has played down Blair's indifferent academic record, so he seems happy to talk up Blair's legal abilities. Blair is remembered by others at the Bar as perfectly able, but nothing more. He was never going to set the legal world alight. A much more talented lawyer, Cherie Booth was always a far better prospect. It is hard to imagine that Irvine was unaware of this. So, when he chose Blair over Booth, Irvine must have been influenced by considerations other than just legal ability.

That is not the only reason Blair owes Irvine a considerable debt, as he told his biographer, Jon Sopel:

> His contribution to my intellectual development was enormous. I was never quite engaged intellectually at Oxford and my schooling was very much the schooling that

gets you through exams. You know, you can pass exams without really thinking . . . He taught me how to analyse and confront problems and how to marshal arguments in debate. He showed me there was no point simply reading a book and reproducing its ideas, what was needed was the confidence to question them.[39]

That praise, though generous, does not tell even half the story. Irvine has been a great deal more than just an intellectual influence on Blair. He has been one of the most powerful forces in Blair's life.

It was through Irvine that Blair met his wife. Indeed, in the run-up to the 1997 election Blair told *The Sun* that it was during lunch with Irvine that he and Cherie Booth realised they were in love. When they married in 1980, Irvine made a toast at the wedding, pointing out the part he had played in bringing the couple together and describing himself as 'Cupid QC'.

Irvine also introduced Blair to John Smith and, through Smith, to the top brass of the Labour Party. In 1981 Irvine created an opportunity for his protégé by suggesting that Blair produce a paper for Smith on the legal aspects of the government's privatisation programme. Smith, then shadow Trade Secretary, was highly impressed and showed the paper to his shadow cabinet colleagues.

This was the beginning of another close and vitally important relationship for Blair. When, in 1982, he was chosen as the Labour candidate for a by-election in Beaconsfield, Smith campaigned for him. Despite this, Blair was trounced, coming in third behind the Liberal and losing his deposit. But even with Smith's help Blair never stood a chance of winning. Beaconsfield was a safe Conservative seat, the Labour Party was riven by internal strife and the by-election was fought during the Falklands War, when Mrs Thatcher was at the peak of her popularity.

Things were soon looking up for Blair, however. At the end of 1982 he had a chance to shine in front of the Labour Party's National Executive Committee. Once again, he had Irvine to thank. When the editorial board of the Trotskyist newspaper *Militant* took legal action in an attempt to prevent their expulsion from the Labour Party, Irvine was instructed to act on the NEC's behalf and he chose Blair as his junior.

The next year, when Blair was asked by the Beaconsfield Labour Party to be its candidate in the general election, he turned to Irvine for advice. Blair was torn. On the one hand, he was anxious to get into Parliament as soon as possible and knew that he had next to no chance of taking a seat as staunchly Conservative as Beaconsfield. On the other hand, he did not want to let down the people who had helped him fight the by-election the previous year.

Irvine has since stated: 'I advised him that sometimes amazing things can happen in politics, and persuaded him to ride his luck, take a chance and say no to the Beaconsfield Labour Party.'[40]

Blair's decision to follow Irvine's advice was to prove one of the major turning points in his life. Just as Irvine predicted, something amazing happened. At the eleventh hour, Blair discovered that the local Labour Party in Sedgefield, a safe Labour seat close to his childhood home in Durham, had not yet selected its candidate.

Blair took a chance and went up to Sedgefield, got himself nominated and then won the day at the selection meeting. No sooner had he done so than he telephoned Irvine from the hall where the meeting had taken place. Blair told Irvine that his recommendation to turn down the Beaconsfield offer was the best advice he had ever been given.

And the relationship between the two men grew even stronger after Blair left Irvine's chambers for Parliament. Blair would phone Irvine on a regular – sometimes daily – basis, seeking his former pupil master's advice on a broad range of subjects.

The extent of Irvine's influence can be seen in the fact that Blair maintained the working practices that had been drilled into him by Irvine. Just as he and Irvine had spent long periods preparing for court, so Blair would make a huge effort before his appearances in the House of Commons. Indeed, so desperate was Blair to make his mark in the Commons that, if a chance of quizzing the Prime

Minister during question time arose, he would call Irvine to discuss exactly how the question should be put in order to make the most impact. Hours would be spent fine-tuning both the question and Blair's delivery.

When, in 1988, Blair became a member of the shadow cabinet, it was Irvine he turned to when he had problems. As shadow Employment Secretary, Blair faced the challenge of winning trade union support for a change in policy, after Labour backed down on its earlier pledge to revoke all of Mrs Thatcher's trade union legislation. In order to alleviate the unions' fears that they would be treated unfairly by prejudiced, Tory judges who knew nothing about industrial relations, Irvine came up with the idea of setting up 'Labour Courts'. The plan, which has never been implemented, was that these would be specialist courts, presided over by expert judges, in much the same way as the High Court's Family Division consists of judges who practised family law when they were at the Bar. Likewise, after becoming shadow Home Secretary in 1992, Blair sought Irvine's advice on constitutional reform.

'Tony quite rightly always had a huge regard for Derry's intellect – he admired it then and he admires it now,' states Maggie Rae, a leading family law solicitor with a firm in Covent Garden, Clintons, and a close friend of both Tony Blair and Cherie Booth. Over the years, however, the relationship has changed. Blair is no longer in awe of Irvine, says Rae, and their friendship has

> matured into a partnership of equals. Tony can say no to Derry and Derry can say no to Tony. It is a partnership, it's a partnership of equals and they listen to each other. Tony will not always take Derry's advice, but he will want it.

James Goudie agrees that Irvine and Blair make a very good team. The two men have very different characters, he acknowledges, but 'They often think along similar sorts of lines. I think they each respect the other's judgement a great deal. And each benefits from debate between themselves.'

Irvine and Blair work well together because they have complimentary qualities, suggests Rae:

> Derry brings to anything a formidable intellect. I'm not saying Tony doesn't have a good mind – he has. But it's not really quite the same kind of mind as Derry's. Tony brings to it huge experience of practical politics and a real ability to listen to ordinary people, pick up the mood of them – what will go and what won't go. Derry isn't in that position, you wouldn't expect him to be. If you marry the two, you get the right answer, usually.

Not everyone agrees. A senior figure in the Labour Party has said:

> John Smith and Derry as a partnership were fine, because John knew where he was going, and he loved the Labour Party. That would have been a good combination. Derry, with all his insecurities, was fine with John, who was very strong. But Tony and Derry are a bad combination.

Top dog

Blair's record of loyalty to Irvine begins in earnest in 1981. In that year, Blair and eight other barristers followed Irvine from 2 Crown Office Row to a brand new chambers, headed by Irvine. The split took place for a number of reasons, but the main catalyst was Irvine's determination to be head of chambers.

Irvine had taken silk in 1978, just 11 years after being called to the Bar. At the time, he was the youngest QC in the country. Perhaps the success went to his head, for it seems that Irvine's thoughts soon began to turn towards taking charge at 2 Crown Office Row. Other barristers would have been happy to wait their turn, but Irvine has always been a man in a hurry. The problem was that several more senior barristers stood in his way, not least

Michael Sherrard QC, who had led 2 Crown Office Row since the middle of the 1970s and was showed no signs of retiring or moving on to the Bench.

Irvine and Sherrard had never hit it off particularly well. The two were highly competitive with each other, suggests a former member of 2 Crown Office Row. Irvine coveted Sherrard's position as head of chambers and felt that Sherrard, though highly successful and respected, was not doing enough to build up the set in the way Irvine felt best. (Certainly, Sherrard was spending a lot of time away from the chambers, working in Hong Kong where a substantial part of his practice was based.) For his part, Sherrard resented the fact that Irvine was becoming a major influence within chambers, getting his own way on most things through a combination of his forceful personality and the support of friends in chambers.

Some of those friends – who were in the main Irvine's former pupils – had their own reasons for wanting change. Christopher Carr was a rising star who wanted to drop employment work in favour of high-value commercial work. Carr feared that his chances of building a successful practice at 2 Crown Office Row were limited because the set did not have a sufficiently strong reputation in the commercial field. He and others wanted to see an improvement in both the quantity and the quality of commercial work and believed that Irvine, who had also taken the decision to build up his commercial practice, was the man to lead the way. Carr says:

> There was a sense, a feeling, that we were not going to realise this ambition of developing the commercial stream of the practice without leadership that was able to drive it, to attract that quality of work and type of work; and that Michael Sherrard, for all his admirable qualities, was not the man.

Others, such as James Goudie, wanted to see a total shift in direction: 2 Crown Office Row was a successful general set, he acknowledges, but times were changing and generalists were on the way out. Goudie suggests: 'Derry and others foresaw, perhaps with more clarity and sooner than most people, that the Bar was moving in the direction of specialisation.'

Irvine and his friends were not the only ones thinking along these lines. Some of the barristers at another set, 2 Hare Court (now known as Blackstone Chambers), were also anxious for change. They included Anthony Lester QC (now Lord Lester of Herne Hill), Michael Beloff QC and David Pannick. Irvine knew Lester well, having been led by him in a trade union case some years previously. In 1980 the two began discussions about creating an altogether new set, taking the best people from 2 Crown Office Row and 2 Hare Court and focusing on strictly limited areas of work.

Beloff explains:

> The plan was to take sections out of each set of chambers and form what we regarded as likely to become a 'super set' in the developing public law field and established employment law field with, obviously, a measure of commercial law involved as well, since both Derry's chambers and indeed ours had persons in that field.

The idea of setting up a super set appealed for a number of reasons. Up to that time, barristers had attracted work exclusively through their reputations as individuals. Now chambers in London were beginning to see the benefits of developing a brand. The stronger the set, the stronger would be the brand.

A new set also meant a fresh start. Chambers to date had not been run like businesses so much as gentlemen's clubs. Barristers came and went much as they chose and did whatever work took their interest. They often shared little more than an address, a clerk and a library. Chambers administration was rudimentary, management systems virtually unknown. Practice development consisted of clerks taking solicitors to the pub for a few drinks on a Friday night.

Christopher Carr and others wanted the new chambers to adopt a more professional and businesslike approach. He was frustrated with the set-up at 2 Crown Office Row. The senior clerk, recalls Carr, was 'old-fashioned, a splendid old man, but a real old-style clerk. Efficiency was not part of his conception of things at all. Fee-collection was a problem.'

Those involved in the 'super set' negotiations were also keen to get rid of some of the Bar's many outdated practices, particularly the ones that cost them money. Although barristers' chambers had grown substantially in recent years, most barristers still paid clerks 10 per cent of their fees, with the result that clerks in some chambers made an awful lot of money for relatively little work. Indeed, some clerks took home more than many barristers in their chambers. A further problem was that the more successful barristers were tired of carrying their less successful colleagues. They were frustrated that, because each member of a set makes a contribution to the chambers' overheads based on his or her earnings, the stronger/more hard-working barristers effectively subsidised the weaker/lazier ones.

But who was strong and who was weak? Beloff remembers that sorting the wheat from the chaff took up a disproportionate amount of the negotiations between Irvine's camp and Lester's:

> There were persons over whom we could not agree. Derry wanted to bring in X, Y and Z and no doubt we wanted to bring in A, B and C. Each of us thought that the other group didn't quite pass the very élite standards that we boastfully had in mind. It's fair to say that we did regard this as [something that was] going to be a real élite meritocracy.

With the benefit of hindsight, a number of the disputes appear comical, suggests Beloff:

When I look at some of the people whom we jibbed at, and their subsequent careers, it just shows how very wrong you can be! I mean they are absolutely at the peak of the profession now and I would be happy to have an association with them.

The negotiations dragged on and on, before eventually grinding to a halt. Lester says he was a little wary of the idea from the very start: 'They, I think, had identified about half a dozen of us as being people they particularly wanted. That meant we would have been a minority in the new set.'

There were other problems, he suggests. Lester and his colleagues were not entirely comfortable with the idea of deserting the other members of 2 Hare Court. They were not certain that the new set would be the kind of chambers they wanted it to be. And the issue of who would lead the new set had still to be resolved.

The loyalty factor was such that Irvine would have had to come up with an extremely attractive package to lure away anyone from 2 Hare Court, says Lester. In addition, the Lester group's philosophy about how the new chambers should be managed was very different from that of the Irvine group. Lester's group wanted what he describes as 'non-hierarchical, modern management'. Irvine, on the other hand, believed that the new set should be based on a more traditional model and should be run by a traditional-style head of chambers, namely himself.

Lester recalls that Irvine was

very keen on being head of chambers. He was junior to me, but I did not mind him being head of chambers, provided that we were confident of being able to run chambers in a modern, democratic way. In the end, we decided we could do better by modernising our own chambers than taking a leap in the dark.

It has not proved a bad decision. Blackstone Chambers is one of the country's leading sets. Lord Lester and David Pannick QC are regarded as among the very best silks in the fields of employment and public law. Michael Beloff left 2 Hare Court around a year after the talks with Irvine fell through, and has since become joint head of chambers at 4–5 Gray's Inn Square and one of the country's most eminent barristers, practising across an unusually broad range of law.

Nevertheless, Beloff admits to some regret that the super set did not come off. Given the quality of the people involved, the new chambers 'would actually have been quite unbeatable', he claims. However, such ideas, says Beloff, have always been difficult to pull off. The fact is that barristers are prima donnas and 'it's very difficult to accommodate a lot of prima donnas'.

Half and half

The failure of the negotiations between Irvine and Lester merely postponed the inevitable. The 2 Crown Office Row set had developed into two camps: those loyal to the head of chambers, Michael Sherrard, and those loyal to their friend and/or former pupil master, Derry Irvine. With the two groups now roughly similar in size, there was, sooner or later, going to be either a power struggle or a split. In the end, there was both.

When linking up with the people from 2 Hare Court disappeared as an option, Irvine and his group began to discuss the possibility of branching out on their own. The issue became urgent when Christopher Carr chose to join One Essex Court, a move that convinced Irvine that, unless he acted, there would be a steady drain of talent from 2 Crown Office Row. Irvine and his friends held meetings in a number of locations away from chambers, including James Goudie's house. Despite these precautions, word of the discussions eventually leaked out.

The people who had not been involved in the breakaway talks were somewhat upset, but things did not turn nasty at this stage. 'It was unpleasant to discover all this plotting had been going on without one knowing anything about it, but they were quite decent about it,' says former 2 Crown Office Row tenant Mr Justice Burton. Those who were staying recognised that there was little point in arguing. Irvine wanted to leave and, given the choice, his former pupils were always going to go with him. One of the senior members of chambers, Brian Capstick QC, was desperately disappointed that his good friend Derry Irvine was leaving, but did his best to keep everyone on friendly terms. This proved an impossible task.

Friction began to develop when Irvine and his camp antagonised their colleagues by failing to specify a date for their departure. They had, in fact, been experiencing problems finding new premises and were hoping to stay at 2 Crown Office Row until they found somewhere suitable. (Space in the crowded Inns of Court has always been at a premium.)

Those who were staying insisted that a departure deadline be set. This was only fair, says Burton, because 2 Crown Office Row had to make plans for the future. In particular, the set wanted to recruit new tenants to replace those who were leaving and have those replacements move in as soon as possible. When Irvine's group refused to name the day, Sherrard's group did it for them, giving them two or three months' notice.

It was now that the real fun began. It occurred to someone in Irvine's faction that, with a little parliamentary-style lobbying, the minority could turn itself into the majority and gain the upper hand. Burton recalls:

> That weekend, after this perfectly reasonable deadline had been imposed, but they hadn't yet found anywhere, they recruited Alistair McGregor, who was otherwise going to stay with us. And they announced over that weekend, I think to Brian Capstick, 'We now have the majority, you're going!' And that was not pleasant. Whether it was meant or not, or whether it was a negotiating tactic, I don't know.

Although McGregor was one of Irvine's former pupils, he had not hitherto been part of the Irvine group's plans. Indeed, McGregor had previously pledged himself to Brian Capstick and Michael Sherrard. The announcement of his defection was followed by an episode straight out of one of P.G. Wodehouse's golf-club stories. Somebody suddenly remembered that there was still one more vote to come. Everyone had forgotten a member of chambers called Eric Falk, who was around 80 years of age and had all but retired. Falk did little more than keep a desk in the room shared by James Goudie and Michael Burton, but his vote could hardly be ignored, not least because his name was on the lease of 2 Crown Office Row – the lease they were now fighting over.

Both sides rushed to see Eric Falk. To the relief of one and the intense disappointment of the other, Falk declared himself to be with the Sherrard camp and everyone was back where they had started. The attempted putsch had failed. 'It was an unnecessary tactic,' states Burton. Until then, the damage caused by the split had been relatively limited, he says: 'Obviously, Michael [Sherrard] was upset and remained upset because he saw it as a personal thing between him and Derry, but he and those loyal to him would have lived with it.' But the weekend's events spoilt everything. 'There were no squabbles about money, but there was this nasty taste which took a long, long time to evaporate. But for that, it would have been a perfectly amicable split.'

Friendships were stretched even further in the years immediately after. Irvine and his team proved highly proficient in putting about propaganda that made themselves look good but which inevitably reflected badly on 2 Crown Office Row. Claiming that they had quit their old chambers because they wanted to create a more focused and more commercial set, they made it appear that 2 Crown Office Row was a rump consisting largely of criminal lawyers.

Burton understands, and understood perfectly well at the time, that Irvine and his group needed to present a positive picture of the split and that ascribing it to their plans for a more focused set was 'a good excuse'. However, in Burton's opinion, the split had nothing to do with focus. There was no one reason for the split, he acknowledges. But he believes that the most important elements were undoubtedly 'Derry's enthusiasm to be head of chambers and the fact that he wasn't prepared to wait'.

A home of their own

Irvine and his group of nine other barristers moved out of 2 Crown Office Row at the end of 1981. At one stage, the search for new premises became so desperate that they considered quitting the Temple for less fashionable Gray's Inn – a radical move for members of a profession obsessed with tradition. However, Irvine's team got the opportunity to stay in the Temple when a few rooms became available at 1 Harcourt Buildings. It was not a perfect solution, but it was better than nothing and they all squeezed together. James Goudie, for example, shared with Tony Blair.

It may have been an inauspicious start, but everyone at the chambers was confident that the new enterprise would prove a success, claims Goudie: 'We weren't in the least fussed that we were small in terms of numbers. I don't think any question arose that we were too small to be viable. It may seem odd now because it would have been terribly tiny in present day terms.'

But, in following Irvine from 2 Crown Office Row, Goudie and the others had taken quite a risk. The new set had just one silk – Irvine. The others were all juniors still in the process of establishing their careers. Thus, they would all rely to some extent on Irvine's reputation to attract work.

The younger members of chambers would also be financially dependent on Irvine. Goudie recalls that, at the beginning,

> Derry was the only QC and his income was half the total income of the whole lot of us. So, we were very, very dependent on him in every sense . . . If he had been knocked down by a bus or whatever, that would have been disastrous.

Fortunately, says Goudie, the new set was 'sufficiently successful, sufficiently soon', that Irvine never needed to support the chambers in any way beyond bearing the biggest share of the overheads, a share that fell steadily as the other barristers became more successful.

Irvine could have quickly taken some of the financial burden from his shoulders by recruiting barristers from other chambers. However, there were, at this stage, two factors operating against such a policy. After the 2 Crown Office Row bust-up, Irvine and the others were reluctant to bring in outsiders. Plus, they simply did not have the space to accommodate new recruits.

The pressure on space was relieved a little when Irvine was able to take a lease of a basement at 10 King's Bench Walk and then a lease of some rooms next door at number 11. However, it was only after several years of cramped conditions and scattered locations that the big breakthrough came, when further space became available at 11 King's Bench Walk and everyone at last worked under one roof.

The move to more comfortable surroundings came too late for one member of chambers, however. Tony Blair entered Parliament at the 1983 election and gave up his practice the following year, when Irvine's set was still stuck in dingy rooms at Harcourt Buildings. Although Blair's name is on the boards outside 11 King's Bench Walk, he never actually practised there.

The new model army

What Derry Irvine wants, Derry Irvine gets. Having torn 2 Crown Office Row apart, Irvine could be sure that the new chambers were run his way. In fact, for most of the next 16 years, Irvine would make nearly all the important decisions worth making. Irvine might easily be described as a 'benevolent despot', says James Goudie:

He always led from the front. He was prepared to see himself that everything got done. He had a clear vision of how it ought to be done and he drove it along very efficiently and effectively, but very much in the general interest rather than his own personal interest, and always with an ear for anybody who wanted to ask for his advice and always being enormously helpful to everyone with advice if ever they had any difficulties.

Former 11 King's Bench Walk pupil Sean Wilken confirms that Irvine really cared about the people in the chambers:

> He loved that set, it was his baby. I think he had great personal affection for members of that set. And so, I think, he always had the best interests of that set at heart. That said, cynics would say it was also his tool for self-advancement, and that may be right, but certainly he was a force for the good for most people at that set.

Nevertheless, Irvine's dictatorial ways were often a source of some amusement at 11 King's Bench Walk. He and others were once discussing the Labour Party's plans to reform its voting system in order to introduce the concept of one man, one vote. 'That's what we've got here,' quipped James Goudie. 'There's one man and he's got one vote.'

However, no one was especially bothered about the lack of democracy, says Tim Pitt-Payne:

> I didn't ever get a sense of resentment that people wanted to be more involved in the running of the chambers . . . I think most of us consider that a rather tedious sideline to the things we're actually interested in, which is giving legal advice and appearing in court. And if other people are dealing with those issues, then on the whole we're fairly happy to let them get on with it.

There was another reason why Irvine was allowed such free rein in running the chambers: he did a great job. Indeed, under Irvine 11 King's Bench Walk became one of the best sets in the country. When founded in 1981, the chambers had just one silk out of a total of ten barristers. When Irvine left in May 1997 there were 10 QCs out of a complement of 28 barristers.

Crucially, Irvine introduced focus and good administration. Unlike 2 Crown Office Row, Irvine's chambers did not cover a broad range of work. Instead, it specialised in just three areas: employment, public and commercial law (the three fields in which Irvine just happened to practise). Although the selection of these work types probably owed as much to luck as judgement, no one is complaining. All three areas – employment and public law in particular – have boomed since the set was founded and 11 King's Bench Walk has boomed with them.

On the administration front, Irvine recruited an excellent senior clerk in Philip Monham and together they ensured that the chambers was run in a highly efficient manner: 11 King's Bench Walk was, from the first, run strictly as a business. Irvine and many of his colleagues may have been Labour supporters, but they fully intended to make plenty of money.

The most important factor in the chambers' success, however, has been quality control. The reason why 11 King's Bench Walk is one of the best sets in the country is that it is home to some of the best barristers. Thanks to Irvine, there are few weak links. He built slowly, but he built well. He declined to take on barristers with established practices. Instead, tenancies were offered only to people who had done pupillages at 11 King's Bench Walk, and then only to those who came up to his exacting standards.

As always, Irvine exerted complete control: each pupil was required to do work for him, so he could make up his mind whether or not they were made of the right stuff. Irvine's methods were not subtle: pupils were thrown straight in at the deep end, with Irvine eager to test their character as much as their legal ability.

Timothy Pitt-Payne's first piece of work for Irvine, he recalls, was 'a fairly big professional negligence case involving some tax consultants. There were about four lever-arch files full of documents. At that stage, I'd never had to deal with that volume of paper.'

Nevertheless, Irvine told Pitt-Payne he wanted more than just a few initial thoughts. Pitt-Payne was to report back to Irvine in two weeks' time when he would be expected to have complete mastery over the papers.

Reporting to Irvine, says Pitt-Payne, was not unlike appearing in front of a judge:

> You'd take him through the basic facts, take him to the key documents and show him what you thought were the key sections in the documents. You'd tell him what you thought the legal analysis was, what the factual issues were and what your views were. So, it was a bit like doing an opening statement in court, and, I suppose, to some extent, he would adopt the persona of a fairly challenging judge who would be asking you questions the whole time rather than just sitting and listening.

Woe betide the pupil who did not produce work that was perfect in every respect. 'When he goes through work with you, you know it's been gone through,' chuckles Daniel Stilitz. 'Everything from the overall structure to the tiniest points of phrasing or grammar he will not let past him.'

Other barristers might make allowances for a pupil's age and inexperience, but Irvine showed no mercy. Sometimes he was brutal. If he decided a piece of work was not up to scratch, he would snap at its author: 'Is this the best you can do?' If he found something he did not like, it was denounced as 'wanking' — something of an Irvine catchphrase.

Praise was rare. More often than not, this comprised no more than a grudging admission that Irvine could find nothing wrong with the pupil's work. Nevertheless, former pupils are quick to applaud Irvine. Some pupil masters neglect their pupils. Irvine, says Philip Sales, took the trouble to teach them as much as he could:

> I think it gave him a kick to impart skills to young people. He would definitely take time to review an opinion you'd written, and say how he thought it could be improved. He'd take time, if you were working on a cross-examination, to explain why he was putting questions in a particular order. And he'd explain how he thought litigation should be conducted.

Irvine always took his role as a pupil master seriously and responsibly, declares One Essex Court's Christopher Carr QC. Irvine's pupils, he says, were not just bag carriers:

> Derry's idea of having a pupil was that the pupil should be totally engaged, totally involved in the practice, knowing about what was going on. When he gave you work, he didn't want you to come back and give him a few pointers or opinions or comments. He wanted you to write a complete, finished, fully documented piece of work. He might throw it away in the rubbish basket and produce his own, but he wanted total engagement and commitment. And, having got it, he would then take the time and trouble to go through it carefully with you.

Towards the end of a pupil's 12-month stint would come the dreaded day of decision. As at all the top chambers, competition for tenancies at 11 King's Bench Walk was stiff. The set usually took on two or three pupils each year, but tended to grant just one tenancy a year if it granted any.

Irvine, who had himself suffered the disappointment of being turned down for a tenancy at the chambers where he did his pupillage, did his best to ensure that the selection process was even-handed. 'He was very fair in that way, I've got no doubt about that,' states Sean Wilken, who moved to 39 Essex Street after completing his pupillage at 11 King's Bench Walk. 'There may have been other people at that set who weren't so fair, but, undoubtedly, Derry was straight down the line.'

Irvine was also at pains not to jump to conclusions about a pupil's ability. If he harboured doubts, he would give pupils a further chance to prove themselves by asking them to do more work for him. The final decision was not made without due consultation of the other members of chambers.

Irvine was very much of the view that chambers is 'not a gentleman's club', says Philip Sales. 'You don't just blackball someone because you don't like them. A healthy degree of tolerance is the order of the day.'

Nevertheless, there was a clear pattern in Irvine's decisions about who did and did not get a tenancy at 11 King's Bench Walk. The people selected by Irvine tended to share certain attributes. They came by and large from humble backgrounds; their university was either Oxford or Cambridge; and they had spent some time teaching. And, of course, they all had first-class degrees.

Indeed, so far as Irvine is concerned, an immaculate academic record is a *sine qua non*. Baroness Smith has acknowledged:

> Marks are terribly important to Derry. He's got it all out of proportion. It's frightening sometimes. For Derry, it's a reassurance that a person's okay if they have got a first. Whatever else about them isn't good, that makes them a good person. [41]

More to the point, it is a reassurance for Irvine that he is okay. Such is Irvine's insecurity that he finds it necessary to surround himself with people who are made from a similar mould. The logic is simple: they are good people, therefore he is a good person.

There are no new Derry Irvines at 11 King's Bench Walk, however. The people at the chambers are refreshingly unassuming, and Irvine could always sleep well at night. None of his fellow tenants was ever going to mount a challenge to his authority.

A major achievement

Irvine is immensely proud of what he created at 11 King's Bench Walk. Shortly before becoming Lord Chancellor he stated: 'You're never self-satisfied. You always want to achieve more. But, if all else failed in life, I would consider the establishment of these chambers as my major achievement in life, leaving aside my wife and children.'[42]

However, Irvine did not achieve everything he set out to achieve. One of his primary goals was to make his chambers a leading commercial set, but this has not yet happened. There are certainly some very good commercial barristers at 11 King's Bench Walk (indeed, some of the younger members of chambers look certain to enjoy glittering careers), but the chambers has never accumulated sufficient commercial weight to take on the 'Big Four' commercial chambers – Brick Court Chambers, One Essex Court, Essex Court Chambers and Fountain Court Chambers. Compared with those commercial giants, 11 King's Bench Walk is not a commercial set so much as a set with a commercial facility.

The irony is that if Irvine had shown a little more patience, he might well have ended up as the head of one of the top commercial sets. The chambers at 2 Crown Office Row was a set simply brimming with potential, declares Mr Justice Burton: 'We weren't one of the top three or four, but we would soon have become so. The very fact that both the two chambers have done so well separately indicates that together we would have done even better.'

Given that Littleton Chambers (as 2 Crown Office Row is now known) enjoys an excellent reputation, it is hard to dispute the logic of this. Irvine and his friends would certainly have found it a lot easier to crack the commercial market if they had held on to Michael Burton and Christopher Carr, both of whom went on to become premier league commercial heavyweights.

But this line of argument ignores a crucial fact. However much a united 2 Crown Office Row might have prospered, Irvine and his friends would never have derived as much satisfaction from the success of 2 Crown Office Row as they have gained from the success of 11 King's Bench Walk. It is *their* chambers: they created it, they made it what it is today. Irvine and the others may have been at fault when they walked out on their colleagues at 2 Crown Office Row, but they were not wrong to want to build something of their own.

The past and current members have every right to be proud of 11 King's Bench Walk. It is a fine chambers; the pre-eminent employment law set and one of the very best public law sets. Solicitors who use the chambers are swift to praise its barristers. Colin Goodier, head of employment in the Birmingham office of the national law firm Pinsent Curtis, has said, 'If you're looking for a top-quality employment service, and you're looking for quality from top to bottom, you aren't going to do better.'[43]

Elaine Aarons, head of employment in the London office of the national law firm Eversheds, has stated, 'There's a bit of an IBM factor with it – you don't let your clients down if you use 11KBW.'[44]

Irvine in particular has a right to be proud. It is the people who make 11 King's Bench Walk and Irvine chose those people. By favouring youngsters from ordinary backgrounds, he fostered talent that might not otherwise have been given a chance. Indeed, a number of barristers at the chambers believe that, but for Irvine, they would not have ended up at a top set.

Likewise, Irvine's bias towards former academics has created a chambers with a warm, civilised feel: 11 King's Bench Walk is not merely a good set, it is a pleasant one. The barristers are, on the whole, relaxed, unpretentious and approachable, making 11 King's Bench Walk one of the most friendly and likeable sets in London.

CHAPTER FOUR

An Old-Fashioned Bully

There are two huge myths about Derry Irvine's legal career. The first is that Tony Blair and Cherie Booth met at Derry Irvine's chambers. The truth is that 2 Crown Office Row was Michael Sherrard's set. The second is that Irvine was one of the best barristers in the business. The truth is that Irvine was good, but not great.

In 19 years as a silk, Irvine was always in demand, did a lot of big cases and made plenty of money. There were always others, however, who were in greater demand, were doing more big cases and were making more money.

The best commercial barristers spend the greater part of their lives in the Commercial Court, the specialist commercial section of the High Court. Irvine 'appeared occasionally in the Commercial Court, but not often', states a former rival. 'Derry was always very able, but I don't think he would have been regarded as being in the top ten.'

That assessment is supported by a survey carried out by the trade monthly, *Legal Business*, in December 1993. The magazine asked more than 100 City litigation solicitors to name the UK's top ten commercial QCs. Not only is Irvine's name missing from that list, he was not even one of the seven runners-up.

There are a number of reasons why the youngest QC of his generation did not reach the very top. First, being a junior is a completely different discipline from being a silk. Juniors at the top sets only do a limited amount of advocacy. They spend the vast majority of their time doing the spadework for leading counsel.

Thus, success as a junior is no guarantee of success as a QC. Indeed, the Bar is littered with examples of barristers whose careers have faded since they took silk.

Second, Irvine only chose to focus on commercial work when he left 2 Crown Office Row in 1981. Thus, he was a late starter at the commercial Bar, the most competitive sector of the legal profession. By then, of course, he already had a reputation as an employment law specialist with particular expertise in the field of trade union disputes. That reputation would have been of no help to him at the commercial Bar. In fact, it was probably a hindrance. Changing tack is never easy in any profession. It is particularly difficult in the law, where the high level of specialisation means that people are very quickly pigeonholed as a expert in one field but not others.

Nevertheless, if Irvine had been truly outstanding, he would have escaped pigeonholing. The legal world is small, says a former head of litigation at one of the best City law firms, and word of mouth still counts for a great deal. He explains that the reason he never instructed Irvine was that

> There just weren't people saying to me, 'You've really got to use this guy, he's absolutely brilliant!' My partners never said it to me, no one from other firms or anyone I had a beer or a gossip with ever said it to me. So, I suppose I stuck with those I knew or those that did get recommended to me.

The tough guy

When people did talk about Irvine, it was not always in complimentary terms. Irvine's superior ways made him plenty of enemies at the Bar. Like a lot of other barristers, Irvine would sometimes take breakfast at Chez Gerrard, a restaurant close to the Royal Courts of Justice. While the others barristers exchanged pleasantries and gossip, Irvine would sit alone.

One barrister remembers bumping into him in Hong Kong in the late '80s, after Irvine had received his peerage:

> Derry was sitting down having tea in the Mandarin Hotel and I came with my solicitor for tea. He went over to Derry and he said, 'Oh Mr Irvine, how nice to see you!' And Derry said, 'Lord Irvine!' It was almost laughable, really. The poor guy was terribly shocked.

Irvine's manners in court were no better. In October 1998 a judge told the *Sunday Times*: 'I remember him saying to one opponent – as a junior, I think – that the answer to [his opponent's] submission was that he had never heard a more abject application by leading counsel. That is not going to endear you to someone.'[45]

What fellow barristers most disliked about Irvine was that he was a bully. One QC has said of Irvine:

> Whenever I was against him in court, as soon as he arrived in the robing room, he'd be leaning on you to settle. Even if he met you outside the building, he'd immediately make snide remarks about the weakness of your case. It was intimidation, and with less confident barristers it might have had some effect. And there was never the slightest sign of a sense of humour.[46]

When on his feet, Irvine was nothing less than a force of nature. 'You wouldn't want to be lying in the witness box when he was cross-examining,' says a barrister who worked frequently with Irvine. 'He has both the voice and the physical presence to be brutal when it's appropriate.'

And perhaps also when it's not appropriate. Irvine showed little lightness of touch, remembers one commercial QC:

> Derry had a very bullying manner as a cross-examiner. It was not a gentle process. There are some people who have

the ability to coax an answer without getting angry and irate and all the rest of it, whereas Derry's tactic was to be repetitive and abrupt and aggressive. Everyone has their own way and, I suspect, for him it worked. I just think sometimes you've got to be a bit more delicate with a witness. I don't think I ever saw Derry being very delicate with a witness, but that was his style.

Irvine's approach was anything but gentle, agrees another barrister: 'It wasn't fencing. It was like watching someone trimming a hedge with a sabre. They know what shape they want it to go at and they're damned if it is going to go any other way.'

Irvine did have the power to dominate a witness, confirms 11 King's Bench Walk's Philip Sales. However, he believes Irvine never abused that power:

> He played hardball, but he played to the highest standards of fairness. He'd be scrupulously fair to a witness. He might feel that the witness was a liar and a cheat and everything, and he'd do his best to catch him out, but he'd never play a low trick on a witness. Likewise, he'd play hardball with other advocates, but he'd never do anything underhand. It seems to me that's the hallmark of being a great advocate – you play by those rules and you play hard. That's what you're there to do.

Irvine was no loose cannon. His aggression was controlled aggression. He knew exactly what he was doing. He knew which were the good points and which were the bad points. He knew exactly how far he could push a judge.

To some extent, Irvine was merely acting out a role. He played the tough guy because it worked. Through aggression he stamped his personality on the case and sought to bend the judge to his will. When a physically large barrister like Derry Irvine goes on the rampage, it takes a very strong judge not to be swayed. 'A lot of judges are mesmerised by it,' confirms a commercial silk. 'I've seen judges overborne by Derry.'

Irvine's style may not have looked subtle, but there was much more to it than mere bravado. Absolutely nothing had been left to chance. Behind each bludgeoning attack lay hours and hours of groundwork. Detailed notes had been prepared on every important aspect of the case. Everything had been referenced and cross-referenced. Key documents had been flagged. The course of every cross-examination had been planned in detail.

Some lawyers prepare for cross-examinations by selecting a number of themes they wish to develop and then leave the rest to the inspiration of the moment. Not Irvine. His approach, suggests Pitt-Payne, was 'a bit like chess. This is my move. If I make this move, what are the possible moves from the other side and how might I respond to them?'

'He wanted every single line chased down,' confirms another barrister. 'I have never seen him be unprepared for court. I did see him once or twice be unprepared for conferences [with solicitors and clients], but for court, never.'

Irvine went to great lengths to ensure that every eventuality was covered, reveals Sales:

> There was one very big case that we did together where we went up to his house in Scotland for a fortnight before it started. We knew that the main task we were going to have was two extremely difficult cross-examinations and that each of them would last two or three days. We spent 14 days going through the files, analysing every question, arguing with each other what the witnesses would say.

The final product of such marathon efforts would be a script or, to be more precise, series of scripts. Whatever the witness said in reply to one of Irvine's questions, one of the scripts had it covered. All Irvine had to do was read the right section of the right script.

This method of working certainly has its virtues. Contrary to the perception created by television and film, few legal cases are won by a barrister's sudden stroke of genius at the right moment. The overwhelming majority of cases are won through plain, old-fashioned hard work by the whole legal team.

Irvine was absolutely right to prepare thoroughly. Barristers who do not know their cases properly will always founder sooner or later. Irvine, however, went to extreme lengths. As a result, his greatest strength was also his greatest weakness. Irvine certainly knew his lines, but he would not – or perhaps could not – extemporise. On occasion, the circumstances of a trial require 'you just to throw the script away', states a commercial QC. Irvine, he says, was sometimes ineffective because 'he wasn't very happy to depart from the script'.

Indeed, once on his feet, Irvine was extremely reluctant to accept even the most minor challenge or interruption. One well-known silk recalls receiving short shrift when he tried to correct a small error in one of Irvine's opening speeches:

> He could be quite prickly. I remember once getting up when he'd simply been guilty of some inaccuracy in his recitation of facts, which I just thought it would be helpful to clarify. It wasn't terribly important. And I got up and Derry said rather sharply, 'The turn will come when my learned friend can make his speech.' Meanwhile, he intended to open the case as he saw fit.

Some barristers recognised that Irvine had an Achilles' heel and attacked it. 'If I was against Derry,' says a highly regarded QC, 'I would try and make a point of going off script – introduce some new case he hadn't thought of, so he had to go outside his notes.'

Whether Irvine was actually able to think on his feet is difficult to gauge, suggests a barrister who has worked with him. 'That was the whole point of preparing everything to the nth degree,' he says, 'there was always an answer somewhere.' He acknowledges, however, that Irvine 'wasn't very intuitive'.

Another barrister has no doubts about the matter, however. He believes Irvine was unable to be spontaneous:

> I don't think he had that sort of feel. He's obviously a very shrewd man, but that wasn't the way he appeared in court. He did not work on instincts and he wasn't subtle. He prepared to the hilt and kept to the script, more or less.

Irvine's real skill, says the barrister, lay in making prepared speeches: 'In terms of the sort of case where he was making a speech in relation to a particular argument or a particular point of principle, I thought he was very good.' But there is much more to being an advocate than simply making speeches. 'I wouldn't,' says this barrister, 'rate him particularly high as a trial lawyer.'

A limited appeal

Like all barristers, Irvine lived and died by his reputation. On the credit side, he was respected for his thorough preparation and his excellent speechmaking. On the debit side, he was seen as inflexible and lacking in instinct. Those limitations did not prevent Irvine from having a highly successful career, but they did stop him from reaching the very top. For the biggest and best cases, solicitors want barristers who can do more than read their lines, however well written those lines may be. They want a barrister who can seize the moment and turn a case on its head in a flash.

A highly regarded commercial QC suggests there is a substantial difference between someone like Irvine and a truly outstanding advocate, such as Michael Burton. The latter, he says,

> would get an answer from a witness and he would just change his entire case within a couple of seconds of getting that answer in order to use it and make something out of it that would help his side. Rather than just seeking to

disprove that answer or continuing his case, he would mould the case as he went along, sometimes to breathtaking effect. That wasn't the Derry style . . . he just didn't demonstrate flexibility or subtlety or particular insight as regards the matters that can be decisive in trial.

Irvine's inflexibility also manifested itself in another way. As an old-fashioned barrister, he retained an old-fashioned attitude towards solicitors. He did not see himself as a member of the team, but as the leader. It did not matter to Irvine that the solicitor was his client, nor that the solicitor paid the bill at the end of the day. Irvine was the boss and everything had to be done his way.

Such an approach was perfectly common when Irvine started to practise. Solicitors were very much the poor relations of the legal profession. Believing it had a monopoly on the best talent, the Bar looked down on solicitors, considering them intellectually and socially inferior. Certainly, the quality of some litigation solicitors at that time left a lot to be desired. Since the 1970s, however, law firms have grown massively, allowing greater specialisation. This, in turn, has resulted in a huge improvement in the quality of solicitors, particularly in the field of litigation. Today, solicitors at the top law firms are no longer prepared to act as barristers' bag carriers. They want to run the case themselves, and insist that their barristers be team players, prepared to make a contribution rather than pontificate from on high.

Irvine made no concessions to this revolution, however. He carried on exactly as before. Speaking shortly before Irvine became Lord Chancellor, a City solicitor said, 'If you've got Irvine on your team, Irvine takes control. He regards himself as the team leader, and he will ultimately decide where it's all going.'[47]

Another solicitor complained bitterly that Irvine was totally old-fashioned. He said Irvine's style was to keep the solicitor and client 'as distant as possible . . . he just doesn't join the team'.[48]

Irvine responded to those charges by insisting that he was a team player. He argued that the contribution he made to the team was leadership:

> If a team system involves all chiefs and no Indians, it won't work. So the fact that I try to provide leadership – if that grates with people, then so be it. Everything I've ever done ... has been in the interests of the client and with a view to winning.[49]

None of this would have mattered one jot, of course, if Irvine had really been good enough. Several of the top commercial silks are notoriously arrogant, rude and insensitive, and yet they continue to be picked for the biggest cases. So great is their ability, solicitors are prepared to indulge them like spoiled children. If Irvine did not enjoy the same licence, it is because he did not enjoy the same respect.

Irvine's prickly personality and high-handed ways led plenty of solicitors to conclude that they could do without him. A solicitor with one of the leading City firms asserts that he and his partners avoided using Irvine because, 'There were sufficient other barristers who were as good, if not better, and he had the reputation of being difficult to deal with.'

That reputation must have hit Irvine's pocket. Certainly, for so senior a QC, working in such a broad field as commercial law, Irvine had a remarkably narrow client base. A very high percentage of his big commercial cases were done for just two City law firms, Ashurst Morris Crisp and Herbert Smith. (Indeed, one commercial silk estimates that work for Herbert Smith may have comprised as much as one third of Irvine's practice.) The City's other leading legal lights, such as Allen & Overy, Clifford Chance, Freshfields, Linklaters, Lovell White Durrant and Slaughter & May, rarely used Irvine if they used him at all.

Luckily for Irvine, there were enough solicitors prepared to tolerate his pompous behaviour and enough cases that demanded a barrister who could steamroll the opposition into the ground. It can be no coincidence that his biggest client was Herbert Smith. Generally regarded as the country's leading litigation practice, Herbert Smith's uncompromising approach to litigation has (somewhat unfairly) earned the firm the nickname of the 'Rottweilers' of the legal profession.

In addition, it was Irvine's good fortune that one of the top litigation partners at Herbert Smith was an old friend. Dr Lawrence Collins, who had been at Cambridge with Irvine, sent a lot of work to 11 King's Bench Walk and encouraged his partners to do the same. Without doubt, the strong relationship with Herbert Smith has been one of the key factors in the chambers' success.

A hard taskmaster

Irvine may have given solicitors a hard ride, but they got off lightly compared with the junior barristers and pupils who worked for Irvine at 11 King's Bench Walk. Indeed, Irvine was infamous for working his people into the ground.

It took a particular breed of junior to survive the ordeal of working for Irvine. In the last phase of his career at the Bar, his favourites were Philip Sales, Timothy Pitt-Payne and Daniel Stilitz. Although the three are very different in character, they share two major virtues: they are bright and they are extremely hard-working.

Sales, Pitt-Payne and Stilitz all acknowledge that Irvine was a hard taskmaster. 'He's very good at getting quality work out of people who work for him,' says Stilitz in a typical comment. 'He works very hard himself and he expects those who work with him to work hard as well.'

If Irvine worked late, the junior worked late. If Irvine worked all weekend, the junior worked all weekend. If Irvine started work at 7 a.m. on a Sunday morning, the junior was expected to be at the chambers when he arrived, ready and able to perform with all pistons firing.

An incident in the weeks leading up to the 1997 general election reveals a lot about how Irvine treated younger members of chambers. He was working at Labour's Millbank headquarters one morning, when the door to his office was unceremoniously kicked open by none other than the party leader. 'Come on, Irvine!' shouted Tony Blair. 'Haven't you finished the work I gave you last night?'[50]

Plenty of Irvine's former pupils and juniors would pay good money to have been in Tony Blair's shoes at that moment. Irvine had made their lives hell, imposing tight deadlines and setting the most exacting standards. Tony Blair was, if anything, understating the case when he once described Irvine as having 'a fairly brutal approach to hard work – if you hadn't done the work, there was no point coming into the room.'[51]

Juniors and pupils were usually given first crack at a new set of papers. Irvine would then inspect the fruits of their labours. Only if the work stood up to his strict scrutiny would Irvine adopt it and improve it. Despite appearances to the contrary, Irvine did not rely unduly on his juniors' work, insists Stilitz:

> Even though he would get juniors to do quite a lot of work, it would all be gone through so thoroughly that, by the end of it, it would no longer be possible to describe it as just his junior's work. It was always his work with initial input from the juniors.

'He was always thoroughly prepared, fully on top of the case when we went into court,' confirms Philip Sales. What really counts, he argues, is not that Irvine worked his juniors hard, but that he made good use of them: 'It's actually a skill of a senior QC to know how to delegate pieces of work and then to know how to take the product of various people's work and blend it into an effective submission.'

If Irvine did sometimes push them to the brink, Sales, Pitt-Payne and Stilitz are too loyal to complain. Their respect and affection for

Irvine is transparent. Working for Irvine may have been tough, but it was also rewarding. Sales readily acknowledges his debt:

> In many ways he is the person who taught me most about being a barrister, in terms of how you structure an argument, how clearly you have to set things out, how to structure a cross-examination and approach a witness as well as instilling in you the importance of what you're doing and the importance of observing the highest standards of integrity and so on. All these things I feel that I had lessons from, in many ways, one of the greatest exponents of them.

In any event, there is much more to Irvine than just work, continues Sales: 'He was a very exciting person to be around. He is larger than life. He had all sorts of dimensions to his life – the politics and the law – and he was an interesting person to talk to.'

It was not all work and no play, confirms Timothy Pitt-Payne:

> He had very good judgement as to how far he could push people. If you were really flagging, you'd go out for lunch together or you'd go out for dinner and you'd switch off the case and talk about art, or talk about politics, or talk about the Bar more generally. And he could be a fantastic companion. He had an enormous capacity for charm.

Irvine was also capable of generosity and kindness. When juniors had been working particularly hard on Irvine's cases, he would sometimes stuff some money in a pocket and tell them he did not want to see them anywhere near chambers for the next 48 hours. If a junior had domestic problems, he could be sympathetic and supportive.

Irvine has always regarded himself as someone who could spot youthful promise and develop it. Certainly, the wealth of talent at 11 King's Bench Walk backs this up. But Irvine's purposes may not have been entirely altruistic. He was a QC who relied heavily on his pupils' and juniors' work. Irvine may have taken great care to polish their efforts, but it was the pupils and juniors who actually wrote his submissions and cross-examinations.

One former rival barrister believes that Irvine relied too heavily on others' efforts: 'When he had pupils, he very much depended on the pupils and, I think, when he had juniors he very much depended on them.' Irvine may have clocked up the hours, he concedes, but, in terms of input, Irvine was much less hard-working than his great benefactor Morris Finer: 'Morris would definitely be much more of a worrier, a terrier in terms of getting his teeth into things and coming up with the bright ideas.'

And, as the years passed, Irvine's reliance on other people's hard work simply grew greater, occasionally stretching the patience of even his most loyal solicitor clients. The barrister whose mantra had been 'preparation, preparation, preparation' was not doing his homework.

Shortly before Irvine left 11 King's Bench Walk to become Lord Chancellor, Ashurst Morris Crisp partner Graham Webb said of him: 'He's somebody who relies a lot on a good junior. You get the most out of him if you give him a good junior, and I think Philip Sales is someone who works well with him.'[52]

Another City lawyer was not so tactful. He stated matter-of-factly:

> Philip [Sales] really came into those chambers as Derry's running mate. Philip is the brains behind the scene ... Derry built those chambers and he now has a towering practice and persona, but I would never use him again because he just doesn't do the work.[53]

Once again, Irvine dismissed the criticism as groundless. He declared:

> When I do a case I am fully involved and do not rely on the work of others. I do it all myself, as well as at the same time accepting help from colleagues, solicitors and juniors. I may

press my juniors harder than they prefer, but that is me doing my duty to ensure that the client gets the full benefit of the team.'[54]

According to one of the barristers at 11 King's Bench Walk, these efforts at self-defence provoked much mirth among the younger members of the set.

A cool million

Irvine's legal career was not about righting wrongs or stamping out injustice, it was about making money. His instructions came from major law firms, not high-street solicitors. His clients were millionaires, local authorities and Stock Exchange-quoted companies, not the poor and the vulnerable.

In 1990, for example, he acted for Hammersmith and Fulham Council in the House of Lords in a high-profile case involving swaps transactions. The next year, he represented the Fayed brothers and the House of Fraser in one of their fights against Tiny Rowland and Lonrho. In 1993 he acted for Mary Moore, the daughter of sculptor Henry Moore in her multi-million-pound claim against her father's charitable foundation.

Given the nature of Irvine's work, there has been considerable speculation in the press about how much he earned while at the Bar. Some newspapers have suggested that Irvine was a member of the so-called 'Million-a-Year Club', the group of barristers who earn £1 million a year on a consistent basis. The case for Irvine's inclusion in this élite is not convincing.

The Million-a-Year Club comprises around a dozen or so of the very best tax and commercial barristers in the country. It includes such people as One Essex Court's Lord Grabiner QC, Essex Court Chambers' Gordon Pollock QC and Brick Court Chambers' Jonathan Sumption QC. But, as an advocate, Irvine was never in the same league as those three.

Nor was he as hard-working. Members of the Million-a-Year Club all work phenomenally long hours – as much as 120 hours a week. Irvine by contrast always had time-consuming interests outside the Bar. During the 1990s (the decade in which barristers first started regularly earning £1 million or more), he was committing a great deal of attention to politics and to Tony Blair in particular. Irvine did probably hit the £1 million mark on at least one occasion, but it seems unlikely that he reached such heights on a regular basis.

It was not for want of trying on the part of his clerk. There is no tougher fee negotiator in the Temple than Philip Monham, 11 King's Bench Walk's senior clerk. Monham has been described as 'like a dog after a bone'[55] and 'extremely tight-fisted when it comes to fees'[56] by solicitors who use the chambers regularly. Another solicitor has said, 'I always feel with 11KBW that I'm going to have a battle over fees . . . They're not as flexible over fees as I'd like or as much as they should be. They must make a killing, that chambers.'[57]

Indeed, 11 King's Bench Walk has a reputation for being one of the most expensive sets in London. 'I would say they're pricey,' states a partner with a City law firm. 'They can ask premium prices and Philip's not afraid of asking.' However, when it comes to racking up fees, he believes that 11 King's Bench Walk is no better and no worse than the other top chambers.

Monham may drive a hard bargain, but he is totally upfront in his negotiations, state a number of solicitors. His philosophy on fees is simple, based squarely on the laws of supply and demand. He knows that he has some of the best barristers on his books, and, if people want the best, they are going to have to pay for it.

Monham certainly produced some great results for Irvine: 11 King's Bench Walk's head of chambers had a reputation for enjoying some very big fees – some surprisingly high for a barrister of his standing. A silk at one of the top commercial sets was pleasantly surprised when he saw his fee note in a case in which Irvine was his opponent. The sum in question was considerably more than the silk usually received for such a case – so much more, in fact, that he thought it best to check with his clerk to ensure that there had not been an error. The clerk told him there was no mistake, the silk was simply getting the same amount as his opponent, Derry Irvine.

Another way in which Irvine ensured that he got his hands on plenty of fat fees was by working abroad. In the '80s in particular, Irvine was a regular visitor to Hong Kong, where fees were generally astronomic.

Some barristers choose to go to Hong Kong in order to support the less lucrative, but spiritually and mentally rewarding, areas of their practices. Doing well-paid work in the Far East gives them the freedom to do legal aid cases or *pro bono* (free) work in the UK. But Irvine did no legal aid cases, and little or no *pro bono* work, so his main motive in travelling to the Far East must have been money.

Irvine's biggest-ever brief fee was indeed for work in Hong Kong. Around the end of the '80s, a law firm there decided that Irvine was the only man for them. He, however, already had plenty of work in the UK and did not fancy another trip to the Far East. So, he instructed Monham to tell the Hong Kong solicitors that he was too busy to take the case.

The problem was, the solicitors refused to take no for an answer. They insisted that they had to have Irvine. Losing patience, Irvine told Monham to get rid of them by saying that Irvine would not take the case for anything less than £1 million. To Monham's and Irvine's surprise, this did not prove any deterrent: the solicitors agreed the fee and Irvine duly packed his bags. This is reputed to be the first £1 million brief fee ever earned by a British barrister.

You rang, sir?

Philip Monham is much more than just a tough-talking fee negotiator. A superb administrator, he is an essential cog in the 11

King's Bench Walk machine. One barrister declares: 'Philip runs those chambers. If it was Derry's baby, he couldn't have done it without Philip. He is a superb clerk. I think he's possibly the best I've ever seen.'

Taken on by Irvine when he quit 2 Crown Office Row, Monham has always been utterly dedicated to Irvine and his chambers. Although his hours have recently tailed off a little, for many years he worked as hard as the barristers, arriving at half past six in the morning and not leaving until eight o'clock at night. Weekends would find him either in the chambers or drumming up new business from solicitors. Indeed, Monham's devotion to 11 King's Bench Walk borders on the obsessive. On one occasion, during a train strike, Monham walked all the way in to the Temple from his home in Bromley.

Nothing, it seems, is too much trouble for Monham, who displays infinite patience with both solicitor clients and barristers. His efforts get a mixed response, however. Some solicitors who regularly use 11 King's Bench Walk positively rave about Monham, describing him as one of the best clerks in the business, but others are uncomfortable with his diffident style.

That style was at its most evident in Monham's relationship with Lord Irvine. This was anything but a typical relationship between a senior clerk and a head of chambers. In fact, Monham was more than just Irvine's clerk. He was effectively his butler too.

Irvine loves oranges. However, because God gave him the hands of a blacksmith, he finds peeling fruit awkward. So Monham did it for him.

Irvine is also awkward with anything evenly vaguely technical. At home, his children change his plugs. At 11 King's Bench Walk, he never learnt how to answer the chambers phone after office hours and never mastered the workings of the chambers microwave. Fortunately, Monham was always there to wet nurse Irvine through the day. No task was too menial: Monham would run Irvine's errands and even cook his food.

With time, the relationship between Irvine and Monham

evolved into a series of rituals. At lunch, for example, Irvine would leave his desk, march past the kitchen next to his room, proceed down two corridors, step into the clerks' room and say one word – 'Soup!' He would then turn on his heel and march back to his desk, where, in due course, he was served by Monham.

The word 'please' did not loom large in Irvine's vocabulary, but there was little that Monham would not do for his master. One bemused barrister recalls:

> I was in the clerks' room talking to Philip, and Derry puts his head around the door and goes, 'Philip! Boot polish!' At which point, Philip moved as though propelled by the hand of God out of his chair, seamlessly grabbing the boot polish and the cloth. The next thing I see, as I toddle past the door, is Derry with one foot on a chair and Philip polishing his shoes!

In some ways, the nature of the relationship between Monham and Irvine reveals more about Monham than it does about Irvine. Monham simply lives to serve. He would, given half a chance, do the same for all his barristers. However, the relationship also reveals something about Irvine. The other barristers at 11 King's Bench Walk would never allow Monham to wait upon them hand and foot. They have too much respect for themselves and for Monham.

The good life

Irvine has never been afraid to enjoy the money he made at the Bar. One friend has said, 'He likes the good things in life and makes sure he gets lots of them . . . He's always drinking claret, he's got all these great pictures.'[58]

So far as eating out is concerned, Irvine regularly visits such restaurants as Orso in Covent Garden and Bubb's near Smithfield Market as well as his club, the Garrick. His favourite dishes include grilled prawns, beef and duck, all washed down with plenty of Burgundy – both white and red.

One of Irvine's friends, solicitor Garry Hart, has told the story of what was obviously a none-too-sober dinner at the Garrick some years back. Having consumed a plateful of cutlets, Irvine called the waiter over to demand why the cutlets were taking so long. Another plateful was delivered – and happily devoured.

Irvine takes his wining and dining seriously. Inviting him to dinner is not to be done half-heartedly, suggests a friend: 'If he comes to dinner, first of all you make sure it's good and secondly, you lay in a few extra bottles. The other side of that, however, is that he's an extremely generous host both in terms of quantity and quality.'

Irvine loves playing host, suggests one barrister: 'Socially, what gives him the most pleasure is having a dinner party where there are a lot of interesting people, and the conversation is very stimulating, with everybody making a contribution.' The guests – frequently politicians, writers and artists – not only get to enjoy Lady Irvine's excellent cooking, they get a peek at the Irvine's fabulous art collection. This includes paintings by Walter Sickert, Sir Stanley Spencer, Sir Matthew Smith, Paul Nash, Euan Uglow and Scottish artists such as J.D. Fergusson and S.J. Peploe. Major works by some of these artists have sold at auction for as much as £500,000. Irvine is reported to have around half a dozen pictures by Sickert (considered one of the greatest British artists of the twentieth century) and an even greater number of paintings by Smith and Uglow.

Art is a real passion for both the Irvines, who sometimes arrange their holidays around major art exhibitions. Although he has a particular interest in twentieth-century art, Irvine enjoys works from numerous other eras as well. He not only reads books about art, but also auction catalogues. So formidable is his memory, he can often recall whether a picture has been in auction over the past ten years or more. He has told friends and colleagues that, if he had not been a barrister, he could have made a living as an art dealer.

Lady Irvine, for her part, has a degree in art from Glasgow University and another in history of art, which she obtained from the Courtauld Institute as a mature student. Not surprisingly, Lady Irvine exerts a strong influence over her husband's purchases. A friend, art dealer Peyton Skipworth of the Fine Art Society gallery in New Bond Street, has stated: 'He and his wife make a fantastic team. He is very intuitive, the way he assesses pictures. Alison is both intuitive and trained. But he always buys within his means.' [59]

The couple, who tend to prefer smaller canvases, enter the market on a frequent basis, constantly refining their collection by selling pictures to buy more. They have a reputation for driving a hard bargain. Their friend Maggie Rae declares, 'Derry and Alison are very shrewd collectors. People, I think, assume that what he did was chuck quite a lot of money at it [the collection]. I've no doubt he did, but it was shrewdly chosen and well thought out.'

The better pictures in the collection are to be found at the Irvines' London home, which they have occupied since they were married in 1974. This is a three-storey Victorian house in South Hampstead, which has been beautifully decorated and furnished. Newspaper reports have placed the house's value at £500,000, but this may be a somewhat conservative estimate.

The collection's lesser paintings are kept in the Irvines' Scottish home, on the banks of West Loch Tarbert on the Kintyre peninsula in Argyll. Enjoying stunning views, this is a converted nineteenth-century farmhouse with sixteen bedrooms and has been valued at £300,000. It was to this home that Irvine used to retire with colleagues to work on his cases. Tony Blair has also been a frequent visitor, not least in the months leading up to the 1997 general election. Other guests have included authors Doris Lessing and Alan Bennett, political commentator Robin Day, SDP co-founder Roy Jenkins and various members of the Cabinet.

Baroness Smith has commented:

> They certainly like to fill the house up with people, and that
> must be their way of relaxing. It's fantastic the hospitality

they put on. Three meals a day and 10 to 15 people. He's just an unbelievable host. He's there every minute of the day, trying to make sure you're enjoying yourself.

Everything about the Irvines – their homes, their art, their food, their drink – is impressive. And there to impress, acknowledges a friend: 'There is slightly the Derry who wants to tell you how much he's achieved. The paintings, which are wonderful, actually speak for themselves. You don't have to say, look, that's a Sickert! And that's a this or that!'

Irvine will not only tell guests the name of the artist, he will also proudly proclaim that a picture is of 'museum quality' and state its value. Those who accuse him of being very New Labour have only got half the story. Irvine is also very New Money.

CHAPTER FIVE

Militant!

During a tour of Australia in the early 1980s, Tony Blair declared: 'Militant is an avowedly Trotskyist group, whose links go back to the Revolutionary Socialist League in the 1960s . . . Militant say that they only sell the *Militant* paper. It is, in effect, a secret conspiracy, a party within the party.'[60]

The Militant tendency's hold on the Labour Party had grown substantially after Labour's disastrous 1979 general election defeat. Militant took full advantage of the party's disarray, recruiting Labour Party members and infiltrating the party hierarchy at all levels. These activities went totally unchecked. The Left and Right were too busy blaming each other for the election defeat to do anything about Militant, while the strains of the Callaghan years had left those at the top tired and unable to give a lead. The fractious state of the party was fully revealed in 1981, when Tony Benn challenged Denis Healey for the deputy leadership and, again, in 1981, with the defections that led to the birth of the Social Democratic Party.

The threat from Militant was, in fact, nothing new. The tendency had been a force within the Labour Party since the 1950s. More recently, in 1975, Labour's national agent, Reg Underhill, had produced a report called 'Entryist Activities', most of which was devoted to the activities of the tendency. However, no action was taken at the time through a combination of left-wing manoeuvring and right-wing apathy.

In 1980, with Militant activity on the increase, Underhill updated his report. Still nothing happened. Michael Foot, who became Labour Party leader that year, was most reluctant to plunge his fragile party into a purge. Former Labour Party leader Neil Kinnock explains:

> In the wake of Reg's 1975 report there were some people who were quiet-lifers and thought: yes, this phenomenon of entryism exists but it's tiny and it may be inconvenient but it will never pose any threat to the Labour Party, so why engage in some great turmoil? Then, secondly, there was a libertarian element, including people like Michael Foot and myself, who said: people have the right to hold opinions, Labour's a broad church, etc., etc., etc. And, of course, for Michael's generation and for mine to a lesser extent there was the memory of the devastating splits of the 1950s. So the mixture of libertarianism and the spirit of unity provided an environment in which nothing effective was done about the Militant tendency.

By the autumn of 1981, however, Foot was left with no choice but to take action. Union leaders were reporting increased Militant infiltration of their memberships and more and more MPs were voicing fears about being deselected in favour of Militant sympathisers. The party had suffered a string of bad by-election results and had slipped behind the SDP and Liberals in the polls. At a meeting of Labour's National Executive Committee (NEC) in December, Foot pushed through a resolution to establish a full-scale inquiry into Militant.

The two men who carried out the investigation, general secretary Ron Hayward and national agent David Hughes, reported back to the NEC in June 1982. Their findings amounted to a declaration of war on Militant.

The report concluded that Militant was not a group formed solely to support a newspaper and that it had a hard core of supporters forming an organisation with its own programme and policy for distinctive and separate propaganda. This meant that the tendency was in conflict with Clause 2(3) of the Labour Party's constitution, which provided that political organisations not affiliated to or associated with the party were ineligible for affiliation if they had their own agenda. Hayward and Hughes went on to recommend that the NEC should set up a register of non-affiliated groups of members that would be allowed to operate within the party and declared that, in the authors' opinion, the Militant tendency was not eligible for inclusion on the proposed register.

At the September 1982 Labour Party conference in Blackpool, two significant events occurred that paved the way for action to be taken against Militant. First, the conference endorsed the Hayward–Hughes report. Second, the balance of power in the NEC shifted to the right. Tackling Militant was still going to be anything but easy, however, because the right wing of the party did not enjoy an outright majority on the NEC and had to depend on the support of left-wing trade unionists who were not entirely committed to the anti-Militant campaign.

The decision was taken that, as a first step, charges should be laid against just five people: Keith Dickinson, Clare Doyle, Ted Grant, Peter Taafe and Lynn Walsh – the editorial board of *Militant*. The main reason for making such a limited initial attack was that proving a case against other members of the tendency was going to be anything but easy. The big problem, states Kinnock, was producing evidence that Militant was an organisation: 'Everybody knew there were Militant full-time organisers everywhere. But, since there were no payments to them, no accounts, it was impossible to prove it.' In the case of the five who had been charged, Labour could at least point to the fact that they had been producing a subversive newspaper.

One of the five charged, *Militant* editor Peter Taafe, complained that the Militant tendency was being unfairly treated and warned that it had taken legal advice. Militant's lawyers, claimed Taafe, had advised them that the NEC's action was unconstitutional and open to challenge in the courts.

The threat struck home. A legal suit was the last thing Labour wanted. The party's leadership had no desire to get embroiled in a time-consuming and potentially expensive action. Worse still, a defeat in the courts would be highly embarrassing and would hand Militant exactly the kind of publicity it was seeking.

The leadership's fears were not allayed by a legal opinion that suggested that members of the tendency would have a strong case if they took legal action. The opinion had been independently obtained by the right-wing Solidarity Campaign, of which John Smith was a prominent member. Smith had turned to his old friend Derry Irvine, who advised that Labour was courting disaster by pursuing selective expulsions. In response to Irvine's advice, the NEC chose to drop all other expulsion plans and to focus entirely on kicking out the five members of *Militant*'s editorial board.

Political dissension

The phoney war ended on 14 December 1982 when the five applied to the Chancery Division of the High Court for an interim (temporary) injunction. Their lawyers asked the court to grant an order restraining the NEC from considering and endorsing a resolution to declare Militant a separate party – a resolution that would, if passed, comprise a significant step towards their eventual expulsion.

With the NEC meeting due to take place the next day, the timing of the court action was clearly calculated to cause Labour as much embarrassment as possible. The same was true of the choice of venue. In the Queen's Bench, applications for injunctions are heard privately in a judge's chambers. But in the Chancery Division such applications are made in open court, so the public and the press are entitled to attend.

The editorial board's legal advisers, solicitors Fisher Meredith and barrister David Altaras, had not missed a trick. Applications for interim injunctions are made *ex parte*, that is, with only the applicants and their lawyers attending the hearing. However, the board's legal team had advised their clients to give notice to the Labour Party. Their reasoning was that, if the injunction were granted, Labour would find it much more difficult to get a judge to overturn the injunction if the party had been given the chance to put its case at the initial hearing.

Nevertheless, having been given only a few days' notice, there was no guarantee that Labour would send along a legal team to oppose the injunction application. And, even if it did, the odds remained in the editorial board's favour because Labour's lawyers had not had much time to prepare.

Fortunately for Labour, the editorial board's team were not quite as organised as they might have been. Militant's managing editor, Lynn Walsh, reveals that he and his colleagues had originally intended to instruct both Altaras and his head of chambers, David Turner-Samuels QC. The senior man, he states,

> had a reputation for being a very strong, sort-of-leftist lawyer. But he was very, very lukewarm about our case and clearly didn't want to do it. And that's why we decided that David Altaras should do it in court. We would have preferred a QC, but . . . we really didn't have the time to go to another QC and David knew the background to the case.

Altaras was more than happy to do the case on his own. In any event, he was not entirely sure that the opposition would show. 'I trolled along to court on the day at the Royal Courts of Justice,' he recalls, 'and to my horror, this lumbering bear-like figure appeared – it was Derry!'

Lynn Walsh was not surprised. A Young Socialists representative on the NEC was feeding the *Militant* editorial board information. Walsh and the others knew well in advance that Irvine would be turning up and that he would not be alone. Sure enough, Irvine brought with him his junior, Tony Blair, and Lord Milner, senior partner of the Labour Party's solicitors, Milners, Curry & Gaskell.

Irvine's most important companion, however, was a rather large pile of affidavits. The affidavits, sworn statements by Labour Party officials, provided a detailed history of the dispute between the two sides. Many had documents (known as exhibits) attached to them, such as the Labour Party's constitution and NEC resolutions. Irvine's aim was to prove that correct procedures had been followed at each stage, that the plaintiffs had been given ample opportunity to put their case and that it was now too late to challenge the Blackpool conference's decision.

Irvine and his team had done a fabulous job in getting both the affidavits and themselves ready. Altaras admits that he had not expected his opponents to be half so well prepared:

> They must have worked overnight to get the affidavits with the exhibits ready, really put a lot of work into it. I suspect Derry was behind it. He was a person who had a reputation of being a very hard worker, not afraid of burning the midnight oil. And, again, he knew the contents of the affidavits so well that I suspect he had a big hand in putting them together.

The hard work had been worth while. Overnight, the tables were turned and the editorial board's lawyers had to struggle to keep up. Altaras believes that the affidavits played a highly significant role in the eventual outcome of the case:

> Of course, if you just give a party notice on an *ex parte* application, you can't really complain if they come along at the last minute and hand you a bundle of affidavits! So, I had this big bundle of affidavits and I think, in retrospect, I would have been better advised to have told the judge that I wanted an hour or two or three to study them.

Instead, Altaras chose to press ahead. He ran into immediate trouble. In his opening submission to the judge, Mr Justice Nourse,

Altaras committed the crime of mispronouncing his opponent's name. Irvine was not best pleased, hissing the correct pronunciation across the courtroom.

Altaras recalls that he did his best to retrieve the situation through a spot of humour: 'I said to the judge, "Political dissension has broken out already – we have some ideological dispute about the correct pronunciation of my learned friend's name!" Nourse thought it was quite funny, but Derry wasn't amused at all.'

Then again, appearing against Irvine was never exactly fun, states Altaras: 'He never struck me as having an enormous sense of humour in court. So, humour was not the high point and I thought it was fun just to prick him occasionally.'

The contrast between Irvine and his junior could not have been greater, suggests Altaras. Tony Blair, he says, had 'a beautiful, easy manner in court and was charming outside court'. Irvine, on the other hand, was 'a disagreeable opponent, as disagreeable as Tony was agreeable . . . he was a forensic bully – he socked it to you . . . he was very intense and quite bitter when he was shooting down his opponent's case.'

Altaras was not the only one who had strong views about Irvine. Lynn Walsh confesses he was completely taken aback by Irvine's behaviour in court:

> I had been involved in various court actions before and it always seemed to me that the courts were surprisingly low key. People would get up and mumble their arguments. There wasn't much heat or exchange. But Irvine wasn't like that at all. He seemed to me to be in the style of advocates you've heard of in the past, like F.E. Smith. He would stride into the court, so the immediate impression is he's a very belligerent, pompous, self-important character. When he spoke he was very loud and bombastic. Even now, I've never heard a barrister speak so loud in court.

Listening to Irvine, he suggests, was like travelling back in time:

It was like something from the days of oratory when there were no PA systems and you had to address 10,000 people with the power of your voice and roll all your words and exaggerate them to be heard . . . He had what I thought was a rather exaggerated, rhetorical delivery. It was almost like an actor playing a barrister in the courtroom.

Irvine was both angry and aggressive, states Walsh:

He glared quite a lot. He used to turn around and glare at me . . . Irvine was savage with Altaras as well. When he was speaking, he used to turn around and glare at him. It was almost like a personal tone: Why are you arguing such a stupid case? This is rubbish! That's not what he said, but that was his tone of voice. Meanwhile, Tony Blair was sitting there. As far as I recall, he didn't say anything. He didn't contribute to the proceedings. He just sat there grinning most of the time.

Although he did not enjoy the experience, David Altaras acknowledges that Irvine put on a fine performance: 'He was impressive. When he was on his feet and arguing, I knew I was losing. I got that sinking feeling and I knew I was going down the pan.'

Every time Altaras raised an issue, Irvine had an answer. When Altaras pointed out that his clients had not been allowed to see the evidence gathered for the Hayward–Hughes report, Irvine countered with a two-pronged attack. He argued that the plaintiffs had never enjoyed a right to see that evidence or to be given particulars of it. Alternatively, if they did enjoy that right, they should have exercised it when they received a copy of the report back in July or, at the very least, before the Labour Party conference in September. He claimed that it was clear all along that the report endangered their continued membership of the party. By failing to act, the plaintiffs had effectively elected to fight the issue at the conference without the benefit of seeing the report's evidence.

The NEC's actions were not open to criticism, suggested Irvine. All it had done was carry out the will of the conference. Furthermore, the NEC was not at liberty to reopen conference's decision, which is what would happen if the plaintiffs were allowed to see the Hayward–Hughes evidence. Their application was an attempt to resurrect a debate they had lost at conference.

Altaras pleaded that the plaintiffs could not act until after conference made its decision because they did not have any legal standing (right of action) before then. He also claimed that the expulsion process could not be said to have started until the beginning of December when the plaintiffs were notified of the proposed NEC resolution that was the subject of these legal proceedings.

Mr Justice Nourse rejected both those arguments. He agreed with Irvine that the threat to the plaintiffs' continued membership of the Labour Party was clear from the end of June and held that the courts would not have excluded the plaintiffs for lack of standing at that date. Nourse declared that he could not ignore the political realities of the situation: it was obvious that the plaintiffs knew what was going on all along and had a very good idea of what the Hayward–Hughes evidence comprised. Finally, the judge accepted Irvine's submission that it would be wrong for him to interfere with the consequences of the Labour Party's decision in conference when the courts could have been, but were not, asked to act before the decision was made.

Irvine's performance had not been pretty, but it had been highly effective. 'Like the good advocate he is, Derry fed him all his judgement points,' says Altaras. 'Nourse just picked up all Derry's arguments, one after another. And that's the sign of a great advocate.'

Altaras recalls that his clients were not surprised by the result: 'I think the Labour Party took it more seriously than the five did. I think the five were always terribly suspicious about the bourgeois court system.' His clients, he suggests, had other things on their minds:

> This was merely one string to their bow, and one they weren't particularly comfortable with. I think for them it was much more likely in their mind that they were going to win through the political medium. I think they were expecting the mobilisation of the grass roots, that they would win that way.

Altaras advised his clients not to bother appealing. There was, he says, no point in doing so: 'I said this is a question of discretion. There's no law involved in it, really. It's just a question of the judge's discretion, and he chose not to [grant the injunction]. It's very difficult to appeal against that when there's no law in it.'

Nonetheless, Walsh clearly feels that this is a case that his side could and should have won. *Militant*'s young barrister, suggests Walsh, was a bit flummoxed by the belligerent show put on by Labour's QC:

> Derry tore into him so much. It was an intimidatory performance, there's no doubt about it. I must say that I felt that Altaras was kind of unnerved by it. My response would have been to be much more combative against Irvine. But he didn't seem to respond to Irvine's arguments and I think that's because he was surprised by the ferocity and the fact that they weren't really legal arguments. He [Irvine] didn't try to counteract Altaras's case, he simply tried to lambaste him.

Irvine's calculated performance covered up the weaknesses in Labour's case, he claims:

> As in other cases, the Labour Party counsel tended to throw up a barrage of arguments. My analogy would be that it's

like anti-aircraft fire – you simply spread it across the sky and the judge picks on what he thinks was the most reasonable out of the case.

A stronger, more active judge might have exposed the holes in Irvine's case, suggests Walsh, but Nourse was disappointingly quiet. He said little and asked few questions. Walsh also believes that Nourse was wrong to focus on the fact that the editorial board had not taken legal action earlier:

> The reason we didn't go to court earlier is because that would have been seen as trying to pre-empt the Labour Party conference and that was before there was any decision on the Hayward–Hughes report. If we'd gone to court any earlier, Irvine would have been in court saying, 'Oh, these people are trying to short-circuit the democratic procedures of the Labour Party.' So you couldn't win.

The most remarkable part of Nourse's judgement, however, was his assertion that he could not ignore the fact that the *Militant* editorial board had probably seen the evidence gathered during the Hayward–Hughes inquiry. Given the many other leaks suffered by the NEC, this may well have been true. But Nourse may have erred in making such an assumption. It would appear to be contrary to the rules of natural justice. It is incumbent on an accuser to give an accused sight of all evidence being used against the accused and a proper opportunity to comment on that evidence. This is made transparently clear in a report to the NEC dated 26 January 1983, a copy of which was leaked to the *Militant* editorial board. The report reveals that, after the injunction hearing, Irvine and Blair advised the NEC that:

> Natural justice requires that each individual against whom an allegation of membership of the Militant tendency is being made, should be given a notice of the resolutions

adopted by the National Executive Committee, particulars of all the facts relied upon to support the allegation that he is a member of the Militant tendency, an opportunity to comment in writing on these particulars, and an opportunity, subsequently and before any decision to expel, to be heard orally by the National Executive Committee.

Irvine knew this all along, of course. However, thanks to his bravado at the injunction hearing, the Labour Party had not been obliged to reveal all of its evidence, most of which was probably weak.

In an attempt to ensure that the problem did not arise again, the NEC adopted – at Irvine's instigation – two resolutions designed to enable the Labour Party to effect expulsions while at the same time protecting the party from accusations of breaching natural justice. The second resolution stated that the Labour Party must act in accordance with the principles of natural justice and that the accused should be given the opportunity to denounce Militant and stay in the Labour Party.

The five members of *Militant*'s editorial board were expelled from the Labour Party at a meeting of the NEC at Walworth Road in February 1983. That action was duly confirmed at the Labour Party conference at Brighton in November. Looking back, Kinnock concedes that the expulsions did not achieve what the Labour Party leadership had hoped:

> Some thought it would have a deterrent effect. Others thought that it would demonstrate that Labour was putting its house in order. Of course, it didn't cut off the head, it just made the head more independent without any form of obligation to the rules of Labour Party membership. It therefore, sadly, proved to be ineffective.

Nevertheless, the legal victory in December was 'critical', acknowledges Kinnock. Defeat at that time would have been humiliating and demoralising for a Labour Party already in dreadful straits. A reverse would also have put the party right back at square one in its fight against Militant. The campaign would have continued, insists Kinnock, 'but we would have had to do it in a different way. We would have had to change the constitution before any form of action was taken.'

This would not have been easy. Indeed, given the divisions between Left and Right, the apathy of some and the excessively tolerant attitude of others, it may well have been impossible. It had been a close-run thing, but Derry Irvine had got the job done.

Not losing

November 1983 was a highly significant moment in the history of Labour's battle with Militant. Apart from the expulsion of the *Militant* editorial board, the party conference saw the emergence of a new leader. Elected on the first ballot with 71 per cent of the votes cast, Neil Kinnock was in a much stronger position to take on Militant than Michael Foot had ever been.

Kinnock did not share Michael Foot's reluctance in tackling the tendency. He relished the opportunity of attacking an organisation that he later described as 'a maggot on the body of the party'.[61]

However, in the years immediately following Kinnock's election as leader, the Labour leadership was not in a position to do much about the Militant tendency. Kinnock explains:

> The problem was we had the miners' strike between March '84 and March '85 preceded by several months of work-to-rule action by the union and followed by some months of reeling from the total commitment of the Labour Party to that strike and all of its massive social implications. So, effectively, the Labour Party was completely engaged with that and not with other things.

Some action against Militant was taken at local party level. However, the Labour Party suffered as many defeats as it won victories and, even when successful, it had little to show for all the energy expended. A local party expulsion would always be followed by an appeal to the NEC. With those in favour of tackling Militant not enjoying a clear majority, the process of getting the NEC to refuse an appeal could be long and very painful.

In any event, few local parties had the heart for such a tough fight, acknowledges Kinnock:

> The difficulty with the very small number of expulsions taken by individual constituency parties was that it did require a particular resolution amongst the broad mainstream of the party to do it, especially since quite a lot of the people in Militant were real sloggers, sympathetic young people who would turn out any rainy night to canvass in a council by-election. They were totally dedicated and they were totally dedicated to the Labour Party, not just to Militant. To drag them before a general management committee in a party that is renowned for its heart and its soul and its 'They're only youngsters, they'll learn' attitude – all features that I love about the Labour Party – required a very, very particular sense of resolution.

The pattern of occasional expulsions by local parties was not sustainable. Kinnock needed to find a bigger challenge that could be fought on the national stage – something that would unite the majority of the party against the Militant tendency. Kinnock knew he had to bide his time for the right opportunity. As it turned out, he did not have to wait too long: events in Liverpool played into his hands.

With its many economic problems and high unemployment rate, Liverpool had long been a Militant stronghold. The city's Militant-dominated council was determined to provoke a confrontation with Mrs Thatcher's government over rate-capping. In 1984 a crisis was narrowly averted when, after concessions were made by the Government, Liverpool agreed to fix a balanced budget. In 1985, however, the council literally went for broke by setting a rate that would result in an illegal 9 per cent deficit.

By the end of August, council officials were warning councillors that the city would be bankrupt by the end of the year and that the councillors would then be on the hook for all the city's liabilities, in particular, its huge wage bill. If the councillors wanted to avoid footing that bill, 90-day redundancy notices had to be issued no later than September.

In a move designed to force the Government's hand, the council decided to declare no fewer than 31,000 redundancies. For some unions, this was a step too far, and they refused to distribute the notices. So, shop stewards from the General, Municipal, Boilermakers and Allied Trades Union (GMBATU) took them round the city in a fleet of 30 hired taxis.

As the councillors had planned, the notices were never to take effect. An agreement between the council and the Government was reached towards the end of November. However, the decision to send out redundancy notices was a huge tactical error on the part of Militant. It laid itself open to attack and Neil Kinnock did not hesitate to seize the opportunity. At the Labour Party conference in Brighton in October 1985, in a moment of great political theatre, Kinnock told the conference that Militant's campaign against the Tory government had culminated in 'the grotesque chaos of a Labour council – a *Labour* council – hiring taxis to scuttle around a city handing out redundancy notices to its own workers'.

Although one left-wing Liverpool MP, the NEC member Eric Heffer, quit the stage during the speech, Kinnock's attack did not immediately spark the confrontation he sought. Much to Kinnock's annoyance, Sheffield Council leader and NEC member David Blunkett brokered a compromise with Derek Hatton, Liverpool City Council's sharp-suited, publicity-loving deputy leader. Hatton agreed to allow a team of independent auditors to inspect the city council's books.

Kinnock admits that Blunkett's action left him 'incandescent'. Kinnock had stoked up the fire against the Militant tendency, only for Blunkett to release the pressure. 'Patently, David Blunkett didn't understand or maybe didn't want to understand – I don't know which – the nature of the beast,' states Kinnock. The Labour Party leader need not have worried, however. The problem created by Blunkett was overcome when the leaders of Liverpool Council rejected the auditors' findings.

The auditors had reported to union leaders Ron Todd (Transport and General Workers' Union) and John Edwards (GMBATU) that the only thing that had prevented Liverpool from finding a solution to its financial difficulties was Militant's determination to confront the Government. After Kinnock encouraged Todd and Edwards to write to the NEC demanding an inquiry, his plans were back on track.

In November 1985 the NEC appointed eight of its members to carry out the inquiry and suspended the Liverpool Labour Party for its duration. Shortly afterwards, the battle moved back into the legal arena and Irvine was again instructed to act on behalf of the Labour Party.

In mid-January 1986 the Liverpool councillors, who were also the defendants in a rate surcharge action, attempted to get the High Court to freeze the inquiry for the duration of the legal surcharge case. Their lawyers claimed there had been leaks from the Labour Party inquiry that might lead to contempts of court. However, Irvine persuaded the judges that the inquiry was private and unrelated to the court proceedings.

At the end of January, lawyers acting for a number of people whose activities were being investigated in the inquiry applied to the High Court for an injunction preventing the NEC from considering and acting upon the inquiry's findings. However, when an affidavit from Labour Party general secretary Larry Whitty was produced, the plaintiffs' lawyers withdrew their application. Whitty's affidavit declared that the plaintiffs' action was premature and misconceived. The investigation was still at a preliminary stage, he said, and the inquiry team had no power to make final decisions about what should be done. It would be the NEC's function to consider the report and decide whether disciplinary action should be taken. If such action were taken, everything would be done in accordance with the rules of natural justice.

The Liverpool inquiry team's report was released in February 1986. It made two main recommendations: the Liverpool Labour Party should be reformed and charges should be drawn up against 16 individuals, including Derek Hatton and Tony Mulhearn, chairman of the district Labour Party and a Liverpool councillor.

In February, the NEC approved the report. However, charges against 4 of the 16 were dropped for lack of evidence.

History then repeated itself. With the NEC due to meet at the end of March 1986 to hear the expulsion charges, the 12 remaining members of Militant applied to the High Court, claiming that they had been denied natural justice and requesting an injunction to delay the hearings. Labour would not have been alarmed by this turn of events. Towards the end of the inquiry, Larry Whitty had obtained legal advice – presumably from Irvine – that the Liverpool inquiry report was bomb-proof.

At the hearing, the barrister for the 12 defendants, Ian Hunter QC, argued, among other things, that the 8 members of the NEC who had sat on the inquiry team should be barred from the expulsion hearings. He claimed they would effectively be acting as prosecution and jury. Hunter then argued – just as David Altaras had done in December 1982 – that his clients should be given an opportunity to challenge *all* the evidence the NEC proposed to use against them. (Through fear of reprisal, some witnesses had insisted that their evidence be treated in confidence by the NEC.)

According to *Militant*'s Lynn Walsh, who attended the hearing and had been advising the 12 plaintiffs, the Labour Party's silk was up to all his old tricks. 'Irvine was even more pompous and steamed up than he was in our case,' he says. 'He was very agitated.'

This time around, however, the judge did not allow Irvine to ride roughshod all over the case. The Vice-Chancellor, Sir Nicolas

Browne-Wilkinson, was made of sterner stuff than Mr Justice Nourse, suggests Walsh:

> There was a lot more to-ing and fro-ing in the exchanges, because Browne-Wilkinson was much more actively involved in the discussion than Nourse. He asked a lot of questions and made a lot of comments. He interrupted all the counsel quite a lot. And Irvine didn't like that. He clearly gets flustered when the judge interrupts his flights of rhetoric. And my impression was that Browne-Wilkinson was irritated by him. Browne-Wilkinson has this reputation for being a very intellectual judge who carefully considers the legal issues and he wasn't impressed by this kind of 'barnstorming tirades' approach and he possibly deliberately would interrupt Irvine and say, 'Yes, but what about this?' and Irvine would have to stop in his tracks and deal with something that he considered trivial or irrelevant.

Browne-Wilkinson was seeking to promote a debate on the real issues. But Irvine seemed incapable of taking part in that debate, says Walsh:

> It's just not his style. He seemed to be annoyed. And it's like in a political argument – if you get annoyed with somebody, you can't think properly. If somebody's getting you angry, you're not able to deal with all the arguments or respond in a flexible way. It's a lack of flexibility, I would think . . . Everything has to be ordered and sequenced and, when it's thrown out, he has to start again and build his pyramid again.

As he had done in 1982, Irvine covered up the flaws in his case by putting up a barrage of arguments. Some of the points he made looked desperate, to say the least. On the issue of the evidence given in confidence, Irvine told Browne-Wilkinson that the NEC was not going to see or hear that evidence. Instead, the NEC was simply going to be told that evidence had been given and that it was adverse to the accused. Irvine suggested that this highly unusual procedure was justifiable in the public interest. He gave three reasons for this: Militant's intimidatory tactics should not be allowed to succeed; Labour should be allowed to root out Militant and its iniquities; and one of the country's major political parties should be allowed to put its house in order.

Browne-Wilkinson threw out those arguments. In his judgement he stated:

> Whatever the public interest involved, there is a major, and to my mind overwhelming public interest in ensuring that decisions are not made affecting the livelihood and future of individuals by domestic bodies without the procedure adopted being fair in the broadest sense ... It is contrary to the rules of natural justice, even in a case such as this, to seek to find a man guilty of a charge having serious consequences for him on the basis of evidence not disclosed to him or even its gist disclosed to him.

On the issue of whether the inquiry members could take part in the expulsion hearings, Irvine argued that the eight people in question had not formed a view on the accused while gathering evidence. He even produced affidavits from six of them, stating that they would be approaching the matter with an open mind.

Again, Browne-Wilkinson had no time for this line of argument. He concluded:

> I can only say as a judge I know how extremely difficult it is, having heard evidence over many days, to put completely out of one's mind the things that one has heard. It is just not possible to put things wholly from your mind. These people have heard this evidence. They cannot help having formed views. In my judgement, a reasonable man would have an

apprehension of real risk of a conclusion or a strong *prima facie* view against them.

The 12 members of Militant did not get everything their own way. Browne-Wilkinson denied their requests that, when appearing before the inquiry, they be allowed to call any witnesses they wanted and that they be permitted to use legal representation. (The 12 were clearly seeking to make the expulsion hearings as slow and difficult as possible.) Most important of all, the judge did not declare that the expulsion hearings should not go ahead.

Browne-Wilkinson's judgement was certainly an embarrassment for Labour, but it was not a disaster. In footballing terms, the result of the March 1986 hearing was a score draw and that was enough to allow the Labour Party to proceed with the expulsions. As Neil Kinnock sums up: 'All that was important about that case, of course, was not to lose it. Winning didn't matter. *Not losing* mattered.'

The expulsion hearings began the day after the legal hearing. Unfortunately for Labour, they did not last long. Seven left-wing NEC members, led by Tony Benn and Eric Heffer, walked out in protest at the way the hearings were being conducted. Already missing the eight members excluded by Browne-Wilkinson's judgement, the NEC was now down to fourteen members – too few for a quorum.

The seven left-wingers strenuously denied that their exit was premeditated. However, their action delivered to Militant exactly the kind of publicity coup it had been looking for. On its own doorstep, Labour had to suffer the huge embarrassment of a group of Militant supporters singing the 'Internationale' and 'Red Flag' with their fists raised in defiance.

This humiliation had been on the horizon for a long time. The Labour Party was in disarray and had not planned the inquiry properly. The party, it seemed, had learnt nothing from the legal action in December 1982 and was again expecting to rely on evidence that was not going to be disclosed to the accused. Nor had the party thought through the obvious consequences of using NEC members to carry out the Liverpool inquiry. Incredibly, none of the party seemed to believe it was unfair to allow the people who had compiled the evidence to participate in the expulsion hearings.

Even the inquiry's objectives were not clear. Neil Kinnock wanted the inquiry to do no more than collect evidence proving membership of the tendency. But Larry Whitty and David Blunkett thought the inquiry should examine possible breaches in Labour Party rules. In the end, Whitty and Blunkett got their way. However, when it came to the expulsion hearings, there was a lack of conclusive evidence to prove that people were members of the Militant tendency.

The party should have called in lawyers to give advice from the start. Instead, it seems likely that Irvine was only called in once the inquiry was almost completed. By that time, it was too late to do anything about the way in which evidence had been collected or about the choice of NEC members to carry out the inquiry. Nevertheless, there is no getting away from the fact that the report was far from bomb-proof and that faulty legal advice was given.

It's got to happen

By the time the expulsion hearings finally went ahead in May, charges had been dropped against another of the accused. The hearings crawled along at a painfully slow pace. After two days, the proceedings had lasted 27 hours and yet only three people had been expelled. Most of the time had been taken up with legal and procedural wrangling.

Derek Hatton, the number one target of Kinnock's purge, was not expelled until mid-June, and then only after a further legal battle. Hatton claimed he could not attend his expulsion hearing because he was too busy with Liverpool City Council affairs. His solicitor Mike Fisher, of Fisher Meredith, was given the opportunity to address the hearing. He tried to persuade the NEC to postpone the hearing until his client could attend. When the NEC opted to go ahead with the hearing, Fisher applied to the High Court for yet another injunction to halt the proceedings.

The judge – Browne-Wilkinson again – granted Hatton a temporary injunction, causing the NEC to break for lunch. Nerves were now fraying, reveals Kinnock:

> I had a conversation with some people over that break. For understandable reasons, they were saying, 'How long is this going to take?' And I said to them, 'Listen, if we never leave this building for the next three months it's got to happen. I don't give a damn how long it takes and I don't think any of you people are just going to turn your back and walk out of the door. And if you do, don't ever even think of coming back in.' And they stayed firm.

That afternoon, Vice-Chancellor Browne-Wilkinson accepted Irvine's argument that Hatton had absented himself from the expulsion hearing merely to be obstructive and revoked the injunction. Free from further interruptions, the NEC confirmed Hatton's expulsion later that day.

The legal victory over Hatton was a big turning point, says Neil Kinnock: 'In some ways, that broke it. Because of the outcome of that case, the [expulsion hearing] restarted, as I recall it, in a totally different atmosphere.'

The expulsions came to an end in September. At the Labour Party conference in Blackpool, Hatton, Mulhearn and five other Militant supporters walked out of the conference rather than defend themselves. Their expulsions were then confirmed by a massive majority.

After the dust settled, Irvine assisted the Labour Party in finally getting its act together by recommending two reforms that were to have major long-term repercussions on how the party was run. First, the party's constitution was amended to introduce the concept of a National Policy Forum. The then leadership was not particularly sold on the idea and the forum did not really come into its own until Tony Blair became leader. Blair has been an enthusiastic proponent, recognising that the forum allows him to exercise much greater control over the party's policy making. Second, the leadership took greater control of shortlists of candidates in order to ensure more loyalty to those at the top.

Although the fight against Militant had been won, Labour was in no position to crow. The tendency had won some significant media victories and had, on occasion, made the Labour Party leadership look foolish. But, thanks to Irvine, the campaign against Militant had never quite ground to a halt. Through sheer force of personality and dogged determination he had succeeded against considerable odds.

Irvine had harboured serious doubts about Labour's chances, reveals Kinnock:

> Derry's advice was that it was dangerous to proceed. And my judgement was that the risks had to be taken. And so the risks were taken. And, in the wake of it all, Derry said to me that I was the most dangerous litigant he had ever represented in his life. They were his exact words . . . But we had to take risks and they were damn big risks too.

Irvine's performance was brave, suggests Kinnock. It was not just the Labour Party that had much to lose:

> He [Irvine] never backed off, even though, in some respects, not only the well-being of the Labour Party was at stake, but, to a degree, his own reputation. And he was willing to invest that. You can't ask more of anybody.

A stranger in the House

Irvine did not charge the Labour Party for his work. Not cash, at any rate. But one year after the last Militant legal action he received a very different kind of reward when he was created a life peer. He took the title Baron Irvine of Lairg in the District of Sutherland in honour of his mother.

There was a second motive behind giving Irvine a title, confirms Neil Kinnock: Irvine was being lined up as a potential Lord Chancellor. Indeed, Kinnock reveals that Irvine would have been his Lord Chancellor in 1992 if Labour had won that year's general election. As it turned out Labour's fourth successive defeat did not damage Irvine's prospects of becoming Lord Chancellor. When Kinnock stood down as Labour Party leader, he was replaced by John Smith, who immediately named his best friend as his shadow Lord Chancellor.

Despite this appointment, Irvine remained an infrequent visitor to the House of Lords. He has blamed his poor attendance on work and family commitments. However, if he was serious about being Lord Chancellor, it is remarkable that he did not make more of an effort to attend the House.

Irvine's and Smith's dream of working together in a Labour government was tantalisingly close to realisation. With a fifth consecutive Tory win looking increasingly unlikely, it seemed only a matter of time before Irvine played Lord Chancellor to his old pal's Prime Minister.

Towards the end of 1993 Irvine and Smith had dinner at Irvine's club, the Garrick. Smith asked Irvine if he remembered a conversation they had held in a coffee shop in Glasgow back in 1962. The two young men had discussed their ambitions, Smith declaring that he wanted to be Secretary of State for Scotland and Irvine staking a claim for Lord Advocate. Smith pointed out that both had subsequently revised their ambitions upwards.

But the dream was not to be. Smith died in May 1994 and later that month Irvine was one of the pallbearers at Smith's funeral in

Cluny parish church in Morningside, Edinburgh. Along with two more of Smith's oldest friends – James Gordon and Donald Dewar – Irvine was asked by Smith's widow, Elizabeth, to say a few words.

Irvine declared:

> He was driven by a set of moral imperatives that owe everything to his inherited conscience. He was born with a compelling sense of public duty to improve the lives of every member of this community, especially the disadvantaged, by levelling up, not levelling down . . . [62]

The public and the private John Smith were two very different people, added Irvine. The media, he said, had given Smith 'the image of the prudent bank manager, the cautious Edinburgh lawyer. Prudent he certainly was, but anyone who has seen John as master of the revels, leading from the front, cannot quite come to terms with the image.' Friends knew a man who had relished the absurd, with a wonderful sense of comedy.[63]

Irvine also told the story of how he had advised Smith not to accept the post of Solicitor-General during Labour's previous period in office. 'The law,' said Irvine, 'was not big enough for John Smith.'[64]

Making speeches at funerals is never easy. However, the fact remains that Irvine's rather ponderous phrases were upstaged by some lines scribbled on the back of an envelope just a few hours before the funeral by Donald Dewar. Irvine's rival spoke from the heart, perfectly capturing the mood when he said:

> Those who saw John as [sedate], dark-suited and safe knew not the man. He could start a party in an empty room, and often did. The people know they have lost a friend, someone who was on their side. They know it, and they feel it.

Smith's death might easily have spelt the end for Irvine's political ambitions. Instead, it was the making of them. John Smith was replaced as Labour leader by another close friend, Tony Blair.

From Irvine's point of view, this was a truly remarkable turn of events. Indeed, Irvine has boasted ever since that he was close to two successive Labour Party leaders. However, this did not happen purely by chance. Irvine had been doing everything he could for many years to progress his former pupil's political career. With Smith dead, he was not going to stop now.

Irvine was heavily involved in Blair's leadership campaign, sending out letters to Blair's friends and supporters, inviting them to donate a minimum of £100 to Blair's cause. This, he said, would enable Blair to present his vision of a Labour government 'of which he will be the Prime Minister'.[65] The fundraising drive proved extremely successful, provoking some Labour Party members to complain that the leadership campaign was not fought on a level playing field.

Irvine was also happy to twist arms, telling people Smith had wanted Blair, not Gordon Brown, to succeed him. Indeed, he later told one of Blair's biographers, John Rentoul: 'During the last six months of his life, John Smith made it clear to me on several occasions that he favoured Tony as his successor.'[66] However, another Blair biographer, Jon Sopel, has written that Elizabeth Smith was keen for Brown to run for the leadership.

The Smiths' close friend Maggie Rae accepts it is possible that Smith changed his mind. However, she is adamant that, a few months before he died, Smith's preferred choice was Brown, not Blair. Rae, who is married to Labour Party Parliamentary Secretary Alan Howarth, recalls:

> Certainly in the summer before, when John and Elizabeth
> spent two weeks with us in France, John thought it should
> be Gordon rather than Tony who should succeed him. Alan

and I both thought the reverse – we thought it should be Tony. I remember having that discussion around our kitchen table in France.

A change of heart on Smith's part seems unlikely because his choice of Brown was based on a point of principle. Rae states:

> John was, by instinct, a redistributor of wealth. If you represented Monklands, you would have to be a re-distributor by instinct. And I think he thought that Gordon was more in that mould than Tony. I think he probably is.

The last lap

In the three years running up to the general election in May 1997, Labour's new leader consulted his friend and former pupil master almost every day. Irvine was in effect an unpaid special adviser, assisting Blair across a broad range of areas.

Such was the strength of Irvine's influence that he was even asked to get involved in the revision of Clause IV – the nationalisation provision in the Labour constitution regarded by some sections of the party as a sacred tenet and by others as something of a millstone. Irvine was responsible for breaking through a number of barriers blocking progress and produced a version of Clause IV that became known as 'Derry's draft'. In the end, however, it was Blair, not Irvine, who produced the wording that was adopted by the party conference.

As the election drew close, Irvine spent more and more time on Labour Party matters. Along with David Miliband, a member of Blair's policy unit, he worked on the final draft of the Labour Party manifesto. The manifesto was criticised in some quarters as bland and lacking in specific commitments. However, given the disasters of previous years, it was argued by many that Labour's priority was to ensure the manifesto did not contain any hostages to fortune.

Judged on that basis, Irvine and Miliband did their job well.

Irvine spent the seven weeks before the election at Millbank, Labour's HQ. Such was his dedication to the cause that he worked 16-hour days. It appears that Irvine was once again on a diet. During his period at Millbank, he ate nothing but plums.

In tandem with Roger Liddle, a member of Blair's policy unit, he rehearsed the Labour leader for television interviews. Liddle threw economic questions at Blair, while Irvine quizzed him on politics. Irvine also led the Labour negotiation team in talks over a proposed live television debate between the party leaders. When the discussions collapsed, the Conservatives blamed Irvine. It seems likely he was instructed to be obstructive, since Labour, with a huge lead in the polls, had little to gain in such a debate.

It was precisely by avoiding such potential banana skins that Labour was able to win power again after 18 years in opposition, with its biggest-ever majority in the House of Commons. On 3 May 1997, two days after the election, Irvine went to Buckingham Palace to receive the Great Seal from the Queen. It was everything he had always wanted and more. Lord Chancellor at last, he would chair a string of Cabinet committees and have a seat on several others. He was given overall responsibility for the twentieth century's most ambitious programme of constitutional reform. Best of all, as a member of the Prime Minister's inner ring of advisers, he would be at the heart of a Labour government that had the mandate and the majority to achieve great things.

His chance had come to go down in history as a great, reforming Lord Chancellor. What could possibly go wrong?

CHAPTER SIX

The Year of Living Dangerously, Part One

It was a time to win friends and influence people. Irvine was not merely a stranger to politics and government, he was a stranger to his own parliamentary party and to some of his new Cabinet colleagues. Naturally enough, many of those MPs and colleagues were suspicious of a man who had arrived so suddenly from nowhere and yet commanded the Prime Minister's confidence like few others.

There was a need to tread gently. Irvine was on foreign ground. His political experience consisted of nothing more than running an unsuccessful general election campaign some 27 years previously. He had a lot to learn and would need time to pick up just the basic principles of political life, let alone the many subtleties of government.

But humility was not on the agenda. Irvine simply could not contain his delight over becoming Lord Chancellor and a valued member of Tony Blair's first Cabinet. A leading journalist recalls that, during his first months in power, Irvine left no one in any doubt exactly how important he now was:

> Everything you attended with him he would say, 'I'm chairing four Cabinet sub-committees,' and list them all. 'I am at the centre of government, I am at the cusp of government.' He said, almost in so many words, 'I am the most important minister – barring the Prime Minister – in government' . . . He said it himself, over and over and over again.

Irvine was also fond of claiming all the credit for the Labour Party manifesto – even though he had only worked on the last draft. In a poor attempt to disguise his boasting, Irvine made a little joke about the manifesto, declaring that it was the only bestseller he had ever written.

Never a team player when he was at the Bar, Irvine was hardly going to start acknowledging the contribution of others once he became Lord Chancellor. Indeed, much to the annoyance of the Scottish Secretary, Donald Dewar, and his department, Irvine would later boast that he wrote the Scotland Bill.

Clearly, this was not the way for Irvine to ingratiate himself with the Cabinet colleagues whose help and support he would need to push through the constitutional reform programme. However, Irvine was oblivious to their feelings. When the Prime Minister and Chancellor of the Exchequer suggested that ministers should encourage pay restraint in the public sector by forgoing pay rises, Irvine simply ignored their recommendation. He chose to forsake the opportunity to express solidarity with his Cabinet colleagues – even though he could well afford to do so. After all those years of coining it in at 11 King's Bench Walk, he was hardly short of a few bob. Certainly, he was now earning a lot less than he had at the Bar, but Irvine was by some margin the highest paid member of the Cabinet. (Irvine started in May 1997 on £140,665, almost £53,000 more than a secretary of state.)

Given Irvine's personality and lack of consideration for others, it is hardly surprising that bitter disputes between the Lord Chancellor and some of his Cabinet colleagues started to occur almost immediately. Just a couple of months after the election, Irvine and Home Secretary Jack Straw were sizing up to each other over the Human Rights Bill. Straw wanted to model the new Bill on the Canadian bill of rights, which gives judges the power to strike out or amend Acts of Parliament. Irvine, on the other hand, favoured the precedent set by the New Zealand bill of rights, which does not allow judges such licence. Irvine had made his views on this subject quite clear on a number of previous occasions, arguing that judges should stay out of politics. (Given Irvine's love of power and domineering ways, it may be that he was arguing on an emotional rather than philosophical level; he just did not want the executive to cede more power to the judiciary than absolutely necessary.)

Around the same time, Irvine was also chairing some fiery meetings of the committee dealing with devolution. Jack Straw, with support from Health Secretary Frank Dobson and Agriculture Minister Jack Cunningham, had argued that the gap between Scottish and English public spending was too great and that Scottish spending should be cut. Rows also broke out over two further issues: the number of Scottish MPs who would sit at Westminster after devolution and whether the Scottish or English parliament should have control over abortion in Scotland.

Straw and the others had been strongly opposed by Scottish Secretary Donald Dewar, with backing from Welsh Secretary Ron Davies and the Leader of the House, Ann Taylor. Somewhat surprisingly, the Lord Chancellor, though a Scotsman, had sided with Straw against Dewar. The committee meetings became so acrimonious that the Prime Minister had to be called in to mediate.

Irvine treated Cabinet committee meetings no differently from a trial. He was his old, aggressive – sometimes bullying – self. This approach had its pluses and its minuses. On the credit side, Irvine got things done. Ron Davies has stated: 'I actually had great respect for him. I thought he was a very brusque, very businesslike chair of a Cabinet committee, but very, very effective and very testing.'[67] Such was Irvine's power that a deal done with the Lord Chancellor was effectively a deal done with the Prime Minister. 'I was absolutely confident that once I'd reached an agreement with Derry, and I had on several occasions, that my proposals would then go through and that's what happened,'[68] said Davies.

On the debit side, not everyone appreciated Irvine's abrasive manner. Davies revealed that:

There were occasions where colleagues looked distinctly uncomfortable. I could certainly see when he was coming towards the end of his supplies of patience, and the warning signs were there, and as a politician everybody should recognise that and be able to gauge the strength. If you have a position which is indefensible, he will unpick it and will expose it. [69]

As before, Irvine was making enemies. This time around, though, his enemies were in a position to do him serious damage. Irvine would eventually pay for his high-handed behaviour.

Not that he needed enemies; Irvine was perfectly capable of making trouble for himself. At the end of July 1997 he gave an in-depth interview to *The Observer* about the Government's constitutional reform programme. On the subject of the Human Rights Bill, Irvine stated that the Government would be adopting the less radical New Zealand model, a move that he claimed was supported by the senior judiciary. He also declared his belief that there would be a rush of landmark civil rights cases after incorporation and that the courts would develop a law of privacy in response to the privacy provisions contained in the European Convention.

He then went on to raise the issue whether it might be better for Parliament to enact a law of privacy rather than allow one to be created by the judges. According to *The Observer*, Irvine threw this point into the discussion 'without giving his own opinion'. [70] However, since Irvine then went on to point out possible advantages of legislation – including giving Parliament, rather than the courts, the power to set sanctions for breaches of privacy by the press – it was not exactly impossible to see where Irvine's sympathies lay.

Irvine's comments went directly against government policy. Tony Blair, who had previously committed himself to press self-regulation, immediately responded to Irvine's pronouncements by rebutting them. There would be no privacy legislation, said Blair.

Thus, within three months of joining the Government, Irvine had earned his first – albeit gentle – rebuke. It was not to be his last.

Over the coming months, the issue of privacy continued to take up a considerable amount of the Lord Chancellor's time. Concerns were growing that the privacy provisions in the Human Rights Bill might erode the freedom of the press. Lord Wakeham, the chairman of the Press Complaints Commission (the main press self-regulation body), warned that allowing the courts to develop a law of privacy would put an end to investigative journalism. Irvine responded by declaring that the press had nothing to fear from the Bill: 'I say as strongly as I can to the press: I understand your concerns but let me assure you that press freedom will be in safe hands with our British judges and with the judges of the European Court.'[71]

Lord Wakeham had a further concern, however. He suspected that incorporating the convention could effectively introduce a privacy law via the back door. He suggested there was a danger that people complaining to the PCC would – post incorporation – have the power to appeal to the courts if they were dissatisfied with the PCC's findings. This, he pointed out, might result in celebrities seeking injunctions to prevent the publication by newspapers of potentially damaging investigative stories.

Once again, Irvine dismissed Wakeham's fears. Indeed, he even went so far as to tell a group of senior newspaper executives that there was no chance of the PCC being affected by the new law. The PCC, he said, was not a public body and, therefore, did not fall within the ambit of the Bill.

Irvine also clashed with Culture Secretary Chris Smith on the subject. When Smith had the temerity to disagree with the Lord Chancellor, Irvine contemptuously dismissed his objections, pontificating that a layman had no right to challenge the opinion of an experienced lawyer.

Irvine, however, was soon forced to change his mind. The PCC sought an opinion from David Pannick QC, an expert in newspaper law. His advice – that the PCC was a public body for the purposes of the Act – was passed to Irvine and the Lord Chancellor was obliged to inform Lord Wakeham that he had reconsidered his position.

This mistake cost Irvine dear, suggests Sheila Thompson, then head of information at the Lord Chancellor's Department. Irvine's admission of error dented his Cabinet colleagues' confidence in his legal ability, she says:

> That was his first slip as a lawyer. I think that shocked an awful lot of people. People had said, 'Oh well, Lord Irvine's not a politician and Lord Irvine doesn't know about this and Lord Irvine doesn't know about that, but at least we can expect him to understand the law.' And he got that thing wrong.

In mid-February 1998 Irvine's embarrassment was complete. The Home Secretary announced amendments to the Human Rights Bill that were designed to protect newspapers from the backdoor privacy law they feared would come with the incorporation of the European Convention on Human Rights. Newspapers, he said, would not be prevented from publishing material provided that the material was in the public interest and the paper had observed the industry's code of practice.

The Government had chosen not to exempt the PCC from the Bill, arguing that an exemption would have left newspapers exposed to the possibility of control by a privacy law developed by the courts. Instead, three amendments had been agreed between the Home Secretary and the PCC's chairman, Lord Wakeham. As a result, judges would not be allowed to grant an injunction preventing publication of a story unless the newspaper was present or represented; courts dealing with privacy cases would be obliged to have particular regard to freedom of expression; and courts would have to take into account the issue of public interest, including whether a newspaper has acted fairly and reasonably and abided by the PCC's code of practice.

Straw's announcement did not win universal support. Some journalists argued that the amendments did not go far enough to protect the press. Nevertheless, they amounted to a much greater concession to the press than Irvine had been willing to make.

What made this defeat so grave for Irvine was that he had fought so long and hard for nothing. The Lord Chancellor had nailed his colours so firmly to the mast, that, when the Home Secretary got his way, Irvine was left looking foolish. To make matters worse, the announcement was made by none other than his worst enemy in the Cabinet, Jack Straw.

The privacy debate certainly cost Irvine dear. He had stepped out of line twice and been given two reprimands, including the worst ticking-off received by any minister to that date. He had given mistaken legal advice and then been forced to make a retraction to both Lord Wakeham and his Cabinet colleagues. Having arrived in the Cabinet with a massive reputation, Irvine's aura of invincibility had quickly begun to fade.

A clash of heads

Unlike some of his Cabinet colleagues, Jack Straw was never intimidated by Irvine. Rows between the two were both bitter and frequent. To some extent, this was inevitable. The overlap between their departments guarantees a certain amount of friction between the Lord Chancellor and the Home Secretary, suggests Sheila Thompson:

> Lord Mackay, who was the sweetest of men, had some serious run-ins with Michael Howard. It's a difficult split of responsibilities ... The same problem always came up: it was the Lord Chancellor's Department that took the rap for things going wrong in the justice system, because, inevitably, the buck stopped with the judge appointed by the Lord Chancellor, sitting in a court administered by the Lord

Chancellor, funded very often by legal aid administered by the Lord Chancellor.

Many of the disputes between Irvine and Straw have had nothing to do with departmental issues, however, which suggests that there is some personal antipathy between the two men. Certainly, Straw, who is hugely ambitious, would not have liked the fact that Irvine held so much sway over the Prime Minister.

Not without reason, Straw resents Irvine being in the Cabinet at all. Straw is a classic Labour Party man, who had to work his way up through the party in the time-honoured way. Irvine, on the other hand, swanned in from nowhere, thanks to his friendship with Tony Blair. To make matters worse, Irvine is not just unelected, but unelectable. Putting his peerage to one side, no local party would ever select Irvine as its candidate. Lacking the common touch, Irvine failed miserably in Hendon North in 1970 and the passing years have done nothing to increase his appeal to voters. In any event, rich barristers who send their children to private school are not particularly popular with local party members.

Irvine and Straw had a particularly nasty spat over the question of whether senior judges should be forced to reveal membership of the Freemasons. The judiciary itself was strongly opposed to the idea. However, Straw argued that, with magistrates and the police being forced to register membership, no special case should be made for the senior judges. Irvine had previously supported the move, but now he chose to oppose it, conveniently claiming that, as head of the judiciary, it was his constitutional duty to reflect the views of judges. Forcing judges to disclose membership of the Freemasons, he argued, would be an infringement of both their privacy and their judicial independence. One government minister described the correspondence between the Lord Chancellor and the Home Secretary as 'colourful, to say the least'.[72] In the end, Irvine got his way, and the senior judiciary were simply requested, rather than compelled, to disclose membership.

No sooner had that situation been resolved, than there was another to deal with. Indeed, tensions between Irvine and Straw seemed to be growing by the day. Straw became angry when Irvine reprimanded a junior minister in the Home Office, Alun Michael, for making a statement in which he stepped beyond government policy. (Michael had promised action to prevent rape victims from being cross-examined by their alleged attackers.) Straw accepted that Michael had gone further than he should, but told Irvine that he had no right to be rebuking one of Straw's ministers.

Another clash occurred over Straw's desire to remove barristers' almost exclusive right to enter pleas in criminal courts. The Home Secretary was anxious to break a practice that he believed caused long delays and was advocating that Crown Prosecution Service solicitors should be able to enter pleas in uncontentious cases. The proposed reform was being pursued as part of a manifesto commitment to speed up the justice system. Irvine, however, fought to maintain the status quo.

In his frustration, Straw wrote to Irvine, reminding the Lord Chancellor that he was unelected and owed his position entirely to the Prime Minister's patronage. Straw pointed out that he, not Irvine, represented the elected government. Once again, Tony Blair had to be called in to mediate between the warring parties.

The relationship between Irvine and Straw had dissolved into a paper war. The two men were barely speaking, if they were speaking at all. Instead, letters and memos flew between the Lord Chancellor's Department and the Home Office. With his excellent command of the English language, Irvine was no doubt well able to defend himself in these written squabbles. However, he had left himself vulnerable to attack in another, less obvious way. Irvine's complete political naïvety now began to show, says his then head of information, Sheila Thompson:

> Lord Irvine was exposed because he didn't have – still doesn't have – a political adviser . . . So he had nobody helping him in that respect. So when Jack Straw, for

example, wanted to spread the word that he was going down one particular road and was finding it difficult because Lord Irvine was opposed to it, he only had to tell his special adviser once and the word would go out. So, you'd read an editorial in *The Economist* which was hostile to Lord Irvine and was pro Jack. These were the guys who knew how to use the system.

Irvine's refusal to take on a political adviser was, to say the least, eccentric. True, his predecessor, Lord Mackay, had done without a political adviser, but Mackay had not played the wide-ranging role performed by Irvine. Thompson recalls:

> Both his permanent secretary [Sir Thomas Legg] and I encouraged him to appoint somebody to fill the usual job description – to be his eyes and ears in the Houses of Parliament and also to give him the kind of advice on issue-handling that civil servants couldn't do. [As civil servants], we were not allowed to make any political observations and we felt that, on some of the issues he was wading into, he needed advice of a more political nature.

But Irvine would not be swayed. He believed that the services of a junior minister should prove sufficient. Thus, even though he had no relevant political experience, Irvine chose to enter the most PR-conscious government in the history of British politics without a political adviser.

The Home Secretary had certainly not made the same mistake as the Lord Chancellor. Jack Straw immediately took on a group of special advisers, who were given a brief to promote both Straw and his policies – a brief they performed with considerable success.

As the number of negative newspaper stories increased, Irvine demanded to know what the LCD's head of information was doing about it. Thompson declares:

This was, of course, one of the fundamental disagreements I had with him. I had to explain to him that these issues were nothing to do with me. It wasn't that I didn't want to protect him, it was just that I knew nothing about them. I hadn't seen the papers, I wasn't sitting beside him at Cabinet and, with the best will in the world, I couldn't help him, because I didn't know. They weren't my subjects and it would have been entirely wrong for me to wade in.

My job was to promote the department and everything he was doing for the department and to do that to the best of my ability. But he thought I was falling down on the job because I wasn't getting him out of these and the other messes.

The man of mystery

During his 30 years at the Bar, Irvine had hardly ever had to deal with the press. Even during his time as shadow Lord Chancellor, he had given no more than a handful of interviews. Thus, when Irvine joined the Government in May 1997, journalists knew next to nothing about him. Frances Gibb, legal correspondent for *The Times*, had interviewed Irvine just once during his time in opposition. She concedes that she did not know much about him: 'He was an unknown quantity because he wasn't a public figure. And although he was the Lord Chancellor in waiting he didn't actually thrust himself into the limelight at all. So, when he arrived, it was like a bolt out of the blue.'

'I knew about him,' states Joshua Rozenberg, the BBC's legal affairs correspondent. 'I knew his background. I'd written about him, I'd seen him around. But I don't think anyone knew him well and I certainly didn't claim I knew him well.'

Less-expert journalists than Gibb and Rozenberg were completely in the dark about Irvine. In February 1996 the *Daily Mail* had laughably dubbed Cherie Booth 'Cabinet-maker Cherie' after she mentioned that Irvine would be Lord Chancellor under a Labour government. The article declared:

> Cherie Blair has raised political eyebrows by publicly nominating a close family friend to her husband's first Cabinet. Leaving herself open to charges that she is behaving like Hillary Clinton as an unelected power behind the throne, Mrs Blair has singled out Lord Irvine of Lairg to head the legal system. She told the Society of Labour Lawyers at a recent reception: 'One thing you can be sure of, Lord Irvine will be the next Lord Chancellor.'[73]

Remarkably, the *Daily Mail* did not seem to know that Cherie Booth had merely been stating the obvious. The newspaper's ignorance that, given the chance, both Neil Kinnock and John Smith would have appointed Irvine as their Lord Chancellor, shows just how low Irvine's profile had been.

The *Daily Mail* article also represented something of a warning. It gave early notice that the press would not be slow to jump on someone who owed his position to the Prime Minister's patronage. But all the evidence suggests that, before becoming Lord Chancellor, Irvine gave no consideration whatsoever to the subject of media relations. Indeed, he was just as ignorant of the press as they were of him.

During his time as shadow Lord Chancellor, Irvine made no effort to get to know the legal or political press or their methods – a situation that came as a considerable shock to Sheila Thompson. Irvine, she says, had done no groundwork:

> I was astonished that he had not made any real friendships with political or legal correspondents. When I was talking to legal correspondents in the months before the election and the weeks after, I just assumed that they knew him, that they'd lunched with him, that they'd seen him at

conferences – after all, he was the Lord Chancellor in waiting. And hardly any of them knew him.

A leading journalist recalls that Irvine was only interested in talking to journalists if there was something in it for him:

> He [Irvine] didn't make it easy for journalists to get him to come out to lunch or anything like that unless he considered it in his interest to speak to journalists – if they had information or if they'd done research on a particular subject or could be of value to him, in which case he made himself readily available.

Even after the general election, Irvine remained reluctant to meet journalists. Sheila Thompson tried hard to persuade him that, in his capacity as Lord Chancellor, he needed to build a relationship with the legal press and that it was up to him to take the first step. She suggested that a press briefing be called at the earliest opportunity so that both sides could start to get to know each other.

Irvine, however, was concerned that he would be flooded with questions about his programme of constitutional reform, a subject which he was not yet ready to broach with the press. Thompson explained that she would only be inviting legal journalists and that she would tell them the Lord Chancellor did not wish to discuss constitutional affairs. She advised him that, if a problem arose, he should simply refuse to answer any questions not relating to Lord Chancellor's Department business.

A month after the election, Irvine finally relented and agreed to a press briefing. The excuse used to call the meeting was the appointment of Sir Peter Middleton, deputy chairman of Barclays Bank and chairman of BZW, whom Irvine had asked to carry out a review of Lord Woolf's civil justice reform proposals and the legal aid system. Thus, in keeping with tradition, the first journalists allowed to meet the new Lord Chancellor were to be legal correspondents. However, Irvine was only interested in meeting journalists from the national media, so reporters from the legal trade press were not invited.

Thompson suggested that Irvine should follow the Prime Minister's example and conduct the press briefing in as relaxed a manner as possible. Given that only half-a-dozen journalists or so would be attending, this made a great deal of sense. However, the Lord Chancellor was not keen to sit among journalists and insisted on having his own table. Irvine simply brushed away Thompson's protests that, by distancing himself from his audience, he would be creating a bad first impression.

Irvine then instructed Thompson to send a fax to each of the journalists who would be attending the meeting, informing them what the briefing was about and making it clear that any questions that went beyond that scope would not be answered. Irvine was, in effect, declaring his rules of engagement.

Thompson warned Irvine that he was in danger of making a serious error. The high-handed fax might end up as a newspaper story in its own right. Again, however, Irvine was having none of it, so Thompson reluctantly sent the fax as ordered.

Sure enough, a story immediately appeared in *The Times*, suggesting that the fax was evidence of 'the Government's attempts to exert a firm grip on the media'.[74] The article described the press briefing as the toughest and most restrictive issued by any minister since the election and declared that previous attempts by press officers to lay down terms for questions had always failed because reporters refused to observe them. There was, it said, an implied threat that any journalist who breached the conditions might have reporting facilities withdrawn.

The article's author, Frances Gibb, argues that there was no need for Irvine to send the fax: 'If you don't want to take questions, you just say so. I mean, Jack Straw does it every day of the week! It shuts people up.'

Irvine's behaviour, says one reporter,

stemmed from his insecurity, really. He was terrified he

might be asked questions beyond what he'd prepared. He's a man who likes to prepare very thoroughly. Unlike many politicians who wing it, he didn't want to be asked questions on matters that he hadn't briefed himself on.

Irvine's fax ended up upsetting everyone, reveals one of the legal correspondents who attended the press briefing:

> First of all it had the effect of alienating those who weren't invited, because it was only sent to a select group. So that was unfortunate. Second, it alienated those who *were* invited because they had to agree to all these stipulations not to ask questions beyond certain limits and all the rest of it, which nobody had been asked to do before. It just set off the whole thing on a very, *very* bad footing.

Those who did attend – Marcel Berlins and Clare Dyer of *The Guardian*, Frances Gibb of *The Times*, Robert Rice of the *Financial Times*, the BBC's Joshua Rozenberg, Terence Shaw of the *Daily Telegraph* and Patricia Wynn-Davies of *The Independent* – decided that they could not let the matter of the fax pass without comment. The BBC's Joshua Rozenberg, who has established a light-hearted tradition of always asking the first question at press conferences, was delegated the task of raising the issue.

Irvine, however, was not interested in what Rozenberg and the other legal correspondents had to say. One of the journalists present says, 'Derry just brushed it aside, really, and thought no more of it. But I think subsequently, from the vibes that must have come back to him, he would have known that it was a massive mistake.'

Throughout the briefing, Irvine sat at his own table 'with a couple of officials, like henchmen, on either side', recalls the journalist. 'It was like a judge and court.'

The entire press briefing, says Thompson, was

the most uncomfortable occasion. There he sat at his little

special table and they trooped in and he treated them like disagreeable schoolchildren who he was forced to spend half an hour with. And they all trooped out again and they could not believe it. It was awful. I didn't know where to look.

For all his devotion to preparation, Irvine had made some fundamental errors. He had failed to think through the consequences of what he was doing. By sending the fax and by keeping his distance, the Lord Chancellor foolishly alienated a group of people with whom he had to work. A journalist suggests that Irvine

> didn't realise at that stage how you have to get on with them [reporters] and how it's important to get on with them – whatever you secretly think and however much you secretly despise their practices and also have no regard for their brains . . . I think he had not appreciated the extent to which you have to humour people in that job. As a politician, you can't just think I'll have nothing to do with him or her because they're a load of rubbish.

A cardinal error

Through no one's fault but his own, Irvine's relationship with the press had not got off to an auspicious start. And through no one's fault but his own, the relationship would soon deteriorate into outright hostility.

A crucial moment in the history of Irvine's long-running battle with the press occurred when Irvine delivered a speech, in October 1997, at the Reform Club on 'The role of the Lord Chancellor in the co-ordination of Government policy'. The speech's theme – which had been chosen by Irvine – may not have held much appeal for some Reform Club members, but it was a subject very close to the Lord Chancellor's heart. There is nothing in this world that

Irvine enjoys more than telling the world how important he is.

Irvine began his speech with a few attempts at humour, before presenting what he described as 'a thumbnail sketch' of the history of the office of Lord Chancellor. After a brief mention of St Thomas à Becket he moved on to the sixteenth century. He said:

> A later Lord Chancellor was Thomas Wolsey, adviser to King Henry VIII. Wolsey was perhaps the most powerful of all Lord Chancellors. Interestingly, he had no legal training. The effective architect of the Court of Star Chamber, Wolsey bestrode English government, politics and religion for 14 years. But he gained a reputation for capricious arbitrariness and gathered enemies. No one wept for Wolsey when he fell into the King's disfavour because he would not support Henry's divorce from Catherine of Aragon. I can compare myself with Wolsey, however, because I too am chairman of a 'Star Chamber', the Cabinet committee called Queen's Speeches and Future Legislation, a mouthful for which the Whitehall acronym is QFL.

Irvine then spoke about Sir Thomas More, reminding his audience that More had been executed in 1535 and canonised 400 years later. He added:

> More modern Lord Chancellors have not usually, I am pleased to say, come to so unfortunate an end. But I wanted to mention some of the earlier Lord Chancellors because they illustrate the fact that, in past centuries, the Lord Chancellor had an important, wide-ranging role, encompassing politics, religion, the economy and even military affairs.

Irvine mentioned the Great Seal, before wheeling into the real subject matter of his speech. He declared:

> The Lord Chancellor became undisputed chief minister in

the reign of Edward I. Frederick Maitland described Robert Burnell, Lord Chancellor from 1274, as 'the architect of Edward's legislative scheme'.

While, as chairman of QFL, it would be going too far to describe me as the architect of New Labour's legislative programme, or as a 'colossus of domestic policy' as a *Times* first leader declared, it is the fact that QFL has a central role in determining the Bills that go into the legislative programme, and how much goes into each Bill. This is a little-known committee. It is, however, hugely important. It gives its chairman the opportunity to be feared and hated in equal measure. But because Lord Chancellors, unlike their other Cabinet colleagues, have no further political ambitions, it seems to me to be an entirely appropriate position for a Lord Chancellor – although I do not believe that any other Lord Chancellor since the war has chaired this committee.

Shortly afterwards, Irvine moved on to the subject of his friendship with Tony Blair. He said:

It is true that I have a closer relationship with the Prime Minister than, I believe, any post-war Lord Chancellor has had . . .

So it can be said that the position I hold in this government is a special one . . . The Lord Chancellor is not the king's conscience any longer, nor is he the Prime Minister's conscience. But he is, once again, one of the principal advisers of the political leader of our country. I think this is as it should be. Let me tell you the reasons why:

The Lord Chancellor is at a number of cusps in government. One is the interface between his department as Justice Department and the Home Office. Another is as the means of communication between government and the judiciary and vice versa.

The Lord Chancellor is also charged with upholding the

rule of law; the independence of the judiciary; and ensuring that people can enforce their rights under the law . . .

I am also the Minister responsible for the Law Commission and the modernisation of the civil law more generally . . .

In addition to chairing QFL, the Prime Minister has also asked me to co-ordinate the Government's whole programme for constitutional change – as chairman of all the Cabinet committees concerned with the development of policy over the whole of our programme of constitutional change – the most ambitious and wide-ranging in the UK this century.

The rest of the speech dealt with the Government's programme of constitutional change and Irvine's role at the heart of that programme. Irvine then argued that there was a need for proper planning and co-operation if the Government's objectives were to be achieved, before concluding with another attempt at humour. He stated: 'I would not want the audience to think of me what Lord Byron said of his mother-in-law and what should never be said of any advocate – "She has lost the art of communication, but not, alas, the gift of speech."'

Here's a copy . . .

Despite the speech's insufferable arrogance, not one word of what Irvine said at the Reform Club appeared in the press the next day, the next week or even the next month. The fact of the matter is that Irvine could have claimed the ability to walk on water and still he would not have been reported. The speech had been delivered under Chatham House rules. (This convention exists in order to allow politicians to speak on special occasions without fear of being reported. Both journalists and the audience are required to act as if a speech has never been made.)

Indeed, when a few details of the speech did become public in December, the Reform Club was horrified. It feared that one of its members had leaked the story to the press and that it would no longer be able to convince speakers that they could talk freely at the club. It need not have been concerned, however. The 'squealer' was not a member. It was the Lord Chancellor himself.

On 4 November, Frances Gibb of *The Times* had conducted her first post-election interview with Irvine. It was just a general chat and the conversation ranged from subject to subject until the two got talking about the machinery of government. Not for the first time that day, the Lord Chancellor turned to his papers. Irvine, says Gibb, is

> a great one for making points and then bringing out a sheaf of papers almost like footnotes – 'Here's the point I'm making and here are the references, 20 of them.' I'm not deriding that, it's just the way he operates. It's a lawyer's way of operating. He talks to notes all the time. So, out came this speech he'd delivered to the Reform Club . . . and he said, 'Look, I've said a lot of my thoughts in this speech, here's a copy of it,' and gave it to me. I said, 'Is this for using?' and he said, 'Yes, you can use that but don't say where I said it because it was a private dinner.'

During the interview with Irvine, Gibb had gathered a considerable amount of information on a wide range of topics. Rather than write one long article covering everything, she chose to write two or three shorter pieces, each dealing with a different one of the areas touched on with Irvine. This is standard practice for journalists on the nationals, where there is always fierce competition for space. (One long piece might never have been printed.) The first piece dealt with Irvine's desire to ditch the Lord Chancellor's traditional costume. However, when she started to write an article about the machinery of government and the conflicts that sometimes arise between ministers, Gibb realised she had a problem. She wanted to include some of the material in the Reform Club speech, but was unsure how to use it. Like all good journalists, it is Gibb's practice to source quotes to the time and place they were made. However, on this occasion, she was under express instruction from Irvine not to do so. Gibb recalls: 'I said to Sheila, the press officer who was present at the interview, "Well, this is a bit awkward, because if I can't say where he said it, how can I use it?" You can't quote from it and then not source it.'

In the end, Gibb took the only course possible – she decided to quote directly from the Reform Club speech as if Irvine had said everything in the speech to her during her interview with him. Gibb informed Thompson that this is the way she would be proceeding.

On 1 December 1997 an article by Gibb appeared on the front page of *The Times* under the headline 'LORD CHANCELLOR'S STRATEGY TO END WHITEHALL FEUDING'. The first four paragraphs explained that Irvine was proposing a new form of collective government to end squabbling among civil servants and that he, as chief adviser to the Prime Minister, should play a key role in creating that new culture. It was the fifth and following paragraphs, however, that got all the attention. These read:

> Of his own position, Lord Irvine said he could compare himself to Cardinal Wolsey, who, as Lord Chancellor to Henry VIII, had an 'important, wide-ranging role, encompassing politics, religion, the economy and even military affairs'.
>
> Like Wolsey, Lord Irvine said, he was chairman of a 'star chamber', a Cabinet committee in charge of Queen's speeches and future legislation. The function was 'entirely appropriate' for the Lord Chancellor because he had no other political ambitions.
>
> Lord Irvine believes no other Lord Chancellor since the war has fulfilled this role, one which exposed him to 'fear and hatred in equal measure'.

He conceded that his relationship with Mr Blair, a former pupil whom he took in as a young barrister to chambers, is closer than any post-war Lord Chancellor has had with the Prime Minister.[75]

In the article, Irvine was also quoted as having described his role on the Cabinet sub-committees dealing with devolution, freedom of information and the European Convention as 'pivotal' and as having pointed out that he was at a 'cusp' of government, being at the interface with the Home Office on justice policy and the chief conduit between the executive and the judiciary. The rest of the piece dealt with the history of the role of Lord Chancellor and Wolsey's life. As Gibb had promised, no mention was made of the Reform Club.

Gibb's article was accompanied by a leader on page 23 of *The Times*. Although this accused Irvine of having 'something still to learn about hubris',[76] the leader was broadly sympathetic, suggesting that Irvine's arguments were 'powerfully made and, for the most part, persuasive'.[77]

Neither piece can in any way be described as sensationalist. Unfortunately for Irvine, however, the same cannot be said of the approach taken by some other newspapers. *The Sun's* headline read: 'LORD UNTO HIMSELF: AN UNELECTED LAWYER WIELDS HUGE POWER FOR TONY BLAIR . . . BUT THE ARROGANT PEER IS MAKING ENEMIES'.[78] The paper's political editor, Trevor Kavanagh, accused Irvine of hypocrisy:

[Irvine] opposes the very concept of unelected political power, especially as enshrined in the House of Lords. Yet today this life peer sits as the unaccountable leader of Her Majesty's Government in the upper house on a £140,000 salary from the taxpayer. He is contemptuous of its pomp and tradition but is ready for his official quarters to be redecorated in nineteenth-century splendour at a cost of £660,000. He scorns its privileges, yet, as Lord Chancellor, he is perhaps the most powerful figure in Tony Blair's government.[79]

A short accompanying piece, meanwhile, described Irvine as 'Lord Ego'.[80] Sheila Thompson recalls that when Irvine saw the coverage he 'hit the roof'.

Downing Street was none too pleased either. The Prime Minister's chief press officer, Alastair Campbell, not only declared that Irvine was 'a very important figure within the government',[81] he attacked Gibb and *The Times* by revealing that the Wolsey comments had been made at a private function. He then claimed, 'The reference to Cardinal Wolsey, as those who were present there would confirm, was a light-hearted way in which the Lord Chancellor compared the Cabinet committee which he chairs, which controls the legislation which goes forward, with Cardinal Wolsey's Star Chamber.'[82]

Campbell's response to her article angered Frances Gibb. The press secretary had ignored the fact that it was Irvine who had insisted that no mention be made of the Reform Club. Gibb had been made to look dishonest. Naturally, *The Times* responded in the only way it could. It printed a brief account of how Irvine had given a copy of the speech to Gibb and told her not to refer to the Reform Club. *The Times* declared, 'The usage of its contents, as well as the method of use, were cleared by the Lord Chancellor's Department on Sunday, which was well aware of its proposed publication in *The Times* on Monday.'[83]

Gibb admits that she still finds it hard to believe that Campbell reacted to her article in the way he did. She says:

> I don't know whether he [Campbell] knew or whether Irvine took fright and said, 'It's all wrong, she's got it wrong – breach of trust,' whatever. Who was behind it, I don't know. But one way or the other a completely misleading and actually erroneous statement was cooked up.

All the same, Gibb chose not to make a big issue of the affair. Irvine, however, refused to let the matter lie. He wrote to *The Times*, declaring, 'I am sorry that my sense of humour was not appreciated and has been subsequently misinterpreted.'[84] The joke, he explained, was that Wolsey 'is widely credited with authorship of the original Star Chamber, the common nickname of a Cabinet committee I chair today.'[85]

If it was a joke, it was not especially funny. A member of the Reform Club who heard Irvine make the Wolsey speech says his fellow members were not laughing. Irvine's big mistake, he says, 'was not to signal entirely clearly that it was a joke.'

Those who were at the Reform Club that night cannot be blamed for taking Irvine seriously, suggests a barrister who has heard him speak. Irvine, he says, is anything but a natural after-dinner speaker: 'He hasn't got a light touch. He can't do after-dinner speaking or that sort of speaking at all. He's not invited to law societies to make speeches. They try him once and that's it. It's appalling.'

In any event, when the speech is taken as a whole, it is simply ridiculous to suggest that Irvine was not being serious. The Reform Club speech – which Irvine has never dared make public – was one long boast. Irvine crowed about his close relationship with the Prime Minister, his 'special' position in the Government and his chairmanship of various Cabinet committees. However, the most telling moment of all came when he was talking about QFL. Even though it was totally irrelevant, he just could not resist mentioning that a *Times* leader had described him as a 'colossus of domestic policy'.

As someone who is wont to shift the blame, Irvine might possibly point the finger at his speech writer. This would be unwise, however, because he should not have been using the Lord Chancellor's Department's speech writer in the first place. It was a speech he was invited to make by the political committee of the Reform Club. Therefore, civil servants were meant to have nothing to do with it. Not only was it a political speech, but it was given under Chatham House rules.

Sheila Thompson comments:

> I knew he was making it, but I had no idea what he was
> going to say, I didn't see it in advance. He did get help from
> his speech writer, but, had there been a political adviser
> around, then he or she would have written it. In my view,
> she [the speech writer] shouldn't have done it.

It was the same old story, it seems. Irvine wouldn't do the leg work
himself and got someone else to do it for him. Instead of a junior,
he used a civil servant. It was yet another mistake in a long
catalogue of errors by Irvine. The real point about the Wolsey
comment, says a member of the Reform Club, is that:

> He probably shouldn't have said it in the first place, but
> certainly shouldn't have publicised it. And once it had been
> publicised, he should have just left it alone . . . Then he
> compounded this by writing a letter to *The Times*, saying,
> 'Can't people tell a joke's a joke?' Which again showed it got
> under his skin.

The man of letters

The letter to *The Times* was not the first time Irvine had written to
the press. Nor was it to be the last. 'I advised him not to write to
the papers,' remembers Thompson. 'I said, "If you write to the
papers, you turn them against you. Just turn a blind eye."' But
Irvine felt he knew better and was always determined to put things
'right'.

In June 1997 the *Mail on Sunday* dared to have a little fun at
Irvine's expense. Under the headline 'THE LORD OF LAISSEZ-
FAIRE',[86] an article in the newspaper's Black Dog column read:

> Over in the House of Lords, I hear ignoble grumbling about

the new Lord Chancellor. Unkind comments are being made that Lord Irvine, who brought Tony and Cherie together, is not focusing on the job. Derry, as he is known to his chums, was never the most visible shadow Lord Chancellor. But there were hopes he would mend his ways. One peer tells Dog: 'Derry is delightful company on a late evening over a few drinks – but hardly inspiring during daylight hours.'

The Lord Chancellor's response was to call in the heavy cavalry. He instructed his old friends at City law firm Herbert Smith to write to the paper. Confronted by the country's leading litigation experts, the newspaper opted for discretion rather than valour and published a light-hearted correction in the same column under the headline 'THE LORD OF HARD WORK'.[87] This declared: 'The ignoble grumbling in the Lords concerning the new Lord Chancellor which I reported last week is well wide of the mark. Far from not focusing on the job, as the gossip-mongers claim, Lord Irvine of Lairg sets himself a punishing schedule.' The article went on to state that Irvine worked from 6.50 in the morning to 8.00 at night with only a 15–20 minute break for lunch and that his private office had been obliged to bring in an extra civil servant to cope with the workload he had generated.

When the correction was published, Irvine was 'cockahoop', says Thompson: 'He got a teeny-weeny little correction on page 37 or something and he called me in and jabbed the paper at me and said, "See! I know what I'm talking about!"'

After that early 'victory' there was no stopping Irvine. 'He wrote to every single paper about everything,' sighs Thompson, 'and I'm told they were long, long, long letters.' Thompson warned the Lord Chancellor that his letters were simply drawing the media's attention away from his work towards him as an individual – but again to no avail. In the end, she had no option but to tell him he was in danger of making a fool of himself. Journalists had told her that editors were laughing at Irvine behind his back, joking, 'What's in the post bag from Lord Irvine today?'

But Irvine was oblivious to the consequences of his actions. According to Thompson:

> I said, 'All these letters are in these office files. They're going to be looked at, they're going to be leaked. The media will love this!' And he persisted. So, every editor in Fleet Street has a thick file of threatening letters from the Lord Chancellor 'putting the record straight'. But they are all on personal things. They're on his divorce, the wallpaper, Wolsey, you name it! It's not, 'You've misunderstood my Access to Justice proposals.' They're all about him!

Irvine takes himself seriously and wants everyone else, including the press, to do the same. He lives in constant fear of being made to look a fool. Nor can he cope with criticism. He is the first to find fault with others, but is himself extremely thin-skinned.

Irvine has claimed that he is not obsessive about his press coverage. But his letters – some of which have been floating around Fleet Street for ages – suggest the opposite. In a letter of 25 November to John Witherow, the editor of the *Sunday Times*, Irvine wrote:

> This letter is not for publication. I trust you will put it in your library and ensure that it is brought to the attention of any other journalist minded to write about me for you. I have also sent a copy to the editors of the other major national newspapers so that it can be put in their libraries and made available to their journalists.

Three days later, Irvine wrote again to Witherow. On 1 December he wrote once more, complaining that he had not received a reply to his letter of 28 November. He then challenged Witherow to publish, unedited, all the correspondence between them. The Lord Chancellor seemed to believe that the editor of the *Sunday Times* had nothing better to do with his time than deal with Irvine's letters. He was also clearly under the misapprehension that the newspaper's readers are so fascinated by everything he does that they would want to read a string of letters that should never have been written.

In any event, the sheer length of Irvine's letters made publication impractical. The letter of 25 November, for example, ran to no fewer than four pages. The first half contained five complaints about a recent *Sunday Times* article. Irvine was not happy about suggestions that: 11 King's Bench Walk was not run on a democratic basis; Irvine and Donald Dewar had 'barely acknowledged each other's existence' during the election campaign; the career of an unnamed Labour MP had nosedived after he made a joke at Irvine's expense at a fundraising dinner before the election; Irvine had paid a premium price for the wallpaper used to redecorate the Lord Chancellor's residence; and that it was incongruous for Irvine's father, a union official, to send his son to a grammar school.

All heart-stopping stuff to be sure. Irvine declared that the *Sunday Times* had been guilty of 'gross factual inaccuracies' and took the paper to task on each issue.

Irvine argued his points like the barrister he is. That is, he presented the facts in the most favourable light to himself, omitting anything that would damage his case. For example, on the question of democracy at 11 King's Bench Walk, he pointed out that the chambers has a pupillage committee and a management committee, but conveniently failed to mention that democratic structures were only introduced in the early '90s, when the set first thought it might lose Irvine to politics.

The second half of the letter complained that 'some press coverage of the refurbishment of the Lord Chancellor's residence has been partial and unfair'. Over two tedious pages, Irvine backed up his defence with quotes from a select committee report, Mrs Thatcher and *Hansard*.

To his credit, Witherow refused to be intimidated. Irvine did not get the correction and apology he demanded and the matter eventually fizzled out after a further exchange of correspondence.

Just what Irvine was hoping to achieve is not clear. Getting an apology would not have changed the public's opinion of him. Nor would it have made journalists less prone to be critical of him. Through his gaffes, he had made himself a target and he was going to have to live with it. Attacking the press would only cause more trouble.

Unable to see this, Irvine allowed his fear of the media to develop into full-blown paranoia. This was at its most evident shortly after Irvine took part in a debate about constitutional reform on Radio 4. Having obtained a copy of the programme's transcript, Irvine discovered that he had not been given quite as much air time as another speaker, the Master of the Rolls, Lord Woolf. Incredibly, Irvine insisted that Sheila Thompson go through the humiliating experience of calling the programme's producer to complain that Woolf had been given five lines more than her boss. Inevitably, news of the complaint got out and Irvine suffered more negative press.

On one occasion, Irvine's irascibility towards journalists even betrayed him in public. In March 1998 he attended the *Times* Law Awards, an essay competition for law students. Like Lord Mackay before him, Irvine had been invited by *The Times* to be guest of honour at the dinner, make a speech and then give the prizes.

On this occasion, the usually loquacious Irvine barely said a word before gruffly handing out the awards to the bemused winners. Towards the end of the evening, guests close to the head table were treated to the unedifying spectacle of the Lord Chancellor engaged in a heated debate with Frances Gibb and her editor, Peter Stothard.

Gibb declines to disclose what was said that night, stating that what took place was a private conversation. However, someone else who was present says the top table was dominated by 'the most amazing row'. Both sides, he says, slugged it out with no quarter asked and no quarter given.

The Lord Chancellor would not have been in the best of moods that evening. Just the previous week, he had been hammered in all the papers for his infamous DIY comments; a couple of days before, the *Daily Mail* carried reports about staff in the Lord Chancellor's Department being unhappy with Irvine's behaviour; and that morning's newspapers had revealed that an early day motion, signed by 50 Labour MPs, was calling on the Prime Minister to axe the post of Lord Chancellor.

A political affair

Even though he may not have liked them, Irvine was fast becoming the headline writers' best friend. Sheila Thompson recalls that journalists thought Irvine was a godsend: 'For the first few months they couldn't believe their luck. He was wonderful subject for caricature with the wig and the gown and all that kind of thing. They loved it!'

Some of the press coverage Irvine received was patently unfair. Shortly after the Wolsey explosion, for example, newspapers reported that Irvine had taken his wife on a trip to Trinidad and Tobago at the taxpayers' expense. This was true, but Irvine had broken no rules. He had been attending the Conference of Commonwealth Speakers and had carried out a number of official functions while in the West Indies. None of the newspapers had criticised Lord Mackay for taking his wife to the same conference in previous years.

The papers had no need to fabricate or embellish. Another good Irvine story was always just around the corner. Journalists needed only to be patient.

At the beginning of February 1998, the *New Statesman* published an interview with Irvine. Talking to the magazine's editor, Ian Hargreaves, Irvine surpassed himself. Not only did he embarrass the Prime Minister by – once again – stepping beyond the bounds of government policy, he also embarrassed one of his senior Cabinet colleagues.

Irvine had told the *New Statesman* that there should be a mechanism that would enable the Press Complaints Commission to stop a story being printed unless the newspaper in question could prove that there was public interest in the story being published. He even revealed that he was putting pressure on the PCC to introduce such a mechanism along with a system of compensation for victims who suffer improper intrusion. Newspapers that breached guidelines would have to pay compensation of up to £10,000.

Hargreaves, a highly experienced and respected journalist who has also been editor of *The Independent*, saw an opportunity for a scoop. Without any real hope of getting an answer, he asked Irvine how such proposals would work in practice and suggested the recent press coverage of the affair between Foreign Secretary Robin Cook and his constituency secretary, Gaynor Regan, as an example. Much to Hargreaves's amazement, Irvine did not dismiss the question as inappropriate. Instead, he replied, 'Robin Cook is a public figure. On the other hand, I am not aware that he has ever lectured anyone about moral values.'[88]

Hargreaves then asked the obvious follow-up question: would the Lord Chancellor have expected the Press Complaints Commission to order the *News of the World* (the newspaper that first broke the Cook–Regan story) not to publish the story about the Foreign Secretary and his mistress? Irvine responded, 'I would hope that that would be the view that the PCC would form in a case like that, yes . . . What public interest is there in disclosing that?'[89]

Irvine's comments were immediately criticised by Opposition MPs who claimed Irvine was advocating a system that would result in a form of censorship through the back door. However, Tory MPs were not half as upset about what Irvine had said as members of his own party. This was not just an own goal, it was an own hat-trick.

Own goal number one was Irvine's breach with government policy. The Prime Minister was clearly furious. He authorised his press office to rebuke the Lord Chancellor in a manner not seen before or since. Irvine was left entirely isolated by a series of statements that made it perfectly clear that he had been speaking out of turn. One of Blair's spokesmen announced, 'The Prime Minister's view, very strongly, is that there will not be a privacy law by the front door or by the back door.'[90] Another Labour spokesman declared, 'We do not have a scheme to gag the press from writing stories that are legitimate. I do not know anyone other than Derry Irvine who thought the Robin Cook story was other than a legitimate one to write.' The spokesman added that even the Foreign Secretary had not referred the *News of the World* to the PCC.

Own goal number two was that, by talking about Cook and Regan, Irvine had dragged the affair back on to centre stage just when media interest was at last beginning to wane. The Foreign Secretary had been given a torrid time by the press and the Opposition and had faced repeated calls to resign. He cannot have been very happy to see the fresh headlines provoked by Irvine.

Own goal number three was that Irvine's comments stole the Prime Minister's thunder. When the *New Statesman* article was published, Tony Blair was on his first official visit to Washington DC since becoming Prime Minister. Never one to miss an opportunity, Blair's chief press secretary, Alastair Campbell, had pulled out all the stops with a view to showing the world's media that his boss was now an international statesman of stature. The trip to Washington should have been number one on the news. It is easy to imagine how the party machinery felt when the first item on the news turned out to be what Irvine had said to Ian Hargreaves about privacy.

Even after being rebuked by the Prime Minister's aides, Irvine remained unrepentant. During a House of Lords debate the day the *New Statesman* article was published, he continued to pursue the line that the PCC should adopt a tougher approach and should be entitled to award compensation. He declared, 'I do hope the press itself will lay down proper standards and procedures to protect the public from illegitimate intrusion into their privacy.' He did not, this time, say anything about prior restraint; nor did he mention the Cook affair.

His bravado did not last long. Irvine got a call from the Prime Minister, which, according to a member of his staff at that time, left him 'shaken'.[92]

The Foreign Secretary himself was no more supportive. During an appearance on the BBC's *Breakfast with Frost*, Robin Cook distanced himself entirely from Irvine's comments, stating: 'I have never complained about that press treatment of my life. I did not complain at the time, I have never complained since . . . I think we should treat the public as adults and not believe that they should be protected from the facts.'[93]

On the same day as Cook's television appearance, Irvine was the subject of a vicious attack in a *Sunday Times* editorial. The article opened:

> Lord Irvine's accelerating self-destruction as a credible member of Tony Blair's inner circle of advisers is good news for democracy. It opens the way for the Prime Minister to rid himself of a man whose political naïvety and pompous self-importance have become an embarrassment.[94]

The editorial then called for the Lord Chancellor to be removed as Speaker of the House of Lords and excluded from the Cabinet. It said: 'New Labour and new Britain have no place for such a relic of bygone days.'[95]

On the subject of privacy, the editorial declared:

> Irvine's call to the newspaper industry to censor itself before publishing accurate reports about the personal conduct of people in positions of power is the latest in a growing catalogue of blunders. His mistrust of the press pervades his attitude to matters that go beyond press freedom and affect basic freedoms of speech and opinion, the right to ask questions and seek the truth. There is much of the autocrat in Lord Irvine's approach to complex issues of freedom and

social responsibility. As with many autocrats, his judgements are based on ignorance and lack of direct experience.[96]

The article concluded:

> Lord Irvine's credentials to sit on nine of the Cabinet's 21 committees should be reviewed. He should be confined to helping the Prime Minister as a backroom adviser, keeping a low profile, especially on matters which affect the lives of ordinary people ... Any talk of his being put in charge of a new justice ministry must be stopped. His sense of what is right and proper has turned out to be a mixture of the absurd and the offensive.[97]

Irvine was paying a heavy price for his unguarded comments to the *New Statesman*. However, he deserved little sympathy. This was not the first time he had stepped out of line on the question of privacy. He had been given a clear warning but had carried on as if nothing had happened. It must also be remembered that, when Home Office minister Alun Michael strayed from the straight and narrow, Irvine lost no time jumping on him.

The problem was – and always will be – that Irvine finds it difficult, if not impossible, to refrain from sharing his wisdom with the rest of the world. Indeed, the *New Statesman* incident was an accident simply waiting to happen.

Sheila Thompson comments:

> The thing about Lord Irvine, which, of course, some people find extremely charming, is that, if you ask him a question, he answers you with his own personal views. So the answers that he gave to Ian Hargreaves that day were, I believe, from his heart.

No tape recorders!

It could all have been so different. The disastrous start to Irvine's relationship with the press did not have to happen. Despite what he may have thought, journalists were not out to get the new Lord Chancellor. 'Why should we be?' says Joshua Rozenberg. 'We hadn't been hostile to Lord Mackay. Even though we may not have agreed with all his views, we were very fond of Lord Mackay.'

There was no anti-Irvine agenda, confirms Frances Gibb: 'Right at the beginning, when he came in, nobody was thinking, you know, let's go for this man. Nobody thinks like that. They want to get on, they want to get the stories, they want to do the coverage. People are prepared to give people a chance.'

Legal and political corespondents cannot afford to have agendas. They operate in relatively small worlds. Everyone knows everyone else and trust counts for everything.

Anyone with the least experience of the media knows this. But Irvine had spent his working life in the highly secluded world of the Bar. Although he had once been a member of the body that appoints the members of the Press Complaints Commission, Irvine did not have the first idea about journalism or journalists.

Irvine's lack of understanding of journalists' working methods was exposed just a year before the general election when Ian Hargreaves interviewed him for the first time. Hargreaves recalls:

> I went to do it at his chambers and pulled out a tape recorder to start the interview and he said, 'Under no circumstances! No tape recorders! I don't allow tape recorders in interviews.' And I said, 'You don't do many interviews, how do you know you don't allow tape recorders?' I simply argued with him and said, if he insisted, I would go ahead and do the interview without a tape recorder, but I couldn't see how it was in his interest. This was probably going to be a long interview and I wanted to record accurately what he was going to say and he was just

cutting his own throat with all of this. And he got very, very arm-wavy about it. And, finally, he agreed that I could use the tape recorder so long as he couldn't see it. So I put it on the chair by where he was sitting.

Hargreaves was bemused by Irvine's behaviour: 'I can't think of a politician in recent years or indeed anybody in the public eye who would refuse to have a tape recorder.'

It does not take a media expert to understand that it makes little or no difference whether tape or shorthand or any other medium is used to record an interview. What counts is how the material gathered in the interview is used. Skilful writers can take the most anodyne quotes and make the speaker look stupid, dishonest or anything else they want him or her to be. A skilful film editor can do the same. The crucial factor is not the medium, it is the journalist. If Irvine did not trust Hargreaves, he should not have been giving him the interview in the first place.

The real root of the problem is Irvine's desire for absolute control, a desire that springs from a deep-seated fear of being made to look a fool. It was that fear that made Irvine send his belligerent fax to the respected legal correspondents who attended his relatively unimportant first press conference.

Irvine got it all wrong, badly wrong. The combination of a disastrous first press conference, his foolish initiative on privacy laws and his endless letters to editors ruined his relationship with the press. Just as he had been hostile to journalists, so they were now hostile to him. Moreover, they were in a much stronger position to do damage. The journalists sharpened their knives and waited for the next Irvine blunder.

CHAPTER SEVEN

The Year of Living Dangerously, Part Two

In May 1997 the Lord Chancellor's Department had been given one hell of a shock. The LCD's new boss was, like his predecessor, a Scot. But the similarities ended there. Lord Mackay had been approachable, unassuming and courteous. Irvine, on the other hand, was brusque, arrogant and irascible. Already facing the considerable challenge of a change of government – the first for 18 years – and a first change of minister in ten years, the LCD could soon see that life was not going to be easy under Irvine.

Like the press, the Lord Chancellor's Department staff had not at first known what to expect. Prior to Labour's victory, Irvine had not been a public figure and, in the months leading up to the general election, he had made little or no effort to get to grips with the new role he would assume when Labour won the election.

Most of the people who would later become Irvine's Cabinet colleagues began to hold talks with their future permanent secretaries in January 1997, but Irvine and the LCD's permanent secretary, Sir Thomas Legg, did not start to have formal meetings until almost Easter. Other future ministers actively sought such meetings, but Irvine was not really interested in talking to Legg, so the two met only rarely.

Unlike Irvine, Legg had given some thought to the transition process. First, he agreed to postpone his retirement in order to help the new Lord Chancellor settle in. Having thought long and hard about the staff who would be working most closely with Irvine, Legg then put together what he considered to be a strong team.

Finally, he took steps to facilitate the bonding process between Irvine and the rest of the department.

Legg was determined to avoid a particular morale problem that had arisen under the previous Lord Chancellor. Because Lord Mackay never occupied the same building as the rest of the department, the LCD staff had felt isolated.

Mackay had preferred to work from his office in the Palace of Westminster. This had the great advantage of enabling him to be on hand to perform his role as Speaker of the House of Lords whenever the division bell rang. Legg assumed that Irvine – for the same reason – would probably spend the greater part of his working day in that office. However, he decided to prepare an additional office suite for Irvine in the LCD's headquarters in Selborne House, Victoria Street, and declared that he would make a strong recommendation to Irvine that he spend at least a little time there too. It would, declared Legg, send a good message to the staff.

The suite was duly made ready and considerable expense incurred in decorating the office and purchasing suitable furniture. However, the effort and money was completely wasted. Irvine turned the idea down flat. He made it clear from the start that the Lord Chancellor's Department staff would come to the Lord Chancellor, not vice versa.

This proved rather embarrassing for Legg, who had promised the LCD staff a new regime. However, Irvine was either oblivious to Legg's position or, more likely, simply did not care. Indeed, it was some months before Irvine even bothered to set foot in Selborne House. The message to the staff could not have been worse.

Irvine's inherent shyness may well have been a factor here. But was it really so much to ask that he do a little glad-handing around the office? Isn't that part of the job?

Irvine's lack of consideration for others even extended to the people immediately around him. The staff in his private office were required to work extremely long hours. A typical day started at 6.45 a.m. and continued until 10, 11, or even 12 p.m. This regime continued day after day for some months.

Irvine was treating his new staff exactly the same as he used to treat pupils and junior barristers back at 11 King's Bench Walk. As before, he wrote rude remarks on submissions, such as, 'This is a very poor piece of work. Do it again. Let me have it again first thing tomorrow morning.'

Once again, those who did not come up to Irvine's strict standards were met with the question, 'Is this the best you can do?' Once again, he was frequently prone to use strong language. And once again, he was obsessed with people's qualifications, asking his staff which university they had attended and what class of degree they had obtained.

For an élitist like Irvine, the Civil Service's system of grading was a dream come true. Irvine was much more interested in his staff's Civil Service grades than their abilities.

Irvine's first private secretary, Liz Hutchinson, was hard-working, efficient and generally regarded as a rising star. She had been specially selected for the job by Sir Thomas Legg, but Irvine decided that she was too junior. Irvine discovered that most of his Cabinet colleagues enjoyed the services of Grade 5 private secretaries and then found out that Hutchinson was only a Grade 7. Through no fault of her own, Hutchinson had to go.

Irvine did develop a rapport with some of his staff. He liked Ian Burns, his director of policy. As a Grade 2 man, Burns had experience and was more used to ministerial changes than most of his colleagues at the Lord Chancellor's Department. Plus, Burns was one of the few LCD staff not intimidated by Irvine. His ability to give as good as he got won Irvine's respect.

Adapting to Irvine's domineering style was not so easy for those who had got used to his predecessor's gentlemanly ways. Lord Mackay, declares a former LCD official,

> was charming to all his officials. He remembered all their names. He encouraged junior members of staff to speak at meetings. He was not at all grade-ist in the way that Lord Irvine is. Lord Irvine only wants senior people around him.

Lord Mackay wanted the people who knew the work. His attitude was very much to consult. A lot of people accused Lord Mackay of taking too long to make up his mind, but his style was to consult as many people as possible and then go away and reflect, and then go for it. Lord Irvine's style was quite different . . . he would just challenge everybody. So, people sitting around the table would just quake for their time when Lord Irvine wagged his finger at them and made them present their best case, which is nerve-racking.

Irvine, suggests the former official, simply did not understand how civil servants work. A civil servant's job is to provide the minister with all relevant information and make a recommendation. It is then up to the minister to make the final decision. Irvine, on the other hand, was constantly challenging his staff to justify themselves, just as he had challenged pupils and juniors back at 11 King's Bench Walk.

At his old chambers, Irvine was always a lot better at destroying than creating, and so it proved at the Lord Chancellor's Department. The former official remembers, 'It was much easier to criticise their work without giving them any idea of what they were meant to do. It was easier to say, "This is shoddy work," than say, "This is what I want."'

Irvine's lack of guidance left staff bewildered. But, to some extent, this suited his purposes. Irvine had made it perfectly clear from the start that he did not have confidence in his staff and was always looking for opportunities to criticise. He demanded to see everything, right down to press notices – even though the Lord Chancellor's Department issues something in the region of 300–400 press releases each year.

This could not possibly last. Despite being a workaholic, the new Lord Chancellor soon had three in-trays piled high with paper. In the end, Sir Thomas Legg had to confront Irvine about the growing backlog. He advised the Lord Chancellor that he had to learn to delegate more, trust his officials and prioritise.

Part of the problem was that Irvine's mind was elsewhere. A former LCD official reveals:

> We got the feeling in the first few months that he thought that being Lord Chancellor was something he could do for an hour or two in the afternoon, and that the real work was being on all these Cabinet committees and driving forward the constitutional reform programme. The Lord Chancellor's department was just a piddly little department. He got a shock when he saw the workload and the breadth of his responsibilities, he really did.

The pressure began to tell on Irvine's staff. Complaints about Irvine began to circulate on the LCD's e-mail system. Then, in early 1998, members of the Lord Chancellor's private office held meetings to consider making a formal complaint about his 'rude and overbearing manner'.[98] They discussed making representations to Sir Thomas Legg about their ill-treatment by Irvine and the long hours they were expected to work.

In March the union for higher civil servants, the First Division Association, called a summit on bullying by ministers. The agenda included a discussion of Irvine's behaviour as well as that of Foreign Secretary Robin Cook, Agriculture Minister Jack Cunningham and the Prime Minister's chief press secretary, Alastair Campbell.

Since then, the issue has died down. It may be that Irvine was ordered to curb his worst excesses. However, the reduction in his workload and the opportunity to assemble around him a private office comprising people who are prepared to put up with his demanding ways are probably equally relevant.

The problem has not gone away. Bereft of any management skills, Irvine is always going to have clashes with his staff. He lacks those skills because he has never had to acquire them. As head of his own chambers for 16 years, he merely had to snap his fingers to get what he wanted. His hard-working and ever-faithful senior clerk, Philip Monham, was always there to wait on him hand and foot, while, on the legal side, Irvine was surrounded by brilliant young lawyers whom he had trained to do things just as he liked them done.

Remarkably, Irvine seemed to believe that when he left the Bar and entered politics, he could carry on exactly as before. However, even he should have been able to see that a government department is not the same as a set of chambers and that civil servants are not the same as pupils, junior barristers and clerks.

There is, in fact, a massive cultural difference. Barristers and clerks have always gone through a tough apprenticeship. To some extent, chambers still resemble old-fashioned public schools, with those at the bottom of the pile being expected to prove their worth by performing the most menial of tasks.

Young barristers and clerks put up with this for two reasons. The first is tradition: they know that their elders and betters went through a similar (if not worse) process themselves. The second is money: if they survive the process, the time will come when they will earn enough money to compensate them for being put through the mill at the start of their careers.

But when would the Lord Chancellor's Department staff ever earn enough money to compensate them for the treatment they suffered at Irvine's hands? A Grade 5 private secretary (such as the one Irvine demanded) earns with allowances in the region of £50,000–£60,000 a year, a mere fraction of what many barristers and senior clerks can take home.

When Irvine became Lord Chancellor, he made no allowance for this. Utterly inflexible, he expected everyone else to adapt to suit him – to work to his hours, to put up with his abrasive manner and to match his standards.

So far he has been relatively lucky with his immediate staff. He trusts his director of policy, Ian Burns, and is devoted to his hard-working and extremely able private secretary, Jenny Rowe. However, both Burns and Rowe are scheduled to move on shortly. Having established such a bad reputation, Irvine is always going to struggle to find people of high calibre who are prepared to work for him.

Hart attack

As the months rolled by, so the problems kept coming. A solicitor, Jane Coker, commenced legal proceedings against the Lord Chancellor over his appointment of another solicitor, Garry Hart, as his special adviser. Hart is an old friend of Irvine (and of Tony Blair) and Coker alleged that, by selecting Hart, Irvine was guilty of sexual discrimination under the terms of the Sex Discrimination Act 1975, a piece of legislation introduced by a previous Labour government. Coker complained that she had not been allowed an opportunity to apply for Hart's position. Instead of advertising the vacancy, the Lord Chancellor had merely handed the job to his friend.

Later the same month, Martha Osamor, a Labour Party activist, legal centre adviser and former deputy leader of Haringey Council, also filed proceedings. The Nigerian-born Osamor went a step further than Coker and alleged discrimination on grounds of both sex and race.

There were also reports that another row had broken out between Irvine and Jack Straw after the Lord Chancellor declared that he wanted to establish a ministry of justice and take over the Home Secretary's law and order functions. The *Daily Mail* stated that Irvine was being criticised by senior Cabinet colleagues for his high-handedness and lack of political skills:

> ... taking on Mr Straw could be his [Irvine's] undoing. The Home Secretary is increasingly seen by the Prime Minister as his most dependable and effective Cabinet 'heavy-hitter'. One insider said last night: 'Jack hasn't put a foot wrong since the election – and Irvine hasn't put a foot right.'[99]

However embarrassing such newspaper reports were, they were as nothing when compared to what was just around the corner.

Papering over the cracks

Newspaper articles about the Lord Chancellor's residence had begun to appear within a couple of months of Labour's election victory. An awful lot of money, it seemed, was being spent on the residence's refurbishment. Some newspapers suggested the cost to the taxpayer was more than £500,000.

As the pressure began to build, Irvine stated in a letter to *The Times* in September 1997 that the renovation of the Lord Chancellor's residence was part of a ten-year rolling programme of building work in the Palace of Westminster begun in 1992. 'The choice is not mine,' he declared, asking *The Times* to 'correct the impression that this refurbishment is taking place because of my choice'. Irvine again disclaimed responsibility in a letter to all papers in November. As a result, the issue went quiet for a while. However, early in 1998 – a little after the Wolsey fiasco – it flared up again.

In February 1998 the *Sunday Times* claimed on its front page that the Official Secrets Act was being used to suppress information about the redecoration of the apartments. Under the headline 'IRVINE'S CURTAINS ARE MADE AN OFFICIAL SECRET', the paper also revealed details of the expenditure, stating that taxpayers were to be billed £145,000 for carpets, curtains and upholstery, £8,000 each for two beds and £25,000 for a ten-person table. The Opposition was quick to seize on this, with Conservative trade and industry spokesman John Redwood suggesting that Parliament should investigate the claim that contractors had been asked to sign the Official Secrets Act.

It was later explained that clauses tying contractors into the Official Secrets Act had been standard in government contracts since 1990. However, that fact was lost in the flood as further details of the refurbishment began to pour out. Lord and Lady Irvine, it was reported, were redecorating the Lord Chancellor's residence in the Gothic style of Augustus Pugin, the man who had redesigned the Palace of Westminster after it was destroyed by fire in 1834.

Nor was this some half-hearted scheme: the Irvines were using the finest craftsmen and materials. Thus, curtains were costing £200 a metre and hand-printed wallpaper £300 a roll. The final bill was estimated to be in the region of £650,000.

Sensing blood, the Opposition went to the extraordinary length of producing *The Derry Irvine Directory*. This five-page dossier branded Irvine 'a huge liability for the Government' and detailed the following expenditures: £21,000 on carpets, £96,000 on soft furnishings, £60,000 on hand-painted wallpaper, £9,640 on a Pugin-style oak table to seat 16, £16,000 on two Pugin-style hand-carved beds, £56,000 on light fittings, £5,000 on ceramic tiles, £5,000 on blinds, £11,000 on domestic equipment and tableware and £20,000 on curtains at £200 per yard.

Downing Street responded that some of the prices had been exaggerated and continued to claim that the renovation was simply part of a bigger programme. However, that defence unravelled when it was revealed that Lord Boston of Faversham, the chairman of Lords committees, had confirmed back in July 1997 that the work being carried out to the Lord Chancellor's residence had been added to the rolling programme only after the election.

Further fuel was thrown on the fire when it became known that Irvine would be adorning his residence with paintings, pictures and sculptures borrowed from various galleries and museums. The Lord Chancellor's office claimed that all the pictures had previously been in store and that the galleries and museums were delighted that they would now be on show. However, reports in some newspapers suggested some gallery officials and curators had been upset by the scale of the loans to Irvine.

In a desperate attempt to stop a campaign by the Tories and press that he believed had become a vendetta, Irvine issued a statement admitting that the redecoration of the Lord Chancellor's residence was authorised only after Labour came to power. However, he insisted that he had not played a significant role in the refurbishment. He said that responsibility lay with three House of Lords committees, both for the works and the choice of materials and furniture. Not surprisingly, Conservative MPs accused Irvine of having previously been economical with the truth.

It was not long before this second defence also came undone. At the end of February 1998 a letter from Irvine was leaked to *The Times*. It was addressed to Black Rod, but was ultimately for the attention of the Lords committee considering the refurbishment programme. Dated 1 July 1997 (a month before the committee approved the works), the letter revealed that, although Irvine had not been the one to instigate the redecoration programme, he was the one who had proposed that the redecoration be carried out on such a lavish scale.

A section of the letter read:

> The palace as a whole is clearly a building of outstanding national importance, and the residence is an historic part of the palace. As such it forms part of our national heritage ... I am, however, concerned at the estimates for the cost of these restoration proposals, which I have just seen. What in my view is, however, plain is that these proposals are only worth implementing to a very high and historically authentic standard. [100]

Acknowledging the high cost of the restoration, Irvine proposed that the works could be staggered:

> I recognise, however, that the committee may consider that the costs of restoration and refurbishment are too high to meet in one go. If the committee so concludes, then what I suggest as a possible alternative is as follows. It could be possible for the renovation to go forward in phases ... [101]

Irvine gave the committee's arm a further gentle twist by offering to make the residence open to the public. He even went so far as to volunteer the services of his art historian wife as a tour guide.

By this stage, the affair was attracting such attention that Tony

Blair was forced to defend his Lord Chancellor during Prime Minister's question time. He told the Commons that the Conservatives had no right to criticise the works when the Tory members of the Lords administration and works sub-committee had not opposed the renovation plans.

Others also lent their support to Irvine, among them SDP co-founder Lord Jenkins of Hillhead. In a letter to *The Times*, the man who had deserted the Labour Party in its hour of greatest need, now sprang to the defence of a Labour Lord Chancellor. Jenkins suggested Irvine's letter to Black Rod had been misrepresented in the press and claimed that 'there is now considerable evidence of a discreditable vendetta spiralling out of control, with obsessive contributions from both the press and too many bereft Conservatives'.

The high-living Jenkins, who has enjoyed Irvine's hospitality at his home in Scotland, made a curious attempt to drum up sympathy for his friend. Jenkins wrote: 'Lord Irvine, who is no commonplace a figure, at once strong intellectual meat and politically unstreetwise, may be a tempting target.' Just how unstreetwise, Jenkins cannot have imagined, but was soon to find out.

A DIY disaster

On 3 March, Irvine appeared before the Select Committee on Public Administration to talk about the Government's policy on privacy and freedom of information. The discussion proceeded along fairly obvious lines until David Ruffley, the Conservative MP for Bury St Edmunds, caused the debate to take a very different tack.

Ruffley said, 'Lord Chancellor, could I raise a question relating to the operation of freedom of information and your own department? It seems to many people that your department and you personally have gone to some lengths to conceal the facts relating to the refurbishment of the Lord Chancellor's residence.'[102] Ruffley then suggested that Irvine's letter to Black Rod proved that Irvine had previously been economical with the truth. He also asked the Lord Chancellor whether it was hypocritical for a minister who claimed to be in favour of freedom of information to include 'in confidence' clauses and Official Secrets Act clauses in contracts for the refurbishment of his residence.

Far from laughing off Ruffley's very obvious attempt to ensnare him, Irvine began a long, detailed and deadly serious defence of his actions. He declared that his press releases had never asserted that the refurbishment works were made part of the House of Lords ten-year rolling programme before the 1997 election. The works had his full support, because the Palace of Westminster is part of Britain's national heritage. All the pictures and sculptures in the residence had previously been in cellars, so the public would benefit from what had been done, as would charities, which were already queuing up to use the residence for functions.

Irvine simply could not stop talking. Eventually, he talked himself straight into a hole. He announced:

> And I also want to say this, to seize the wallpaper charge straight on the chin, we are talking about quality materials which are capable of lasting for 60 or 70 years. We are not talking about something down in a DIY store which may collapse after a year or two. What is intended is a durable refurbishment of an historic part of our national heritage in a way that will give satisfaction to future generations.[103]

Ruffley then drew Irvine's attention back to the seemingly forgotten subject of gagging clauses. Irvine stated that the contracts signed by the contractors had nothing to do with the Lord Chancellor's Department but were standard form contracts of a type used by the House of Lords for years.

Andrew Tyrie, the Conservative MP for Chichester, then opened a second front. He asked the Lord Chancellor, 'When you wrote your letter to Black Rod, did it occur to you there might be some political embarrassment about it?'[104] Irvine answered no and continued to insist that the £650,000 was money well spent. 'Future generations,' he stated, 'will agree and will regard this as a remarkable storm in a tea cup.'[105]

When Tyrie mockingly announced, 'So it can be summed up as, if I may coin a phrase, "*Je ne regrette rien*,"'[106] Irvine replied, 'I certainly do not think any apologies are due. On the contrary, I tend to side with the commentators who have said, "Three cheers for this being done in Parliament and three cheers for the House committees that decided to do it."'[107]

Before the discussion finally returned to the real issues at hand – privacy and freedom of information – a bemused Mike Hancock, the Liberal Democrat MP for Portsmouth South, could not resist a little sarcasm. He said, 'I feel the first question I ought to ask you is, would you care to give us all some advice on what to avoid at B&Q?'[108] Laughter erupted, but not from Irvine, who looked confused. It appeared that he did not know what a B&Q store is. After consulting an aide, he mumbled, 'Very amusing.'[109]

Still, when the select committee hearing finally ended, Irvine walked away a happy man. He believed that his performance had been nothing short of a triumph. Such is Irvine's lack of feel, it was not until he saw the next day's newspapers that he realised that he had another disaster on his hands.

The Sun's headline was 'WHAT'S B&Q? DERRY HASN'T GOT A CLUE: HE SNUBS DIY STORE WALLPAPER'.[110] The article offered the Lord Chancellor ten DIY tips on B&Q, including: 'They are huge warehouse-type buildings with large orange signs outside – saying B&Q.'[111]

In an accompanying article, political editor Trevor Kavanagh wrote:

> When he stopped studying his fingernails, Lord Irvine actually claimed future generations would be grateful for his indulgence. It was a virtuoso performance by a man who

regards the rest of us as mere mortals – but Tony Blair could not bear to watch it. Instead, aides witnessed every second of the two-and-a-half-hour grilling and reported back. The best they could say was his lordship survived. But he failed to show any trace of the humility or humour which might have ended this embarrassing fiasco.[112]

The *Mirror* devoted a two-page spread to Irvine under the headline 'GIVE ME THREE CHEERS'. DIY stores, it revealed, were less than happy with the Lord Chancellor's comments. B&Q said: 'This is absolute rubbish. The types we stock will last just as long as the Lord Chancellor's.' Sainsbury's Homebase said: 'Our range is value for money and designed to give our customers a long-lasting finish.' Do It All said: 'You don't have to pay a fortune for quality.'[113]

Both Ruffley and Tyrie took the opportunity to turn the knife. Ruffley told the *Daily Mail* that he was 'appalled at the sneering, dismissive and condescending tone of the Lord Chancellor . . . his attitude told us all we need to know about the Lord Chancellor. It was the most revealing moment of an arrogant and high-handed performance.'[114] In the same newspaper, Tyrie accused Irvine of 'breathtaking arrogance'[115] and said the Lord Chancellor had made 'a huge political misjudgement'.[116]

No riff-raff

A few days after his appearance before the select committee, Irvine announced details of the access he would be allowing to the Lord Chancellor's residence. These proposals were far more generous than those set out in his letter to Black Rod, and were, in all probability, an attempt by Irvine to take some of the heat out of the situation. However, his effort backfired. Once it became known that the apartments would only be open for 90 minutes twice a week, and then only upon written request, Tory MPs again called for Irvine to quit or be sacked.

The furore finally began to subside after the Lord Chancellor's Department's head of information, Sheila Thompson, organised a day for the press to come and see what all the fuss was about. Further details of the expenditure on the residence continued to leak out and cause Irvine embarrassment, but the worst was now over.

At the end of May 1998, Irvine finally adopted a more conciliatory approach, telling the Royal Academy summer banquet that the wallpaper saga had taught him 'many lessons'.[117] He even confessed that the affair might have been better handled, declaring, 'Of course, it is possible to make mistakes in attempting to explain a policy of authentic restoration and an increase in public access for enjoyment.'[118] Nevertheless, Irvine was clearly unrepentant about spending so much taxpayers' money. 'We must,' he said, 'battle against those who view such investment as somehow élitist, a luxurious add-on and not in the public interest.'[119]

Irvine would, in fact, be best advised to give up this particular fight. There is little to support his claim that he will be thanked by future generations for what he has done, while there is plenty of evidence to suggest that by far the most significant beneficiaries are Lord and Lady Irvine. True, the Palace of Westminster is a very important part of the nation's heritage. True, until relatively recently, it has been badly neglected and, at times, abused. However, the fact remains that £650,000 is an awful lot of money to spend on private apartments that few people will ever see.

Taking parties of up to 25 people around the residence two or three times a week is a very thin definition of public access. He claimed that he was enthusiastic for people to be able see the residence in its restored condition, but, in the letter to Black Rod, he suggested two options for controlling admission:

> The first would be to limit access in some way to those with
> a bona fide interest in historic buildings and art, such as art
> historians and critics, directors and staff of major galleries,
> and art and architecture colleges in this country and

elsewhere. This approach would require some means of assessing the authenticity of requests received to visit the residence . . .

In addition, parts of the residence could be opened up to the public for, say, one or two afternoons a month. The arrangement would be that peers or MPs could bring groups of acquaintances/constituents, signed up in advance as for tours of the palace.

Irvine's snobbery could not be more transparent. He was also, initially, highly selective with regard to the media. When Sheila Thompson recommended that the residence be thrown open to the press, Irvine wanted to keep the number of invitations strictly limited. Thompson recalls:

I advised him that when it was finished, he had to show the world what it looked like, what the taxpayer had got for their money. He reluctantly agreed that this could happen. But he only wanted people like *Country Life* and *Interiors*. And I said, 'No, we have to have everybody – TV, radio, papers, magazines.' And he said, 'What, even *The Sun*?' And I said, 'Especially *The Sun*.'

Amusingly, Irvine would later swallow his pride. In December 1998 he endeavoured to soften his public image a little by giving a rare interview in which he talked for the first time in detail about his childhood and the break-up of his first marriage. The lucky newspaper on which Irvine bestowed this scoop – and which gave him a very sympathetic hearing – was none other than *The Sun*.

Much ado about nothing

The work done to the Lord Chancellor's residence has been much misunderstood. Most people believe that the residence was decorated to the Irvines' – especially Lord Irvine's – personal taste. It was not. What the Irvines were trying to do is to return the residence to the way it might have looked back in the 1840s.

So, what do the lucky few see when they visit the Lord Chancellor's residence? There are some exquisite paintings, including the portrait *Beata Beatrix* by Dante Gabriel Rossetti, and some fine etchings by Giovanni Battista Piranesi. However, for most people, the main attraction is, of course, the infamous wallpaper.

Sadly, the wallpaper, like much of the residence, is something of a disappointment. It may have been hand printed; the manufacturers may have used separate pearwood blocks for each colour; and it may have cost a packet. However, barring the expense, it is hard to see what all the fuss has been about. Indeed, some of the designs are positively garish. Likewise, there is little to say about the £8,000 beds and the £10,000 table. They may be attractive, well made and functional, but, at the end of the day, they remain nothing more than reproductions.

Everything has been done with great attention to detail. The design of the chandeliers is based on that of a chandelier in the residence of the Speaker of the House of Commons. The carpet designs are copied from others in the palace. The fabric for the blinds has been reprinted from a scrap of an old blind found by chance when work was being carried out in the early 1970s. No expense has been spared to achieve authenticity.

Nevertheless, there remains a huge and fundamental flaw in the Irvines' grand scheme. Visitors are not seeing the Lord Chancellor's residence as it might have looked in the middle of the nineteenth century. There was no such residence at that time. In fact, no Lord Chancellor lived in the Palace of Westminster until as recently as 1923. At that date, a residence was carved out for the then Chancellor, Lord Cave, by giving him Black Rod's apartments and a drawing-room that used to belong to the Lords' librarian. Thus, the renovated Lord Chancellor's residence is in reality a very expensive Gothic fantasy on the part of Lord and Lady Irvine.

Still, the Irvines are happy. They got what they wanted. Courtesy of the taxpayer, they now occupy a beautifully appointed residence in a prime London location. Nothing less was ever going to do.

When Irvine first became Lord Chancellor, he had no intention of using the official residence. As revealed by his letter to Black Rod, it was only upon the promptings of his then permanent secretary, Sir Thomas Legg, that Irvine came round to the idea of living in the Palace of Westminster. The problem was that the residence had been decorated some years before by Lady Havers, the wife of former Lord Chancellor, Lord Havers. Lord and Lady Mackay had bravely put up with Lady Havers' taste. But, as committed Presbyterians, they are not ones to grumble. Lord and Lady Irvine, on the other hand, are used to living in the lap of luxury.

Thus, the letter to Black Rod contained a thinly veiled threat:

> Neither my wife or family have any need to live in the residence, although it would be convenient for the reasons I was advised. We live in Central London in the house which has been our family home for the past 25 years and, whether or not we were able to reside at the residence, we would retain and maintain our family home. At the time I arrive at my office in the morning, my journey by car takes a mere 15–20 minutes. [120]

The inference was clear: unless the apartments were restored in the grand manner he wanted, Lord and Lady Irvine would not be taking up residence. In true Irvine fashion, it was either going to be done his way or not at all.

The letter also showed that Irvine had been choosing his words very carefully. On a strict interpretation, his protestations that the decision to renovate the Lord Chancellor's residence had been taken by others may have been true, but they created the false impression that Irvine had played no part in the decision process.

Remarkably, Irvine has never done anything to correct that

impression. During his appearance before the Select Committee on Public Administration, Irvine reasoned:

> I do not accept that the letter [to Black Rod] has resulted in two-thirds of a million of public expenditure any more than I would accept that when an advocate appears in front of a court and succeeds in his argument that he is party to the decision of the court. What I was doing was not even submitting an argument to the committee. I was setting out the facts as dispassionately as I could with the pros and cons of what we intended and I regard the decision as a decision for the committees and I believe that it is their decision and their decision alone and not mine.

But Irvine's letter was anything but dispassionate. Since when did barristers offer their wives' services as tour guides?

Irvine did at least admit that the refurbishment of the residence did not become part of the ten-year rolling programme of works to the Palace of Westminster until after the general election. However, he only did so when evidence was produced that cast his earlier comments in a different light.

Irvine also claimed that all decisions were taken by others, right down to the choice of materials. Again, upon a strict interpretation, this is entirely true. However, the House of Lords committees were in reality doing little more than signing the cheques. Lord and Lady Irvine were the real driving force behind the redecoration programme. Irvine even attended some meetings of the redecoration team. The members of the team were delighted by his enthusiasm and impressed by Lady Irvine's knowledge of the period and the contacts she brought in to give advice.

Perhaps even more remarkable than Irvine's lack of candour is the fact that Irvine never stopped to think about the repercussions of what he was doing. It never occurred to him that spending £650,000 on a private residence might convey an unwelcome picture of both himself and the newly elected Labour government.

The programme could have been put on hold for a while or carried out in stages, but Irvine strode straight ahead.

Before he knew it, members of the House of Lords works office were talking to the press and documents were being leaked. His response was to panic. He put out a flurry of press notices, claiming the redecoration programme was nothing to do with him. Such was his concern to shift the blame, he even overlooked the fact that he was using Lord Chancellor's Department resources and Lord Chancellor's Department press notice paper for a House of Lords matter.

A vow of silence

Alastair Campbell was not a happy man. From a public relations perspective, Labour's first year in government had been a spectacular success: the Government was still riding high in the polls, while Tony Blair was the most popular prime minister in British history. But Blair's chief press officer had a headache: what was to be done about the Lord Chancellor?

Campbell faced two problems. First, Irvine was ruining all of Campbell's good work. The Lord Chancellor had proven a remarkably gaffe-prone member of a relatively gaffe-free govern-ment. Second, Campbell was heartily sick of Irvine and his demanding ways. Infuriatingly, Irvine was not willing to take much, if any, advice from his own head of information, Sheila Thompson. Instead, he turned all the time to Campbell, only to be told again and again that he should follow the advice he had already been given by Thompson. It was Minister without Portfolio Peter Mandelson, meanwhile, who had to bear the brunt of Irvine's refusal to appoint his own political adviser. Thompson says, 'I had a very good relationship with Alastair. He was absolutely delightful to me. He was supportive, understanding, made time for me. He was absolutely great. He said, "Listen, we all understand what you're going through."'

Patient though he was, Campbell was not always able to contain his frustration. On one occasion when Thompson approached Campbell for some advice about a press strategy for the Lord Chancellor, he bluntly replied: 'It consists of just two words. Shut up!' [121]

But Irvine would not, or could not, shut up. So, when the Lord Chancellor talked himself into the wallpaper fiasco, Campbell decided that he had had enough. Even if he was the Prime Minister's old bosom buddy and mentor, Irvine had to be stopped. Another warning – such as the one given after the *New Statesman* article was published – would not do. Irvine, concluded Campbell, had to be taken out of circulation.

What happened next is without precedent in British political history. At the behest of a press secretary, a senior minister was ordered not to speak to the press at all for the foreseeable future. Irvine was not sacked, nor told to avoid certain subjects when talking to journalists. He was gagged.

Irvine had irritated the wrong man. During his Wolsey speech at the Reform Club, the Lord Chancellor had boasted of his close relationship with the Prime Minister. However, Irvine is not the most powerful unelected member of the New Labour regime. That particular honour belongs to the Prime Minister's senior press secretary, who enjoys Blair's confidence to a far higher degree than any minister.

Campbell talked to Blair and Irvine got a call. The Prime Minister gave Irvine a serious ticking-off. He was told not to open his mouth. The order was absolute: Irvine was not to speak to any journalists about anything, not even legal issues.

Irvine was not the only person put out by this turn of events. The BBC's legal correspondent, Joshua Rozenberg, who was due to interview Irvine on 4 March about his legal aid green paper, only learned at around 11.30 that morning that the man he was supposed to be interviewing for that afternoon's news would not be turning up.

Rozenberg could see that this was a news story in itself. Turning to the notes he made at the time, he relates:

In my report on the one o'clock news that day, I said, 'The last occasion on which Lord Irvine gave a television interview was before Christmas. It was expected the Lord Chancellor would do interviews this afternoon, following publication of his consultation paper on legal aid, but it has now emerged that he won't be speaking to reporters today at all.' And then I said, 'The Lord Chancellor's comments to MPs yesterday are thought to have influenced the Government's decision that he should not give interviews. A public relations firm acting for his department had invited bids from reporters. Today's decision adds to speculation that, in Downing Street, Lord Irvine is no longer seen as a safe pair of hands.'

As on the occasion of *The Times'* Wolsey report, the Number 10 press office quickly moved into action. Alastair Campbell gave a briefing to lobby journalists and on 5 March a report appeared in the *Daily Mail*. This read:

Relations between the BBC and Downing Street were further strained last night following an attack on coverage of Lord Irvine's legal aid reforms. The Prime Minister's spokesman was furious after the BBC's one o'clock news reported that the Lord Chancellor had pulled out of interviews on the new law package.

Branding the report 'lies', 'an outrage' and a 'disgrace', Mr Blair's spokesman denounced the BBC's respected legal correspondent Joshua Rozenberg.

He accused him of basing his report on 'facts that are completely untrue' and insisted Lord Irvine had never agreed to any interviews and was not, therefore, avoiding them.

Campbell's response had been swift and savage. It was also totally over the top. After all, Rozenberg had not exactly launched a major attack on the Government. When he dared to mention that Irvine had been forbidden to give interviews, he was merely reporting the facts as he saw them.

Rozenberg was no more happy about what the chief press secretary had said than Frances Gibb had been about Campbell's response to her Wolsey article. Unlike Gibb, however, he was not prepared to let the matter lie. Rozenberg explained the position to Campbell, who wrote back making it clear that he was not accusing Rozenberg of lying.

Pointing the finger

This series of press disasters was bound to lead to repercussions for the Lord Chancellor's Department. Someone had to get the blame – but it wasn't going to be Irvine.

Towards the end of 1997, the LCD head of information, Sheila Thompson, got a call from Irvine's private office. She was told that Irvine had called a meeting at which his permanent secretary, Sir Thomas Legg, and his policy director, Ian Burns, would also be present.

When the day came, Thompson, Legg and Burns sat around Irvine, with a secretary taking a note of proceedings. The Lord Chancellor declared his disappointment with the way he had been looked after by the departmental press office. He was concerned about three events in particular: his failure to get any of the credit for the passage of the Human Rights Bill, the Wolsey fiasco and the press coverage over the refurbishment of the Lord Chancellor's residence. Although his criticisms were all clearly directed at Thompson, Irvine did not look at her once while he spoke.

When Irvine finished, Thompson asked for, and was given, a right of reply. She told Irvine:

> The Human Rights Act was a piece of Home Office legislation. You happened to take it through the House of

Lords, but it was Home Office legislation. I saw none of the papers, I saw none of the draft legislation, I attended none of the meetings. The Home Office were responsible for that. There was a Home Office press officer in the House every single day.

They had discussed the Cardinal Wolsey affair before, pointed out Thompson, reminding Irvine that he himself had given the speech to Frances Gibb. Thompson had never mentioned the speech to any of the press because it was made under Chatham House rules. She had not read the speech in advance. Gibb had asked Irvine on what basis she could use the speech. Thompson had written down Irvine's answer at the time. Gibb had subsequently checked with Thompson several times before she wrote her story. Gibb had done nothing wrong.

Likewise, the wallpaper was nothing to do with the Lord Chancellor's Department; it was a House of Lords matter. When Thompson explained that she had been spending her time promoting LCD initiatives, Irvine declared that he did not think much of the way she had handled that work either.

Thompson brought her defence to a conclusion by advising Irvine once again that the issues he was concerned about should have been handled by a political adviser. Indeed, her Civil Service rules of employment prevented her from engaging in certain areas.

Legg and Burns now chipped in their tuppenceworth. Legg confirmed that the boundaries between political and departmental public relations should not be forgotten, while Burns made a rather irrelevant plea for more money and resources. Irvine then concluded the meeting by announcing that it had been good to clear the air and asked Legg, Burns and Thompson to put together a media plan.

The next week, however, Burns informed Thompson that Irvine had instructed Legg to appoint a Grade 3 director of communications over her head. The decision, it transpired, had been taken before the meeting with Irvine.

When an advertisement was placed for the new role, the LCD was not exactly inundated with applications. Around eight were received, but then two or three of those were withdrawn. Of those remaining, one was an internal application, one was a senior official from another department and one was from Allan Percival, who got the job.

Percival, who had previously been deputy press secretary in the Prime Minister's office, asked Thompson to stay on, but she chose instead to join the private sector, quitting the LCD in May 1998. It was a cruel ending to the 17-year Civil Service career of someone whom Frances Gibb of *The Times* describes as an 'excellent' press officer who brought the Lord Chancellor's Department press office into the Whitehall mainstream. Gibb explains:

> She really professionalised that department, because, when she came, it was still quite a small backwater. She boosted the department, made it more professional. She also took on the job of handling PR for the judiciary. She set that whole thing up so that the judges as well as the Lord Chancellor had good public relations. She turned it around.

Thompson is remarkably philosophical about her departure from a job she held for almost eight years, pointing out that she was not the first nor the last Whitehall press officer to move on after the election. Indeed, in the months following Labour's election victory, at least half-a-dozen departmental public relations heads moved on, suggesting that Labour has very definite ideas about what it wants from its PR advisers.

The problem with Irvine, on the other hand, was that he did not have definite ideas. He knew what he wanted – good press – but did not have the first clue how to get it. This made advising Irvine a virtually impossible job. His lack of experience of the press, his thin skin and his refusal to take even the most obvious advice made for a dangerous combination. In the end, Irvine chose to learn the hard way and paid the price with a serious of public setbacks.

Those setbacks made Thompson's position untenable. After all, Irvine is not the type of man who takes well to being reminded of his own mistakes. He must have become absolutely sick and tired of Thompson saying, 'I told you so!'

Few friends

Blaming Sheila Thompson for his problems may have helped Irvine to live with himself, but it was never going to save him politically. What saved him was Tony Blair's loyalty. Any other minister with a record half as disastrous as Irvine's would have been dumped long before. But, even after the Wolsey fiasco, Blair stood by his friend and former pupil master.

Maggie Rae, a close friend of the Blairs for many years, declares that the Prime Minister is not the type of man to desert his chum in an hour of need:

> Tony is not a fair-weather friend. If Tony's your friend, Tony's your friend and he will stick by you through thick and thin. He also knows that politics is rough. He has a very clear appreciation that politics is rough and that you can expect this sort of thing.

However, few, if any, other ministers stood by Irvine at this time, suggests a former senior civil servant:

> When he was going through his very difficult patch, a lot of his colleagues were rubbing their hands with glee, waiting to see him fall from grace. Because he hadn't made friends with any of them, there would have been no helping hand to pick him out of the gutter.

In his political life, Irvine was a very lonely man, says the former civil servant: 'I don't know who his friends were in the Cabinet. He was always so scornful of how everybody else behaved.'

Irvine had not only failed to make friends, he had made plenty of enemies. Many of his fellow ministers thoroughly disliked the Lord Chancellor, states the former civil servant: 'An awful lot of his Cabinet colleagues were very, very fed up with the way he behaved – this arrogance, this high-handedness – "I'm cleverer than the rest of you put together."'

When questioned in a May 1999 Channel 4 documentary, Lord Richard, who was Leader of the House of Lords in Blair's first Cabinet, could not disguise his feelings about Irvine. He said, 'It's not a question of admiring or liking the man. It's a question of whether, in fact, he got the job done. On devolution, he did get the job done.'[122] When asked if he had reservations about Irvine, Richard pointedly replied, 'Well, he was a colleague of mine and I respect him for his abilities. You haven't got to like your colleagues, thank goodness.'[123]

Irvine can have no cause for complaint. He had made it transparently clear to Richard and his other Cabinet colleagues that he considered himself their intellectual superior – and by some margin. His treatment of them had frequently been brusque and sometimes brutal.

The most notorious instance of this came when Irvine was used by PX, the committee on public spending, as a prosecuting counsel to probe for weaknesses in ministers' budget proposals. In an interview for *The Independent*, Donald McIntyre put it to the Lord Chancellor that he had treated Defence Secretary George Robertson like a prisoner in the dock. Irvine did not specifically deny it. Instead, he replied that he and Robertson were

> absolutely the best of friends . . . But if PX is to do its job properly, if there's any merit in questioning assumptions and received wisdoms, then it's got to do its job professionally and vigorously. All my Cabinet colleagues have broad shoulders.[124]

Irvine was in his element when cross-examining ministers before PX. But, if he had stopped to think about it, he would have realised that there was a major difference between what he was doing now and what he had done throughout his career as a barrister. Back then, having demolished someone in the witness box, Irvine could walk away and consider it a job well done. There was no walking away now, however. He was going to have to face his Cabinet colleagues again.

Irvine's excessive aggression was bound to make him enemies. Perhaps he did not care. Irvine may even have planned it, suggests the *New Statesman*'s former editor, Ian Hargreaves:

> One gets the impression that Irvine entered government, on the one hand impressively, as a man who had a much better idea than many other ministers of exactly what he wanted to achieve in the first five years. And he could speak to this agenda, just roll it out. He also entered, I think, as a novice in politics feeling that if people were going to take him seriously, he'd better break a few bones in the first few weeks. I think he set out to do that and that was probably a mistake.

It is now absolutely clear, he says, that Irvine 'should have listened to the people who were there who could have helped him, found others to help him and tempered his assertiveness with more guile and subtlety'.

Guile and subtlety were never two of Irvine's more prominent qualities, however. Indeed, aggression has always been his response to every challenge, whether it be in court or in Cabinet. Someone who witnessed the battles between Irvine and Jack Straw has said of the Lord Chancellor:

> He has the most curious way of dealing with people. He argues an extreme position. When he is forced to retreat, he does so in page after page of the most pompous argument. He never uses a word where he can use a sentence, or a

sentence when he can use a paragraph, or a paragraph where he can make a speech. A politician would be pragmatic and cut his losses. But he has to make these tortuous arguments to try to justify any retreat. He does it with a total lack of grace, and never acknowledges the strength of the opposing argument.[125]

What makes Irvine's behaviour so inappropriate is his insistence on behaving like a barrister when he is in fact supposed to be a politician. Irvine argues extreme positions because he is used to doing that in court. Barristers think nothing of it. It is their job to win the case and, provided it is within the rules, they will try virtually anything to come out on top. In the real world, however, arguing extreme positions has only resulted in Irvine looking ridiculous.

It may be that, after a lifetime at the Bar, Irvine knows no other way of settling a dispute than through an adversarial joust. However, it seems equally likely that Irvine chooses to hide behind a barrister's persona. Irvine is not good at dealing with people. He suffers from a chronic lack of self-confidence, which he covers up with excessive displays of assertiveness. It is those displays that have created an image of Irvine as a man who is pompous, arrogant and aggressive.

At the Bar, Irvine could get away with it. Indeed, his time as head of chambers at 11 King's Bench Walk, where he was rarely if ever challenged, served only to foster that side of his nature. However, politics and public life are far less forgiving worlds than the Bar and Irvine's inability to develop anything other than dysfunctional relationships with his Cabinet colleagues has left him badly exposed.

As has his lack of judgement. Picking fights is one thing. Picking the right fights is another. At the beginning, Irvine seemed to think he was invincible, but his defeats at the hands of Home Secretary Jack Straw proved otherwise. Nor was Straw the only senior minister to best Irvine.

While chairing QFL – the committee for future legislation referred to in his Wolsey speech – Irvine refused to include in the next Queen's Speech a Bill to reform the regulation of the privatised utilities. Irvine adopted his stance knowing that both the Treasury and the Department of Trade and Industry were keen to see the Bill become law as soon as possible. In the end, Gordon Brown was forced to intervene and Irvine was overruled by the Prime Minister. The incident confirms that Irvine had no feel for his position in the Cabinet pecking order. It is clear that Irvine believed that only Tony Blair ranked above him.

There have been numerous other examples of Irvine's lack of judgement. However, they all pale when set against the 'Big Three'.

Irvine could not see that his Wolsey speech was outrageously arrogant and blithely handed a copy of it to *The Times*. He could not see that his remarks about Robin Cook's affair with Gaynor Regan would rebound on him and the Government and happily delivered a scoop right into the *New Statesman*'s lap. Most incredible of all, Irvine could not see that his performance before the House of Commons Select Committee on Public Administration had been a complete and utter disaster.

His approach could not have been more wrong. Instead of attempting to show that he was aware of, and sensitive to, people's concerns about so much money being spent on the Lord Chancellor's residence, Irvine behaved like a barrister with an unbeatable case. His style of delivery – alternatively smug and aggressive – may once have helped Irvine to destroy his opponents' case in court, but, before the committee, it made him look both arrogant and insincere.

A man who had just spent £650,000 of public funds should have been picking his words extremely carefully. It is truly remarkable that he failed to foresee that his comments about DIY products would cause offence to DIY stores and leave him open to ridicule.

Perhaps he would have got it right if he had been given the time to prepare a speech (although the Wolsey affair suggests otherwise).

However, the appearance in front of the select committee exposed all of Irvine's old weaknesses. When challenged, his natural reaction was to attack, not defend. And, without a script, he was lost. He babbled, and as he babbled the actor's mask slipped and the world saw Irvine for what he was: out of touch, self-obsessed and a snob.

CHAPTER EIGHT

No News is Good News

As Tony Blair's first Cabinet reshuffle approached, many predicted that the biggest head to roll – in more senses than one – would be Irvine's. However, come July 1998, the axe failed to fall.

Clearly, Tony Blair's loyalty to his former pupil master played a huge part in Irvine's survival. Yet the Lord Chancellor was also starting to show one or two signs that he was getting his act together. He had even started making jokes about his recent misfortunes. In March 1998, while hosting the first event at his refurbished residence, Irvine told guests, 'Here we all are in the River Room. I'm not going to ask you what you think of it. Someone once said you have to suffer for your art – and it is not even my art!' It was not a great joke, and probably not his own, but it was a start.

Another, more significant, development was that the boasting died down. Irvine no longer told everyone within earshot that he was at the centre of government, playing a pivotal role. 'He doesn't says that any more,' concedes a journalist. 'That doesn't mean he doesn't think it! But he's got the sense not to say it.'

The Lord Chancellor had not suddenly discovered humour and humility. He had simply gained a special adviser. From now on everything would be done differently. Garry Hart's arrival at the Lord Chancellor's Department proved a turning point in Irvine's fortunes.

Irvine and Hart are friends. They are close in age, share a passion for the good life and enjoy drinking. However, their personalities could not be more different. Where Irvine is self-conscious and suspicious, Hart is relaxed and outgoing. Where Irvine is pompous and aloof, Hart is self-deprecating and fun to be with.

Hart has the ability to put people, including Irvine, at their ease. Indeed, like Lady Irvine, Hart is able to work a transformation in Irvine. When Hart is about, Irvine lightens up and begins to enjoy himself. So great is the change, even people who know Irvine well are surprised. A journalist who attended one of the LCD's press receptions recalls that 'he sat with Garry on that bench seat – in the River Room – and they were just joking and laughing. I'd never, ever seen him look like that.'

The pair first met when Hart was a partner at Herbert Smith, the City law firm that instructed Irvine so frequently during his time at the Bar. Hart first briefed Irvine to act on behalf of some developer clients who had run into a planning dispute over a proposed development at Coin Street on London's South Bank. The recommendation to use Irvine had come from their mutual friend Tony Blair. Like Irvine, Hart is godfather to one of Blair's children (in Hart's case, Kathryn; in Irvine's, Nicky). Until the Blairs moved into Downing Street, Hart was a neighbour and a member of the so-called 'Islington mafia'.

It is as a friend that Hart's true value to Irvine lies. Because Irvine has genuine respect for Hart, he listens to Hart in a way he would never listen to a civil servant. Because Hart has Irvine's trust, he can talk to Irvine in a way that no civil servant would ever dare.

Hart is an 'expert' rather than a 'political' special adviser. His role has nothing to do with politics, confirms a former LCD official:

> I think he was there purely and simply to be Derry's personal confidant and adviser, someone who would shore him up, a mate. It's lonely being in government. You're surrounded by strangers who profess to be there to help you, and if you're neurotic you think they're giggling about you behind the door.

Hart has been described on occasion as a spin doctor. However, this is a complete misinterpretation of his function. He was not taken on to provide damage limitation or to make Irvine look better than he really is. He is there to be a sounding board and to provide some much-needed common sense.

In a rare interview since becoming Irvine's special adviser, Hart has declared:

> I do not regard myself as a spin doctor. I regard myself as an adviser who is there to help him. But the prime purpose of mine is not to spin images, and in my view he does not need spinning in that way because the talent of the person will be seen in the work he is doing. [126]

Hart has also declared that, since taking up the role of special adviser, his admiration for Irvine has only increased. He has even dismissed Irvine's problems in his first year of office as nothing more than a problem of perception. He said:

> I don't think he ever got things wrong. But it takes a little while for policy to be formulated and put forward in, for example, the Access to Justice Bill, and it is only when you actually see what he has produced that the public and commentators can begin to form judgements. In the early days, he was busily preparing for legal and constitutional reform. I don't think he got sufficient recognition for what he was seeking to do. [127]

Hart's claim that Irvine has not made mistakes was well meant, but it may be carrying loyalty a little too far. Down to earth and practical, Hart is not blind to Irvine's faults. Indeed, he knows them well and is thus usually able to counter them before they cause a problem. In fact, if Hart had been on board at the Lord Chancellor's Department from the start, Irvine's first year in office might not have been such a disaster.

Irvine was, in fact, keen for Hart to join him long before his actual starting date in March 1998. However, Tony Blair was curiously reluctant to let Irvine appoint a special adviser. Correspondence between the Lord Chancellor and the Prime Minister in autumn 1997 reveals that Irvine had to beg to be allowed to take on Hart. In a letter to the Prime Minister dated 25 September, Irvine wrote:

> I refer to my letter to you of 21 August 1997, to which you have not formally replied.
>
> When we last spoke on a number of issues in the garden of Number 10, you gave me an indication that your mind was moving in a favourable direction on my request.
>
> I would be most grateful if you could read this letter yourself now and give me your decision. I am becoming embarrassed by my inability to be positive with Gary [sic], who has ascertained from his partners that they would be understanding if he took early retirement . . .
>
> I simply do not think that it is fair that all of my Cabinet colleagues should have two special advisers, and perhaps more in some cases, when I have none. If for any reason you think Gary is inappropriate, and I can see none, I will of course accept your decision and report it to Gary diplomatically. If that were your view, then I would like you to tell me what your position in principle is in relation to my having any special advisers. [128]

In the end, it took four months of similar pleading by Irvine to get Blair's permission to appoint Hart in the role of special adviser. It was a most unfortunate delay, argues Sheila Thompson: 'Life would have been different for Lord Irvine, I think, if Garry had been appointed right at the beginning. He would have seen so many of those banana skins.'

Life might also have been different for the people at the LCD. Hart 'endeared himself to the department very, very quickly', she recalls, and provided a much-needed line of communication between a distant Lord Chancellor and his staff.

However, not everyone greeted Hart's appointment with enthusiasm. As soon as it became known that Hart had no previous political experience and was close to both Irvine and Blair, accusations of cronyism and 'jobs for the boys' were made once more — just as they had been when Irvine was appointed. Irvine's choice of Hart was also attacked on the basis that Hart had only joined the Labour Party shortly before the 1997 election and that he had been a regular contributor to Labour Party funds.

Some of the criticism has struck home. Hart has admitted:

> I am stung by this. What you have to do is examine if there is any substance in the charge that somehow or other somebody has been appointed to a post without any talent to fulfil that role.
>
> I did give money to the Labour Party. But I have also given money to the Almeida Theatre. I have supported a lot of charities and I intend to go on supporting a lot of charities . . . I see no difficulty in trying to give money to help the party succeed.
>
> The suggestion seems to be that I gave money to the Labour Party in order to get a job which forced me to take an 80 per cent cut. That is not the mark of cronyism, it is the mark of lunacy. [129]

Hart has not allowed the criticism to deflect him from his task. Indeed, he has done a remarkably good job. It is no coincidence that, after Hart became Irvine's special adviser, the stories of rows between Irvine and his Cabinet colleagues began to dry up, as did the stories of staff bullying. Most important of all, there were no major gaffes. As a result, press coverage began to focus on the Lord Chancellor's work rather than just his personality. Newspapers continued to take the odd pot shot at Irvine, but there was nothing to compare with the repeated, and sometimes vicious, attacks

Irvine had been forced to endure during the storms over Wolsey and the wallpaper.

The secret of Hart's success with Irvine is remarkably simple. He has got the Lord Chancellor to calm down a bit. Hart has revealed to Irvine that he can achieve a lot more by taking a more considered and less aggressive approach.

Allan Percival, Irvine's director of communications, and Sir Hayden Phillips, Sir Thomas Legg's replacement as the Lord Chancellor's permanent secretary, must also take some credit. However, the suspicion remains that the main reason as to why they have done a good job is that – unlike their predecessors – they have been allowed to do a good job. Thanks to Hart and some harsh lessons, Irvine now listens to his advisers far more than he used to.

The extent of Hart's influence over Irvine was clearly seen in an interview the Lord Chancellor gave to *The Guardian* in March 1999. Irvine implied that he had learnt much during his time in office, stating:

> The notion that, because you have acted for household names for 20 years, the whole range of human behaviour and reaction is within your knowledge, and therefore you have nothing to learn from politics, is the opposite of the truth. Politics, I think, is an extremely startling experience. [130]

This rare confession of human frailty was followed by an even less characteristic bout of insight. Irvine declared, 'Perception, what people perceive to be the truth, is in itself a fact . . . there's an enormous danger that the truth, the sacredness of facts, is lost behind the perception.'

This was a truly remarkable turnaround for a man whose life-long philosophy had been 'Take me as I am'. It is inconceivable that Irvine would have made such statements during his first year as Lord Chancellor. There was, at that time, no place in Irvine's world for public admissions of doubt.

Not known

Irvine has an awful lot to do if he is going to change people's perceptions of him. His public image remains very negative. People know Irvine for his gaffes (Wolsey and the wallpaper in particular); they know him as Tony's crony (the man who only got where he is because he is an old mate of the Prime Minister's) and they know him for the breeches and the stockings. And that is about all that they do know.

Part of the problem is that the public has not been given the opportunity to see Irvine. He has never done a major interview on TV and, given his bad record when being interviewed by newspapers, is never likely to. As a result, he remains, so far as the public is concerned, a distant and somewhat shadowy character who, like Alastair Campbell, wields huge power behind the scenes.

Another factor is that the little positive media coverage Irvine has received has been lost in the flood of negative press. The bad publicity has been a lot more memorable, because it has been a lot more entertaining. For most people, Irvine the bungler has, quite naturally, proved a far greater attraction than Irvine the Cabinet committee chairman.

The Lord Chancellor's greatest difficulty at the present time is that he does not have a lot to show the public for all his hard work in the first two years of the Labour government. Much to his frustration, this situation is not likely to change much in the foreseeable future. Like everyone else, politicians can only be judged on results and, in politics, results can take a long time to come through.

The Human Rights Act provides a perfect example of this. At press time, the Act was stalled. A confidential Whitehall audit had revealed that many existing laws could be open to legal challenge once the Act comes into force. (To give but one example, the honours system might be open to attack because awards are made on a discretionary basis rather than through open competition.) In order to give officials an opportunity to knock regulations into shape, the decision was taken to postpone the Act's implementation until perhaps as late as mid-2001.

This situation immediately presented the Government with a dilemma. The new Scottish, Welsh and Northern Ireland assemblies are committed to act in accordance with the European Convention on Human Rights, which means that England now stands alone as the only part of the United Kingdom without such a commitment. In its rush to be seen as radical, the Government chose to effect its reforms in a piecemeal way and appears to have made a real mess of implementing one of the key elements of its programme of constitutional reform.

How successful the Human Rights Act will prove once it finally comes into force is, at this stage, anyone's guess. Concerns have been expressed that there will be increased conflict between the Government and the judiciary, which will have the job of interpreting how the introduction of the European Convention affects both legislation and the common law. Given the Blair government's controlling ways and the strong will of some members of the senior judiciary, sparks seem set to fly sooner or later.

Likewise, it is too soon to give an appraisal of Irvine's contribution to the devolution programme. Certainly, Irvine and the Blair government deserve credit for delivering devolution to Scotland and Wales, but will it be workable?

It is already obvious that the most important parts of the devolution legislation will be those provisions dealing with disputes between Westminster and Scottish parliament and Welsh assembly. Indeed, those provisions will be all the more relevant now that Labour has failed to achieve an outright majority in either the Scottish or Welsh parliaments. If the drafting of dispute resolution clauses is not right, there will be chaos.

As for reform of the House of Lords, that still has a long way to go. The Government has achieved its manifesto commitment to remove the speaking and voting rights of hereditary peers – but only after a massive struggle.

Just as there had been rows in the Cabinet committee dealing with devolution, so there were, in the early months of 1998, fierce arguments in the committee dealing with Lords reform, which was also chaired by Irvine. No sooner had the committee been formed than it split over whether reform should be effected in stages or in one go.

On one side were Irvine, Lord Richard (Leader of the Lords), and Lord Carter (Chief Whip). On the other were the Commons members of the committee – Richard's and Carter's counterparts Ann Taylor and Nick Brown, plus Irvine's old sparring partner, Home Secretary Jack Straw. The MPs argued that it was impossible to consider Lords reform in isolation from the impact that reform would have on the House of Commons. They were concerned that a reformed House of Lords might be a more powerful body and thus pose a threat to the authority of the Commons.

After the decision was made to press ahead with a piecemeal programme – a victory for the MPs – the committee still faced the challenge of finding a means of excluding hereditary peers without provoking their hostility. Irvine instigated secret talks with Lord Cranbourne, the Tory leader in the House of Lords, and other senior Tory peers.

The first meeting took place at Lord Cranbourne's house, but details of the talks leaked out, to the especial embarrassment of Irvine, who had appeared to imply to the Commons Public Administration Committee that the reform programme was proceeding without other parties being consulted. Indeed, some members of the committee went so far as to complain that Irvine had misled them.

It took until the beginning of December 1998 to achieve a breakthrough and then only through highly unconventional means. Displaying considerable pragmatism, Irvine persuaded Lord Cranbourne to accept a deal whereby nearly 100 hereditary peers would stay on in the House of Lords until a fully reformed second chamber was in place. However, the most remarkable aspect of the deal was that it was done without the sanction of Conservative

Party leader William Hague. Upon finding out what had happened, Hague immediately sacked Cranbourne. But too late. The Irvine–Cranbourne agreement had garnered considerable support among Tory peers, leaving Hague high and dry. It was quite a triumph for Irvine: House of Lords reform was back on track and he also had managed to embarrass the leader of the Opposition.

With the first stage of Lords reform effectively done and dusted, the second stage was placed in the hands of a royal commission. Chaired by Lord Wakeham, the commission has been charged with the task of producing a blueprint for the new House of Lords. Nothing will come of the commission's report for some time. In September 1998, at a meeting at Chequers to finalise details of the then imminent Queen's Speech, it was decided that the creation of a new second chamber would have to wait until after the next general election. The excuse given for postponing Lords reform was that there was a danger of constitutional overload. However, Tony Blair has never been particularly devoted to the issue of constitutional reform, which he inherited from John Smith. It seems likely that the Prime Minister thought it was time that the Government's efforts were directed elsewhere.

All guns blazing

Irvine's key role in constitutional reform has tended to attract attention away from his work in the legal field. However, it could be argued that Irvine's record since taking charge of the legal system provides a better insight into his political ethos than anything else he has done. Irvine is determined to stamp his mark on the legal system and has proved aggressive, ruthless and unafraid to make enemies.

Ironically, the Bar greeted Irvine's arrival as Lord Chancellor with relief. It was more than happy to see the back of Lord Mackay. An outsider plucked by Mrs Thatcher from the Scottish Bench, Mackay had not proved a friend. Far from protecting the profession, he had introduced reforms exposing barristers to greater competition, and cut back on legal aid at every opportunity.

Everyone assumed Irvine would be different. He was one of them, a true son of the Bar who had made a fortune while in practice. Nor was there much in Irvine's record as Labour's shadow Lord Chancellor to cause concern. True, at the last Bar Council conference before the general election, Irvine had declared that a Labour government would set in motion a review of legal aid and the civil justice system and had warned that Labour would cut the high fees paid to barristers in the most expensive criminal cases. But those are the kind of noises politicians always make before an election, especially when they are members of a party desperate to show that it is financially responsible and worthy of the nation's trust after 18 years in opposition. In any event, Irvine had seemingly made clear his commitment to legal aid when he declared, 'Supporters of legal aid must never cease to emphasise that it is a highly successful public social service.' [131]

As it turned out, the Bar's complacency proved to be mistaken. Just ten weeks after Labour's victory, Irvine attacked his former colleagues in a way that antagonised just about every section of the Bar. While speaking in a House of Lords debate on whether rising court fees were denying ordinary people access to justice, Irvine announced:

> To argue that court fees act as a deterrent to litigants is rather like arguing that people are deterred from buying a new car by an increase in vehicle excise duty. Fat-cat lawyers railing at the inequity of court fees do not attract the sympathy of the public . . . Top lawyers easily earn at least four times what top surgeons earn. The main deterrent on going to law is not court fees but the price at which lawyers value their own services and, so far, have succeeded in charging. [132]

For a man who had until recently commanded massive fees and whose clerk had always been prepared to wring an extra penny out of clients, this was one hell of U-turn. Indeed, at the Bar conference in 1996 Irvine himself had blamed the press for the fact that the public saw all lawyers as 'fat cats'.

Irvine's conscience did not trouble him, however. During his House of Lords speech, the poacher-turned-gamekeeper smugly declared:

> I have to acknowledge that, until recently, I had what I think I can fairly describe as an entirely satisfactory and rewarding practice at the Bar so that, to some, my calling attention to incomes of this order might bear comparison with the conversion of St Paul. [133]

Irvine's comments were targeted at a strictly limited number of barristers who earn big fees from legal aid work. But, because he did not make that clear, his remarks were reported as an attack on the Bar in general. Indeed, the newspapers had one of their regular 'lawyer bashing' days, producing headline after headline about 'fat-cat' lawyers earning £1 million a year.

As usual, the majority of the press was oblivious to the realities of life at the Bar. Only a tiny handful of barristers make £1 million a year. Those that do are at the top of their profession through dint of immense hard work and tremendous ability. Their clients are private companies and PLCs well able to afford their fees. And however great the top barristers' earnings may be, they seem reasonable in comparison with the money made by countless other people in the City and in industry.

Naturally enough, barristers were upset to receive such negative and inaccurate coverage, especially since it had been provoked by Irvine. They felt he had no right to point the finger.

Irvine was 'quite the wrong bloke to turn around and start firing shots like that', says former Bar chairman and legal aid lawyer Anthony Scrivener QC. 'If the bloke had done his fair share of legal aid work like everybody else – which he didn't – then fair enough, he could have had a crack.

The Lord Chancellor also managed to offend barristers in fields that have nothing to do with legal aid. Irvine should have expressed himself more clearly, says a top commercial silk. Instead, he went in all guns blazing and everyone got shot down. The newspaper articles that appeared at the time, complains the barrister, conveyed the impression that

> we were all milking the legal aid fund, and I was rather upset by that . . . I haven't had a legal aid fee in a very long time and nor have any of the people I know that practise in the same kind of work that I practise in.

Irvine's blunderbuss attack bruised the Bar's already fragile reputation and also ruined the opportunity for a proper debate on an important topic. The issue of rising court fees was totally lost in the rash of 'fat cat' headlines. (In fact, Irvine later bowed to pressure and exempted people on state benefit from paying court fees.)

Undeterred, Irvine continued to draw attention to barristers' earnings. In December 1997 he revealed that, during 1996–7, 35 barristers had received £270,000 to £575,000 from the legal aid fund for criminal work, while another 20 received between £203,000 and £411,000 for civil work. He complained:

> A High Court judge earns £112,011. A lord justice of appeal earns £124,511. Many hospital consultants earn £56,000–£70,000 a year. Judges and hospital consultants all work hard over long hours . . . The lives of many people depend on their professionalism. Yet almost 1,000 barristers earned more from legal aid last year than hospital consultants are paid.

Naturally, Irvine's comments excited considerable interest. Journalists were particularly keen to discover the identities of the barristers on the list. A couple of days after Irvine's speech, Alan Jones QC, who had led the defence of Kevin Maxwell, was 'outed' by *The Guardian* as the biggest earner.

In April 1998 the guessing was over. In answer to a parliamentary question that had probably been planted, Irvine's representative in the House of Commons, Geoff Hoon, produced lists of the top 20 earners from civil legal aid and the top 20 earners from criminal legal aid.

Again, many barristers were furious. Irvine, however, defended the lists on the grounds that, 'We believe in freedom of information, and we believe in freedom of information about what people earn from legal aid as well.'[134]

However, the information put out by the Lord Chancellor's Department cannot be taken at face value, warns Scrivener. Some of the fees included in the list had been earned by the barristers in question over a period of several years. On some occasions, he claims, the LCD's figures 'were just plain wrong . . . they had to withdraw one set of figures because the individual barristers checked with their accountants and told them they had to retract'.

Not that Irvine would have minded. He had achieved his goal. The 'fat cats' bombardment had prepared the way for the Government's attack on the legal aid system. As Scrivener points out, having a go at 'fat cats' is 'the usual thing they do to try to soften up the opposition, because any barrister who stands up and tries to protect legal aid can always be condemned as a "fat cat" thereafter.'

A Tory in Labour clothing

When the attack on legal aid came, it took many by surprise. People had known it was coming, but they had not envisaged the scale. It transpired that it was not Irvine's intention to shake up the civil legal aid system so much as to dismantle it.

In October 1997 Irvine announced at the Law Society's annual conference in Cardiff that from April 1998 legal aid would no longer be available for any claim for monetary damages. (Aid would still be available for criminal, housing, immigration and social welfare cases and for family and divorce cases where money was not the remedy being sought.) Litigants would instead have to use an American-style 'no win, no fee' system. That is, people would have to find a lawyer who was prepared to handle their case even though the lawyer would only get paid if the case were won. Litigants would be expected to take out insurance to cover the cost of defeat.

Irvine told the conference:

> Civil justice is too expensive and too exclusive. The very rich and the very poor have access, but middle-income Britain is left out in the cold – and middle-income Britain is the overwhelming majority of people in this country . . . [135]

> Legal aid must be refocused. It must be a tool to promote access to justice for the needy, not seen by the public as something basically keeping lawyers in business. It is the people's needs which justify our having legal aid in the first place. [136]

Irvine's announcement signalled a turnaround in Labour Party policy every bit as drastic as Irvine's decision to join the ranks of the Bar's critics. During its many years in opposition, Labour had steadfastly resisted the Conservative government's attempts to prune the civil legal aid budget, which had escalated from £682 million in 1991 to £1.47 billion in 1997, a rise of some 115 per cent. Incredibly, Labour was now attacking a pillar of the welfare system – one of the sacred cows of party policy – and doing so in a far more radical manner than the Tories had ever dared. Left-wing lawyers, such as Anthony Scrivener, were shocked.

'This isn't a Labour government,' he complains. 'It's a farce to pretend it is. It's a Conservative government. I rather suspect that if Ken Clarke took over the Conservative Party, he'd be much more left wing than this lot.'

If the Blair government has its way, access to legal services will no longer be available through the welfare state, says Scrivener:

> They want to keep taxation down. They want to pursue a Conservative Party policy. And the only way they can do it is by cutting down in some area or another, and so they've cut off law from the welfare state. That's what's happened. And if I'd known that, I wouldn't have voted for them. I certainly wouldn't have given them 5,000 quid to help them on their way. Every time I get a letter to go to dinners now, I have a very short reply!

Scrivener's complaints comprise just a small part of the criticism against Irvine's proposals. A number of action groups have argued that, far from opening up the legal system to more people, the reforms will only result in more people being excluded. Poorer litigants will not be able to afford the insurance premiums or the cost of the initial report required to evaluate whether or not the case could be won. Lawyers will only agree to take on simple and cheap cases that can be easily won and litigants with difficult or complex cases will be left out in the cold.

The Government has countered that law firms, rather than litigants, should bear the early expenses, such as the insurance premiums and report costs. However, the policy's opponents have complained that small law firms will not be able to bear those expenses and would risk going bust if they did.

In the end, opposition to Irvine's proposals proved such that he was obliged to tone down his reforms. In March 1998 a consultation paper called *Access to Justice with Conditional Fees* stated that medical negligence actions would continue to be eligible for legal aid, at least in the short term. In July Irvine reiterated his commitment to his 'no win, no fee' programme but then announced that he was postponing his plans to withdraw legal aid from accident cases until October 1999 at the very earliest. Irvine had apparently bowed to pressure from the Law Society, the Bar and consumer groups that his reforms should not be introduced until it was clear that the insurance market would be able to provide the cover for 'no win, no fee' cases. Irvine said that he now accepted that, in replacing legal aid with conditional fees, there needed to be a 'measured approach'. [137]

This back-pedalling was in part the price Irvine had to pay for rushing the reform process. In particular, Sir Peter Middleton's review of the legal aid system had taken place with indecent haste. Just five months separated the date on which Irvine announced the review and the date on which he declared its results, leaving not very much time in between for proper consideration of a highly revolutionary set of reforms.

No one should get too excited about the fact that Irvine has made some concessions, warns Scrivener:

> Mackay used to do the same thing. You'd make such a fuss about it all, he'd postpone bits. But he [Irvine] is going to bring them in later and he'll find them easier to bring in later. It's all part of an overall stratagem . . . He wants to appear to have listened to reason, but he's a bloke who'll never listen to reason. He's a chap who always thinks he's 100 per cent right. He's not a person to listen to the other side's view at all.

Certainly, the concessions only made so much difference. Irvine's December 1998 White Paper, *Modernising Justice*, still spelled out the biggest reorganisation of the legal aid scheme since its introduction in 1949. The White Paper declared:

> The justice system is top heavy – it is dominated by lawyers, courts and outdated legal practices and jargon. But our legal system should be for everyone. The Government will refocus legal aid spending on social welfare cases and expand the role of voluntary advice agencies, so helping to correct this imbalance.

In order to effect this revolution, the Government would be setting up two bodies: the Community Legal Service for civil disputes and the Criminal Defence Service for criminal cases. The Community Legal Service would only use approved lawyers and advice centres working under contract and would operate as a national network of GP-style legal surgeries. The Criminal Defence Service would use a combination of approved law firms and its own salaried lawyers with the result that those facing a criminal prosecution would no longer enjoy unlimited freedom in their choice of lawyers.

Lawyers would not be paid according to the amount of work they handled. Instead, they would work to strictly controlled budgets. They would also have to meet quality standards. The Legal Aid Board would be replaced by a Legal Services Commission, which would monitor the allocation of contracts on the basis of local needs.

Civil actions would not be backed by public funds if they were deemed suitable for mediation nor if they could be funded in another way, such as through a contingency arrangement. Likewise, no case would get backing unless it was considered that a reasonable person would spend his or her own money on it. Changes would be made to the legal insurance market in order to encourage 'no win, no fee' work.

Heather Hallett QC, chairman of the Bar Council, attacked the proposals. She argued: 'What the legal aid system needs is cost control, not state control.'[138] Hallett recommended that the best way to achieve this would be through fixed-fee schemes rather than block contracts, which might result in lawyers developing a 'sausage machine mentality'.[139]

She also suggested that the Criminal Defence Service might backfire without proper funding. The lawyers employed by the service, she said, 'may not be so fearless if they have the state on their shoulder and a financial disincentive against properly preparing their case'.[140]

Irvine, meanwhile, stated his side of the case in an interview he gave to Frances Gibb of *The Times* shortly after the White Paper was published. He declared that he had every confidence that his proposals would meet with general approval. He said the Community Legal Service would amount to a 'more rational, joined-up whole'[141] than what had previously existed. He added, 'I would be surprised if there was opposition to it.'[142]

Irvine accepted that his reforms would result in a sharp reduction in the number of law firms providing legally aided services. However, he believed that quality was a more important factor than quantity and that a loss of choice was preferable to cases being handled badly. He stated:

> At present, if you are eligible for legal aid, the solicitor can take on your case from beginning to end, regardless of expertise. The classic area is medical negligence. I take the view that if the State is going to fund these very difficult cases, the State should point people in the direction of specialist lawyers.[143]

As for the Criminal Defence Service, Irvine declared that there were no plans to move towards an American-style public defender service in either the short or long term. Although the Access to Justice Bill would provide for the use of some salaried lawyers, Irvine said that he confidently expected the great majority of criminal defence work to be handled by independent lawyers.

A sick joke

In January 1999, Irvine made yet another concession, when he agreed to withdraw his plans for conditional fee arrangements in divorce disputes involving money or property. He had been persuaded that such arrangements would make it more difficult for couples to achieve amicable divorce settlements (a goal enshrined in government policy).

At the end of the month, Irvine was defeated in the House of Lords, which narrowly rejected his attempt to give solicitors and employed barristers the right to appear in the higher courts. (A coalition of cross-benchers, judges and Conservatives got together to argue that only independent self-employed barristers should have the right.)

In mid-February Irvine was defeated in the House again, when peers voted against his plan for a Criminal Defence Service that would employ salaried lawyers. A clause was also voted into his Access to Justice Bill, which introduced new overriding aims into the Bill with a view to protecting access to justice. Irvine dismissed the clause as 'a gimmick', much to the annoyance of its backers, such as the Bar and the Law Society, and pledged that the clause would be removed. He insisted that a proposed hardship fund would ensure that vulnerable people, including children, the old and the disabled, were not disadvantaged.

However, the new Bar Council chairman, Dan Brennan QC, argued that the clause should be retained. He said, 'The Lord Chancellor says that these are the very people who are protected under his legal aid reforms. If that is the case, why not put it in the Bill?'[144]

At the end of April, Irvine showed all his old irascibility when he allowed himself to get sucked into an unseemly row with the Law Society. The Lord Chancellor was enraged by an advertising campaign run by the society against his legal aid reforms. He described the ads, which complained that the reforms would reduce access to justice, as 'irresponsible scaremongering'.[145] Next, he released to the press a letter he had written to the Law Society in which he accused it of 'propagating untruths'[146] and suggested that the £700,000 spent on advertising might have been better used in tackling the backlog of complaints against solicitors. For good measure, he wrote to *The Guardian* criticising the Law Society ads appearing that week in the newspaper. He declared:

> The advertisements are a travesty of the facts. The Access to

Justice Bill does not propose cutting legal aid – the Government plans to spend more on legal aid over the next three years than the previous Government intended. The Bill will help focus legal aid money on the areas of greatest need; it will encourage a wider range of legal services; it will cut restrictive practices among lawyers and get value for money for taxpayers. It will increase access to justice, putting the public first, not the legal profession.

Beside Irvine's letter, the newspaper published one from human rights solicitor Louise Christian. A founding partner of Christian Fisher, she spoke for a lot of legal aid practitioners when she wrote:

The truth is that a Labour government is doing to legal aid what, in opposition, it criticised the Tories for doing to the health service. Not only will a false internal market prevent us from doing our jobs through untold bureaucracy, but civil justice is to be almost completely privatised . . . Many important cases now brought successfully will no longer be taken. When Lord Irvine decided to call his Bill the Access to Justice Bill, he was indulging in a sick joke.

Then in May came what can only be described as a highly vindictive move on Irvine's part. He wrote to the Law Society stating that he proposed to ban it from using any of the income it receives from solicitors' practising certificates for 'trade union' activities. (The fees paid by solicitors for such certificates forms the bulk of the Law Society's annual income.) The ban would mean the society could no longer afford to run the kind of advertising campaign that had inflamed the Lord Chancellor. Irvine, it seems, had once again grown tired of debate.

No passion for politics

A Harris poll conducted at the end of April 1999 showed overwhelming support for the Law Society's stance on legal aid. No fewer than 93 per cent of those surveyed said that legal services should be provided as an entitlement to those who cannot pay for them.

Despite such public support and despite the considerable opposition his proposals provoked, Irvine is pressing ahead with reforms that will, in due course, result in the virtual destruction of the legal aid system. The Bar, the Law Society and various action and consumer groups will, no doubt, continue to make a lot of noise, but they know they are fighting a losing battle. The sad fact is that the public is not especially interested. People may say that they are in favour of free legal services, but few, if any, of the Harris poll's 93 per cent are ever going to do anything about it.

Herein lies the key to the Government's strategy. The Government is not attacking legal aid simply because the legal aid budget has spiralled in recent years. It is attacking legal aid because public apathy makes legal aid an acceptable target. The Government would never dream of mounting such an assault on education or health.

The public must take more interest in Irvine's proposals before it is too late. There is a genuine danger that those in most need of assistance will be isolated. Furthermore, a fundamental human right is being threatened: a man or woman faced with criminal charges must enjoy the freedom to instruct the lawyer of their choice. If Irvine has his way, the Government will enjoy the right to select any lawyer to fight its case, while the defendant will only be able to pick a lawyer approved by the Government. And that is only the beginning of it.

Irvine has insisted that he has no plans to create a public defender service. However, his decision to limit defendants' freedom of choice cannot be seen as anything other than the first step towards an American-style system. Anyone who has ever seen the Crown Prosecution Service in action will know that this would be a disaster. Because attracting high-quality lawyers is extremely difficult, the overall standard of lawyers employed by the CPS is woefully low. There is no reason to believe a public defender service would have any more success in recruiting the best. In other words, defendants will have to rely on second-rate advice from second-rate lawyers.

Irvine might adopt a different approach if he had some direct experience of criminal justice. He would then be aware of the incompetence that pervades the system and the lower courts in particular. However, during his legal career, he was far too busy making money to trouble himself with legal aid work. And, since becoming Lord Chancellor, he has remained preoccupied with other things. A former LCD official recalls:

> It took the [Lord Chancellor's] Department almost a year to get him to go and look at courts. He thought they were boring visits. He was shy about meeting court staff, but he didn't seem to have any interest in what it was actually like to go through the system that he was responsible for reforming.

Irvine's indifference begs the question: does he actually care about those at the sharp end of his reforms? The former official, for one, thinks not:

> When Lord Mackay was working on his reforms, you always got the feeling that he really, really cared about what it was like for people to go through the court system, whether as a victim or a witness or somebody standing in the box accused of a crime. You always got the feeling that he really cared about them and wanted things to get better for them. You never got the feeling that Lord Irvine did.

Irvine would deny this. In October 1998 he told the *Independent on*

Sunday that his political motivation is 'to make the lives of ordinary people better'.[147] However, there is little or no evidence to back up this claim.

Although both his father and grandfather were committed socialists, Irvine is not a conviction politician. His lavish lifestyle hardly bespeaks socialism, nor does his decision to send both his sons to a private school. Irvine's loyalty to the Labour Party is purely inherited. He supports Labour because it is in his bones, not because it is in his head. When asked by the *Independent on Sunday* whether he considered himself a socialist, he paused before replying:

> I attach very little importance to labels, but, to the extent that it has a contemporary meaning, not in the Marxist–Leninist sense, but in the British tradition, then, yes. I think that New Labour is a natural development of socialist tradition.[148]

Around the same time, the *Sunday Times* asked Irvine to define the Blair government's *raison d'être*. He answered:

> I don't think there are any easy 'isms' or 'ologies'. But there is nothing wrong with what the Prime Minister says: modernising and reform. To look at the whole of our institutions with a view to rationalising them and modernising them. That seems to me to be a very sensible but hugely ambitious set of objectives.[149]

Irvine's responses sum up his lukewarm attitude towards politics. He has never shown any real passion. He could not even be bothered with politics at school or university, while his efforts at Hendon North in 1970 look distinctly half-hearted. Despite being shadow Lord Chancellor, he was for years a virtual stranger to the House of Lords. He has never attended a Labour Party conference.

It is obvious that Irvine's real interest lies not in politics, but in political office. He has been telling friends for many years that he wants to be remembered as a great, reforming Lord Chancellor. The allusion to Cardinal Wolsey was no joke: Irvine wants a place in history. As Baroness Smith has declared:

> The Cardinal Wolsey stuff had a lot in it. He thought he would be a different kind of Lord Chancellor. And I never quite understood, because he used to say it before he got appointed . . . he had all these plans. They were all good things he wanted to do. But he kept saying, 'I'm going to be different.' The idea was that he was going to stamp his mark and go down as a great, reforming Lord Chancellor. He knew how he would go down in history before he ever got there. And that's not political. That's got no sense of what history is. History is written afterwards, not before. [150]

Sounding the retreat

Legal aid is not the only topic over which Irvine has scrapped with the Bar. In June 1998 – during his first press conference for a year – he announced proposals to dismantle its near-monopoly of work in the higher courts. He said the move was intended to abolish 'antiquated restrictions' [151] that pressure people into using two lawyers – a solicitor and a barrister – when only one is needed.

Irvine claimed that change was long overdue:

> The perception has grown that the legal system is dominated by the interests of lawyers, rather than the need to provide justice for the people . . . I have one clear aim: the establishment of a modern and fair system which will promote quality and choice for those who need the help of an advocate while, at the same time, providing value for money. [152]

Irvine's proposals were set out in his White Paper, *Modernising Justice*. This not only contained reforms opening up the higher courts, it provided that barristers and legal executives would, for the first time, be allowed to prepare cases for court. Irvine was – with good reason – determined to finish off Lord Mackay's programme of destroying the legal profession's restrictive practices. These have been allowed to continue for far too long, thanks in the main to the strength of the legal lobby.

The Bar Council has in the past been guilty of opposing virtually every recommendation for opening up the provision of legal services. On this occasion, it confined its objections to a specific point. Throwing open the doors of the higher courts was all well and good, the Bar suggested, but doing so would allow CPS lawyers to run cases in the higher courts, giving the State far too much control over prosecutions. The Bar said that the use of independent barristers in criminal prosecutions can prevent abuses of justice.

Irvine rejected that argument. He declared:

> The Government does not accept the arguments that it is improper, dangerous or unconstitutional for Crown prosecutors to have such rights ... If, as has been claimed, it is wrong in principle for someone to be prosecuted by an employed lawyer, how is it that we tolerate this practice in the magistrates' courts, where over 95 per cent of criminal cases are tried?[153]

Irvine was not going to allow the Bar to frustrate his plans in the way it had frustrated Lord Mackay's. *Modernising Justice* announced that the Lord Chancellor was to be given a power to impose rule changes on the legal profession, with the senior judges' right of veto over rule changes being removed.

The Lord Chancellor's new powers would not be entirely unfettered. As a safety guard, he would not be able to exercise them without Parliament's approval. Nevertheless, the proposal attracted considerable opposition, not least from judges, who suggested that giving the Lord Chancellor such powers was unconstitutional and violated the separation of powers.

Irvine answered his critics in December 1998. Having been forced by the Wolsey and wallpaper fiascos to adopt a less aggressive approach, he had now reverted to his belligerent best. Indeed, he told *The Times* that criticisms of his proposals were 'spurious'[154] and an attempt to 'bolster and lend dignity to a weak case'.[155]

Even though it was perfectly in character, Irvine's decision to take such an aggressive stance was surprising. When making those comments, he knew very well that his plans faced massive opposition from the judiciary. Back in October more than 100 Court of Appeal and High Court judges had responded to Irvine's consultation paper by expressing grave concerns over his proposals and one of the country's top judges, Lord Steyn, had used the opportunity provided by the 1998 Kalisher Memorial Lecture to make a public attack on the Lord Chancellor's plans. In his speech, Steyn declared:

> The proposals of the Lord Chancellor seek to concentrate in his hands the power over rights of audience . . . In the consultation paper the Lord Chancellor states that he would be acting as the head of the judiciary. But he is hardly a neutral and impartial figure. The Lord Chancellor is a member of the Cabinet and he chairs a number of Cabinet committees. He is a member of the executive carrying out the party political agenda of the Labour administration. He is a politician . . .
>
> To entrust to a Cabinet minister the power to control the legal profession would be an exorbitant inroad on the constitutional principle of the separation of powers.[156]

Steyn was also scathing about Irvine's proposal to allow CPS lawyers greater rights of audience. He stated:

Prosecutions in the Crown Court by members of an independent Bar place a brake on the executive. It is no answer to say that CPS lawyers already prosecute in the magistrates' courts. The important cases where tensions between the liberty of the citizen and the interests of the executive arise are heard in the Crown Court. It is an illusion to believe that CPS lawyers work in the same culture of independence as barristers in private practice. Inevitably, CPS lawyers have to display a loyalty to the organisation which employs them and that imposes direct and indirect pressures on them. Failure to fit into the corporate culture of the CPS may result in dismissal or denial of promotion. [157]

Such criticism of a Lord Chancellor by so senior a judge is, to say the very least, uncommon. Nor was Irvine in a position to shrug off Steyn's comments as those of a blinkered reactionary who was only concerned with protecting the Bar's and the judiciary's turf. Not only is Steyn highly respected, he is one of the most liberal judges to have sat in the House of Lords in years.

In any event, Steyn was not alone. In January 1999 a report produced by the House of Lords select committee that scrutinises proposed legislation attacked Irvine on two fronts. First, it complained that the Bill did not set out policy objectives, national principles, nor the criteria for how the Lord Chancellor should exercise his powers over the Legal Services Commission. The report said the Lord Chancellor's directions would be crucial to the running of the civil and criminal justice systems and yet 'the power of the Lord Chancellor is almost untrammelled. We view this with considerable concern.' [158] It was pointed out that Irvine's predecessor, Lord Mackay, had said that such criteria should not be left to directions but should be part of primary legislation.

Second, the report criticised Irvine for seeking such broad powers over the legal profession. The committee said there had to be strong justification for requiring a professional body to change its rules of conduct. It recommended that the Access to Justice Bill should be amended to provide that the Lord Chancellor could only intervene if the legal profession acted unreasonably and suggested that any power granted to the Lord Chancellor should be exercisable only with Parliament's permission.

Irvine must have realised he had gone too far. Shortly after the report came out, he conceded the day and told the House of Lords that he would accept curbs on his proposed powers over the justice system and the legal profession. Irvine agreed an amendment tabled by a retired Law Lord, Lord Lloyd of Berwick, which provided, among other things, that people should not be denied access to justice or the machinery of justice because of their means; that legal services would ensure that disputes are settled expeditiously; and that a strong, independent and self-regulating profession would be preserved.

Given that Irvine had only shortly before described his opponents' case as spurious, lacking in dignity and weak, this was quite a climbdown. However, it is precisely the kind of climbdown Irvine is likely to have to make throughout his political career, because he insists on arguing his points as if he were still a barrister in court. He needs to temper his aggression. A government minister should encourage debate, not constantly try to kill it.

There must be serious doubt over whether Irvine will ever be able to do this. He has never been one to debate issues. Once he has come to a decision, he tends to stick to it through thick and thin. As the Culture Secretary, Chris Smith, and many others have found out, Irvine does not like his authority to be challenged.

CHAPTER NINE

The End of the Line?

Power is everything to Lord Irvine. His love of control contributed to the break-up of 2 Crown Office Row and led to his being installed as an absolute, albeit benevolent, monarch at 11 King's Bench Walk. Irvine's desire to give himself unprecedented powers over the legal profession suggests that he has not changed his ways since entering politics. Furthermore, he has proved most reluctant to yield any reduction in the Lord Chancellor's authority.

Labour came to power with a long-standing commitment to create a judicial appointments commission. The idea was that the commission would assume the Lord Chancellor's responsibility for the selection of judges and would, in order to win public confidence, include a number of lay members. In an article published by *The Guardian* in March 1992, Irvine wrote: 'There is growing dissatisfaction with the outdated, secretive and élitist arrangements for the appointment of judges and the composition of the judiciary . . . There can be no argument against a shake-up in the judicial appointments system.'[159]

However, in October 1997 Irvine announced that the idea of a judicial appointments commission had been indefinitely shelved. The reason he gave for this decision was pressure of work, generated in particular by his legal aid and civil justice reforms. There were, Irvine suggested, more pressing issues to be dealt with. He added that, in the meantime, 'Appointments will continue to be made strictly on merit, after the independent views of the judiciary and the legal profession have been taken into consideration by the Lord Chancellor.'[160]

But it is clear that a lack of time is not the only reason why the setting-up of a commission will have to wait. Irvine declared in February 1998:

> I'm in principle now quite hesitant about it, particularly because of the arguments put around by some, that the result of the European Convention will be to politicise the judges and that their political views and social views should be criteria in determining whether to appoint them. [161]

Irvine went on to state that he was 'very hostile to the idea of a politicised judiciary'. [162] He also revealed that, as an alternative to creating a judicial appointments commission, he was considering appointing an ombudsman to take complaints about unfair decisions.

Irvine's dramatic change in policy since entering government is a serious disappointment to those people who have long campaigned for greater transparency in the appointment of judges. Judges still continue to be chosen after secret 'soundings' by the Lord Chancellor, a situation which many people consider nothing short of a disgrace.

What these soundings actually comprise is anyone's guess. Indeed, it is suspected that successive Lord Chancellors have done little more than have a cosy chat with lawyer friends over brandy and cigars at the end of a good dinner. In his book *Judges*, David Pannick QC wrote that the soundings system resembles 'a pre-1965 Conservative Party leadership contest or a papal conclave rather than the choice of law-makers in a modern democracy'.

In opposition, Irvine was the first to complain about the excessive secrecy of the soundings system, but now that he is in power he expects everyone to trust his decisions. Perhaps Irvine deserves our trust, but that is not the point. The public cannot be expected to have more confidence in the judiciary until there is greater transparency in judicial appointments.

Irvine's record of appointments since becoming Lord Chancellor serves only to strengthen that argument. He has – quite rightly – not refrained from appointing as judges people who happen to be friends and acquaintances. (Since Irvine was a practising barrister right up to the day he became Lord Chancellor, this situation was always going to arise.) Most of these appointments look excellent; one or two, however, have raised eyebrows within the legal profession. It may be that Irvine's judgement will, with time, be shown to have been excellent. However, no aspersions could be cast if judicial appointments were removed from the sole gift of the Lord Chancellor.

This issue is not going to go away. In December 1998 the House of Lords decided to set aside its own recent ruling in the extradition case involving former Chilean head of state General Pinochet because one of the judges, Lord Hoffmann, had links with one of the parties in the case, Amnesty International. That decision resurrected the debate over the appointment and vetting of judges.

In an interview with *The Times*, Irvine conceded that judges will come under greater public scrutiny when the Human Rights Act comes into force. However, he declined to go further than suggest that he might consult over setting up a judicial appointments commission. He defended the present system on the basis that it is preferable to the system used for the US Supreme Court, where judges are chosen to represent a particular interest group, race or gender.

This is a good point, but there is no reason why a British judicial appointments commission should take the US system as its model. Irvine has once again muddied the debate. Thus, it seems that, for the foreseeable future at least, there will be no change and Irvine will stay in charge of judicial appointments.

This suits Irvine very well. He may want to go down in history as a great, reforming Lord Chancellor, but he has no desire to reform the office of Lord Chancellor.

Time for change

Irvine can only resist for so long, however. The case for reform is unanswerable. It should have happened long ago. As far back as 1918 a report suggested that the Lord Chancellor's duties were too great for any one man. The report was produced by a committee chaired by Lord Haldane, who had been Lord Chancellor from 1912 to 1915 and would briefly reassume the office in 1924. It recommended that the Lord Chancellor should no longer act as a judicial member of the House of Lords nor as its Speaker. It also advised a radical overhaul of the administration of justice, with one minister being given control of both the civil and criminal legal systems. This new Minister of Justice, who would be responsible for the state of the law and for the promotion of reforms, would sit in the House of Commons.

The Lord Chancellor, meanwhile, would be the Cabinet's expert on legal and constitutional questions and would be able to assist in the preparation of government legislation. He would also continue to be responsible for appointing the higher judiciary. Haldane felt strongly about this issue, arguing that judicial appointments should not be under the control of the Minister of Justice because the minister was bound to come under political pressure when making appointments.

Since it was completed, the report has done nothing more than collect dust. The Lord Chancellor of the day, Lord Birkenhead, opposed Haldane's findings. He argued that the office of Minister of Justice could not be filled effectively by a layman and that the post would not attract the best lawyers. He also claimed that the Lord Chancellor served an important function as a link between the executive and the judiciary.

However, it was not Birkenhead's antipathy that killed the Haldane report, it was generalised apathy. No one had the appetite to pick up the report's recommendations and drive them through Parliament.

A few of those recommendations have, in fact, since been

adopted. But, as so often before, chance played the main hand in changing the Lord Chancellor's role. The threat of German bombs, and the arrival of central heating in the House of Lords, proved far more effective than all Lord Haldane's hard work.

During the Second World War the House of Lords took the decision to begin its sittings at 2.30 p.m. rather than 4.15 p.m. in order to finish daily business before the blackout. This presented the Lord Chancellor with a dilemma: he now had to choose between taking part in judicial hearings and fulfilling his role as Speaker in the House of Lords. By choosing to sit on the woolsack, the Lord Chancellor had to accept a drastic reduction in his judicial role.

In 1948, a clear distinction between the upper chamber's legislative and judicial responsibilities finally appeared, with the establishment of the House of Lords appellate committee. This was intended to be a temporary measure, forced on their lordships while a new heating system was installed. But the convenience and obvious good sense of a separate judicial body were immediately recognised and the appellate committee became a permanent fixture.

Since the Second World War, the chancellorship has lived a charmed life. The main reason for its survival is that post-war Lord Chancellors have maintained a relatively low profile. They did so by confining themselves in the main to legal matters and by not making a series of headline-grabbing errors. Irvine has changed all that. He has put the chancellorship back in the spotlight, leading many to question its place in a modern democracy.

In one way, Irvine's timing could not be better. The House of Lords is undergoing the most radical reform process it has ever seen. If for no other reason than consistency, it makes sense to a lot of people that the chancellorship should be reformed at the same time.

In May 1999 the human rights group Justice recommended to the Royal Commission on Reform of the House of Lords that the Lord Chancellor should cease to be head of the judiciary in England and Wales, and should no longer sit as a judge in the

House of Lords. It also advised that a Supreme Court should be established to replace the House of Lords judicial committee.

Justice said that the purpose of its proposals was to achieve 'wider and clearer separation of the functions and powers of the judiciary from other branches of government',[163] before declaring that reform is 'not a luxury but an urgent necessity'.[164] Its report was signed by a number of eminent lawyers from across the political spectrum, including Lord Alexander of Weedon QC, Lord Lester of Herne Hill QC, Professor Jeffrey Jowell QC, Baroness Kennedy of the Shaws QC and Lord Scarman.

The report explained that the Lord Chancellor should no longer hear legal cases because his office had become more and more political in recent years. Justice was careful to state that it did not doubt Irvine's ability to act independently when sitting as a judge but then said:

> In view of his powerful political role as a Minister of Justice in charge of a large spending department, the appearance of independence and impartiality is reasonably open to doubt, particularly in the wide range of cases where the executive is directly or indirectly interested.

Since becoming Lord Chancellor, Irvine has sat only infrequently as a judge. Like most post-war Lord Chancellors, his other commitments have limited his opportunities to hear cases. Indeed, in his first two years in office, Irvine found the time to hear just three House of Lords appeals.

Nevertheless, the danger of conflict as envisaged by Justice remains a very real one. In early 1999 Irvine was due to sit as one of five judges in a House of Lords case, but was obliged to stand down after objections by a barrister acting for one of the parties in the case. Nicholas Blake QC argued that the Lord Chancellor should not hear a case concerning police liability for the suicide of a man in police cells because his clients, the dead man's family, would not get a fair hearing by an independent and impartial tribunal, as guaranteed by the European Convention on Human Rights.

This affair was seriously embarrassing for Irvine, because it followed quickly on the heels of the furore over Lord Hoffmann's involvement in the Pinochet trial. In December 1998 Irvine had written to Lord Browne-Wilkinson, the senior Law Lord, stating that, in the light of what had happened in the Pinochet case, judges should, prior to a trial, always consider 'whether any of their number might appear subject to a conflict of interest'.[165] By writing that letter, Irvine was imposing a very heavy burden on the Law Lords: their lordships now had to consider not simply whether a conflict might arise, but whether the appearance of a conflict might arise. But Irvine clearly had not subjected himself to the same test and it took Blake to point out that a member of the Government should not be sitting on a case concerning a death in police custody. After all, the Government controls both the police and the funds from which any compensation is paid to a victim's family.

In view of the serious danger of conflicts and the many demands on his time, losing the right to sit as a judge would not appear to be a huge sacrifice on Irvine's part. However, the Lord Chancellor does not approve of Justice's recommendations, according to the Liberal Democrat peer Lord Lester:

> Derry doesn't agree at all. In fact, I think he's a bit cross. He believes that his empire should not be diminished in any way. He understands the arguments, but believes that any concession will mark the beginning of the end of his office. As a result, he will not surrender any of his powers. He is not willing to share power over the appointment of judges, even with an advisory committee made up of judges. And he is not willing to declare that he will refrain from sitting, even on cases involving devolution and human rights, or where the other Law Lords ask him not to sit. I respectfully disagree, as do many judges and lawyers.

To date, the senior judiciary has refrained from speaking openly on this subject. However, Irvine may not be able to count on their discretion for much longer. There is serious antipathy between Irvine and some of the other Law Lords, who do not like Irvine as a person or as a Lord Chancellor. They find him patronising and interfering. Some have reservations about his ability as a judge.

But Irvine shows no sign of making concessions. Instead, he continues to argue that the Lord Chancellor acts as an important buffer between the Government and the judiciary. In July 1999 he told the Worldwide Common Law Judiciary Conference in Edinburgh that constitutional reforms only made the need for a strong Lord Chancellor greater. He declared that his role as 'effective guarantor of judicial independence' required him to sit on important appeals from time to time.

A very awkward mixture

Irvine's stand against reform of his office looks forlorn. Other than the Prime Minister, his Cabinet colleagues are hardly going to rally around him. Nor will he find much support in the parliamentary Labour Party.

In March 1998 an early day motion sponsored by Robert Marshall-Andrews QC, the MP for Medway, requested that the Prime Minister axe the post of Lord Chancellor in favour of a Secretary of State for Justice within a Department of Justice answerable directly to the House of Commons. The motion immediately drew 50 signatories and was eventually signed by over 100 MPs, a figure that would have been much higher had Tory MPs not been refused permission to sign.

Although the move came when Irvine's fortunes were at their lowest ebb, Marshall-Andrews declared that the motion was the result of concern over the Lord Chancellor's constitutional role and was not intended as an attack on Irvine as an individual. He said there was 'a sense of unease that this is a very powerful public figure who is not elected . . . It is, frankly, an anachronistic post.'[166] He suggested the situation could very easily be remedied as part of the Government's constitutional reform programme.

The early day motion was certainly not to Tony Blair's liking. He made it very clear during Prime Minister's question time that he would not abolish the Lord Chancellor's role. Meanwhile, the government whips moved into action, putting pressure on Labour MPs who had signed Marshall-Andrews's motion to withdraw their names.

In the end, nothing came of Marshall-Andrews's efforts. (Early day motions have little chance of being adopted and are effectively no more than a means by which backbench MPs can express their views.) But at least one of the motion's signatories remains keen for action to be taken. He says:

> We have got to abolish this office. I feel very strongly about patronage – many Members of Parliament do. Obviously, we're elected and we don't like people who are appointed. That's where it comes from. And there is no greater example of patronage than Lord Irvine.

Irvine's behaviour since becoming Lord Chancellor has only reinforced the case for reform, adds the MP:

> If you bring to this role a conspicuous vanity – in other words if you start to liken yourself to Cardinal Wolsey – then you are bringing that to a role that is already steeped in patronage and anachronism. Now, that is a very awkward mixture.

The general mood of backbench Labour MPs is evidenced by the fact that the Labour whips did not enjoy much success in persuading signatories to withdraw their support to Marshall-Andrews's motion. But then the whips had not been given a very strong case to fight. The signatories had not acted contrary to party policy. Indeed, it could even be argued that they were merely following it.

Labour's 1997 election manifesto was silent on the question of reforming the Lord Chancellor's role – hardly surprising given that Irvine had had a hand in its drafting. However, the 1992 manifesto had declared:

> We will appoint from the House of Commons a Minister for Legal Administration, who will initially be part of the Lord Chancellor's Department. We will go on to create a department of Legal Administration headed by a Minister in the Commons who will be responsible for all the courts and tribunals in England and Wales.

In June 1994, Paul Boateng, then Labour's legal affairs spokesman in the High Court, reasserted the party line on this issue when he announced, 'Labour will take executive functions away from the Lord Chancellor and give them to a Ministry of Justice headed by an MP.' [167]

Within a matter of months, however, his tune had changed. Or, more likely, it had been changed for him. In March 1995 he stated:

> We are not really going to get hung up on the issue of the Lord Chancellor, whether or not he should be in the Cabinet, or anything like that . . . We have a very considerable constitutional agenda anyway. There's always a danger of constitutional overload. [168]

The normally verbose Boateng was at a loss to explain why Labour had abandoned the commitment it had made so unequivocally in 1992. But he could hardly declare that his new leader had unilaterally dropped the issue perhaps because he wished to appoint one of his best friends as the next Lord Chancellor.

A huge error

There must have been times when Tony Blair has seriously regretted his decision to appoint Irvine as his Lord Chancellor. As 'Tony's crony', Irvine's gaffes have caused Blair acute embarrassment and made him a frequent target for ridicule.

The Prime Minister, however, deserves little sympathy. He is the one who chose Irvine. He is the one who made Irvine one of the most powerful members of the Cabinet. He is the one who failed to exercise sufficient control over Irvine until it was too late.

It is not as if Blair did not know what he was getting. As Irvine's friend, former pupil and fellow chambers tenant, he knew Irvine's character and its faults. He knew how Irvine behaved in court, he knew how Irvine ran 11 King's Bench Walk and he knew how Irvine treated his juniors, pupils and clerk. Thus, Blair should have foreseen that Irvine would have ferocious rows with his Cabinet colleagues and that his high-handed behaviour would upset the Lord Chancellor's Department staff.

As one of the most media-conscious prime ministers in history, Blair should also have foreseen that Irvine would struggle with the media; and as a barrister himself Blair must have realised that it was asking an awful lot of any barrister – let alone one as set in his ways as Irvine – to step from the insulated world of the Bar into front-line politics.

Remarkably, no one, including Blair, took the trouble to ensure that, in the run-up to the election, Irvine was given even basic media training. And yet he was the one who needed it most. He had only stood in an election once – way back in 1970. He had never had a constituency to nurture. He had never had to go out and press the flesh and do interviews. He had never had the opportunity to hone his media skills while sitting on the back benches. And then, suddenly, he was launched upon the world in a senior Cabinet post and expected to drive forward an important part of the manifesto.

Why Irvine was not given such training remains a mystery.

Perhaps Blair actually believed the myth about Irvine being so clever that he can do anything. However, if Blair did believe it then, he certainly does not believe it now. For all his undoubted ability in certain areas, Irvine has demonstrated that he has distinct limitations in others.

Bringing Irvine into the Cabinet and giving him such wide powers was a huge error on Blair's part. Irvine did not possess the basic people skills needed to be a successful politician and it was ridiculous to believe he was suddenly going to acquire them.

Irvine is not a politician and never will be. He should have been left where he was – at the Bar. Blair could have gone on using Irvine as one of his close advisers just as he had for many years; or perhaps appointed Irvine formally as a special adviser. With all his experience and ability, Irvine might have filled such a role with distinction. Either way, he should have been kept behind the scenes and not exposed to the harsh realities of political life.

Given time, it is possible that Irvine's stock will rise again. But Irvine will find opportunities to turn his fortunes around strictly limited. Devolution has been delivered, constitutional reform is no longer high on the Government's list of priorities and his role on the various Cabinet committees is much reduced. Indeed, with little more to handle than his legal brief, Irvine has begun to resemble a conventional Lord Chancellor.

The problem with conventional Lord Chancellors is that they are expendable – particularly when there is a ready-made replacement in the wings. For years, Irvine faced little competition for the chancellorship, but the rapid rise of Lord Falconer has changed that.

Falconer shares several things with Irvine: he is a life peer; before joining the Government, he was a highly successful barrister, practising out of one of the country's top sets (in Falconer's case, Fountain Court Chambers); and, most important of all, he is an old and trusted friend of Tony Blair's.

Ennobled by Blair in 1997, he was made Solicitor General and then promoted in 1998 to the Cabinet Office as a junior minister responsible for pushing through the Government's programme of legislation. After the downfall of Trade Secretary Peter Mandelson at the end of that year, Falconer was handed responsibility for the Millennium Dome, a hot potato that he has, so far, handled with aplomb. Even if he were to slip up, Falconer would never attract the kind of media mauling suffered by Irvine. He may be another of Tony's cronies, but 'Charlie' Falconer is widely regarded as a much nicer man, relaxed and friendly as Irvine is stiff and superior.

In mid-1999, Blair gave himself further options when he made Peter Goldsmith QC and Tony Grabiner QC working peers. As two of the very best commercial silks in the country, both are well qualified to take on the role of Lord Chancellor should Blair decide to keep Falconer in the Cabinet Office.

None of this will matter, of course, so long as Irvine retains Blair's loyalty. However, he can no longer count on this. Any debt Blair once owed him has long since been repaid. Not only did Blair give Irvine the chancellorship, he stood by him through the *New Statesman*, Wolsey and wallpaper débâcles. Having stretched Blair's friendship to the limit, Irvine could be just one big gaffe away from losing the chancellorship.

The Prime Minister might even sensibly choose to cut the ties before they break. Blair has shown he can be ruthless when necessary, not least when he went back on his promise to Gordon Brown not to stand against him in a Labour Party leadership contest. For all the loyalty he has shown Irvine in the past, Blair may yet use the next general election as an opportunity for Irvine to stand down without attracting undue attention.

This would suit one of Blair's long-term goals. Like Irvine, he wants his place in history. Blair will want to be seen as his own man, not as someone forever tied to his mentor's apron strings. If he is going to achieve that, Blair will have to distance himself from Irvine.

It may be that this process has already begun. Blair has failed to support Irvine in his battles with Jack Straw, leaving the Lord Chancellor looking increasingly isolated. This was never more apparent than in May 1999 when it was announced – after a string of delays – that the Freedom of Information Bill would not be appearing in the form envisaged by its White Paper. With Irvine's full support, this had declared that information would be made available unless it would cause 'substantial harm' to the Government or other public bodies. However, Straw was concerned that police and intelligence work might be compromised and managed to achieve a significant change to the draft Bill with the effect that information will now only be handed over if it does not 'prejudice' the Government.

Irvine looks distinctly out of favour. It is Straw who now commands the Prime Minister's confidence. That must be a very bitter pill for the Lord Chancellor to swallow.

No regrets

Since the possibility of more gaffes can never be ruled out, it may be that Irvine will not last as long as the next general election. Worryingly for Irvine and his advisers, there is little or no evidence to suggest that he has learnt from his mistakes. His sometimes vicious attacks on those who dare to oppose his views show that he remains as intemperate as ever, while his claim to have written John Smith's essays at Glasgow University reveals that he still cannot refrain from the occasional boast.

The reason Irvine has failed to learn from his mistakes is that he refuses to acknowledge them. In October 1998, the man who had been through the Wolsey, Robin Cook and wallpaper fiascos told the *Sunday Times*:

> I don't feel really any disappointments. Let me think very hard ... No, I think that the part of the legislative programme for which – for the policy development of which – I am responsible is a success story. I would be disappointed by failure, but I genuinely can't identify any ... I've realised that

all you can do is your best in the circumstances and, my goodness me, I've learnt that in politics. It is the art of the possible. No, I've no sense of failure at all. On the contrary, I mean, I've got quite a considerable sense of achievement. I haven't really known failure.[169]

On the plus side, Irvine's second year in office passed much more quietly than his first. But, despite keeping a much lower profile and Garry Hart's useful guidance, the period since May 1998 has not been entirely without its problems.

In March 1999 an employment tribunal gave its ruling in respect of the discrimination proceedings brought by Jane Coker and Martha Osamor over Irvine's appointment of Hart. The tribunal found there was no case for direct or indirect discrimination against Osamor, who did not have the necessary political qualifications for the job. It also held that Coker had not been the subject of direct discrimination. However, the tribunal declared that the Lord Chancellor and his department had indirectly discriminated against Coker on the grounds of gender.

Remarkably enough, the evidence that caused most damage to the Lord Chancellor's case came from his own staff. The tribunal chairman, Ian Lamb, stated:

> The further the departmental staff went in showing how good their [recruitment] procedures were, the more it put into sharp relief the inadequacy of the Lord Chancellor's personal way of proceeding in employing a person as his special adviser. It should have been apparent to the Lord Chancellor and all ministers that open recruitment enhances the prospect of obtaining a person of the highest ability.[170]

The employment tribunal's decision must have taken Irvine by surprise. In the run-up to the hearing, he adopted an aggressive approach, describing the women's case as mischievous and political and announcing that he would not dignify the action by appearing at the hearing to give evidence. Irvine felt, no doubt, he had done nothing that had not been done many times before. Indeed, the employment tribunal was told that nearly all the Government's special advisers had been hand-picked by ministers without any advertisements being placed. In response, the tribunal chairman warned the Government that ministers should in future take greater care to avoid discrimination when appointing special advisers.

Irvine, who has indicated that he will make an appeal, will hope he can reverse a decision that has embarrassed him in several ways. As an expert in employment law, he should know what the law requires of an employer when recruiting staff. As Lord Chancellor, he should follow the letter of the law, not adopt the attitude, 'Well everybody else does it, why shouldn't I?'

Worse still, Coker has claimed that there were 'glaring contradictions'[171] within the evidence given by Irvine. In his submission, Irvine had declared that, when considering Hart's appointment, he had not consulted anyone beyond one Lord Chancellor's Department official. However, Irvine's letter to Tony Blair of 25 September 1997 shows that he consulted the Prime Minister. Irvine had also claimed that Hart was the only candidate considered. However, an earlier letter to Blair revealed that other candidates were looked at.

Coker told the *Sunday Telegraph*:

> If these contradictions in his evidence are just mistakes, he should say so. But if they are deliberate untruths, it is appalling. What you have here is court proceedings where the highest law officer in the land does not appear to have been honest.[172]

An LCD spokesman responded that it was incorrect to accuse Irvine of being economical with the truth. The employment tribunal, he pointed out, had not made these criticisms.

This is not the only occasion on which Tony's crony has himself been accused of cronyism. In early 1998 Josephine Hayes, chairman of the Association of Women Barristers, commenced an action against the Attorney-General, John Morris QC. She suggested that Morris had broken the law by not advertising the post of First Junior Treasury Counsel, Common Law (better known as 'Treasury Devil'), before awarding it to Philip Sales, a member of Irvine's old set, 11 King's Bench Walk.

The position of Treasury Devil comes with a guarantee of plenty of good government work and is thus highly valued at the Bar. No one has ever doubted Sales's ability. Indeed, he is generally regarded as an outstanding prospect. However, questions were asked about his credentials to be Treasury Devil. At 35, he was considered young for the post, had been on the official panel of government barristers for only a few months, and, having previously specialised in commercial cases, had only limited experience of public law work, the Treasury Devil's primary field of business.

Not unnaturally, perhaps, many barristers thought that Irvine had played a part in Sales's recruitment. They included Hayes, who, in her witness statement, declared she had never heard of Sales before he was appointed Treasury Devil. She also claimed that, at a Law Society function held shortly after Sales's appointment, a number of solicitors in government departments had told her Sales had been put on the Government's list of approved counsel in July 1997 with instructions to use him in preference to those already on the list.

Full details of what actually happened may never be available. In June 1999 Hayes's case was settled with the Attorney-General giving a number of undertakings as to future appointments.

Irvine, for his part, has stressed that he was not the one who appointed Sales (he took a similar line when responding to questions about the refurbishment of the Lord Chancellor's residence). But, if Irvine did play no part in the affair, it is the most stunning coincidence that Sales should get the job. It is perfectly possible, therefore, that the settlement, which came just days before the employment tribunal was due to sit, saved Irvine considerable discomfort. Certainly, a number of newspapers were taking a keen interest in the case and were, no doubt, disappointed to be robbed of the opportunity to launch yet another attack on Irvine.

Both those employment tribunal cases arose from decisions made before Garry Hart joined the Lord Chancellor's Department, which again illustrates what a good job he has done. But Hart can only do so much. He watches Irvine like a hawk (at public functions he is rarely more than inches away from the Lord Chancellor), but he cannot be with Irvine all the time and he cannot control everything Irvine says and does. Furthermore, Hart knows that danger is always close at hand.

Since his days as a student, Irvine has been known as a man who likes – and can take – his drink. Some have even dared to make jokes about it. Prior to the 1997 general election, Irvine and his former pupil Cherie Booth attended a fundraising dinner which was addressed by Robert Marshall-Andrews QC. Marshall-Andrews told the audience: 'Today we have a Lord Chancellor who is a Scotsman and a teetotaller. After 1 May, we'll have a Lord Chancellor who is a Scotsman and, aye well, a Scotsman anyway.' [173] (Neither Irvine nor Booth laughed at the joke.)

In recent years, however, some people have begun to doubt Irvine's seemingly infinite capacity for alcohol. In February 1998 the historian Paul Johnson wrote in *The Spectator*: 'His lordship likes a wee dram and, when thus emboldened, he speaks his thoughts. His post-prandial comparison of himself with Cardinal Wolsey was a classic example of in *vino veritas*.' [174]

Johnson went on to reveal that, prior to Irvine's appointment as Lord Chancellor, he had approached Tony Blair to suggest that

> since Irvine had developed the practice of going into training for important cases, he should extend it, and forswear drinking 'for the duration'. Blair was uneasy about demanding such a promise, and evidently did not exact it; or, if he did, it has not been kept. And the media, who have

long been compiling dossiers on Irvine, are eagerly waiting for the great man to fall into their hands. [175]

Johnson is in no way guilty of scaremongering. The press *is* waiting for Irvine to slip up. Sheila Thompson recalls that she received several enquiries from journalists about whether Irvine was drinking during the working day:

> There was a perception that he was drinking. I got a number of calls from journalists trying to persuade me to confirm that he wasn't capable of doing any work in the afternoon because he drank so much at lunchtime. But I knew that was not true. There was no drink in the office and I observed him having lunch and he had a very frugal lunch and drank water. So it was very easy for me to say, 'No you're all on the wrong track.' But when I had these three separate journalists ringing up and telling me that they had seen Lord Irvine drinking a fair bit in restaurants or coming out of restaurants somewhat the worse for wear, I felt I had to go and tell Alastair [Campbell], first, of these allegations and, second, that there was a perception he was drunk. I was denying it, but there was a kind of head of steam, an expectation, that was taking root and I felt it was my duty to warn Alastair that they were on the lookout.

Campbell acknowledged Thompson's warning. Since there has been no discernible change in Irvine's drinking habits since he became Lord Chancellor, it appears the warning was either not passed on or ignored.

Two traits

Drink is not the only danger. The bad news for the Lord Chancellor is that the press is always watching and waiting for any kind of slip-up. He may not have been getting so much bad press of late, but this does not mean the newspapers have changed their view of him. Getting less bad press is not the same thing as getting good press. Indeed, some newspapers will never pass up an opportunity to have a go at Irvine.

In March 1999, for example, it was reported that Irvine had used government writing paper to invite friends to a private drinks party at his London club, the Garrick, and had allowed his department to pay the postage. A spokesman for the Lord Chancellor's Department claimed that an official had mistakenly used departmental, rather than House of Lords, stationery and the postroom had inadvertently franked the envelopes. Whatever the truth of the matter, this episode proved Irvine's continuing newsworthiness. Although it was not a particularly important story, it made the front page of *The Times*.

Irvine's family and friends cannot understand why the press has taken so strongly against a man they consider charming, kind and generous. Christopher Carr QC, for example, pays generous tribute to his former pupil master:

> Derry has enormous human qualities. He is an intensely loyal, decent, humane, liberal and understanding man. As a matter of substance, those are his qualities. People say he's bullying, overbearing, pompous and so on. These are just superficial mannerisms. The man himself, I think, has formidable human qualities. Maybe people don't see those in the political sphere or in the forms of relationship they have with him in his political life. But I know the man and I know those are his qualities.

Carr's comments are not untypical. There clearly exists a 'good Derry' who commands both affection and respect. But only the chosen few get to see this Irvine. The face he presents to the world at large is very different. At some stage, Irvine decided his best chance of getting ahead lay in playing it tough. As one old friend acknowledges, 'He's a hard man. He's always been a hard man. Why that is so, I don't know.'

The answer probably lies in the two dominant traits of Irvine's character – overweening ambition and chronic insecurity. It is a most unfortunate combination. Irvine has accomplished a great deal, but incidentally caused great unhappiness to others along the way. Everything in his life has been a fight, a constant battle for supremacy. If, instead of forcing his will on others, he had possessed the ability to carry people with him, Irvine might have achieved so much more – both at the Bar and in his political life.

Losing the chancellorship will hit Irvine hard. He loves the power and prestige of the office. Most of all, he still desperately wants to go down in history as one of the great Lord Chancellors. When, in October 1998, the *Independent on Sunday* asked him if he could imagine being Lord Chancellor for ten years, he replied: 'If the Prime Minister wants me to and God willing, the answer is enthusiastically yes. Why stop at ten years?' [176]

It seems most unlikely that Irvine will last that long. And yet he could have bought himself ten years or more quite cheaply. The price was no more than a little tact, a little sensitivity and a little humility.

References

1. Select Committee on Public Administration Third Report, Volume 1
2. Ibid.
3. Ibid.
4. *The Sun*, 2 December 1998
5. Ibid.
6. Ibid.
7. Ibid.
8. Ibid.
9. Ibid.
10. *Sunday Times*, 18 October 1998
11. Ibid.
12. Ibid.
13. Ibid.
14. Ibid.
15. Ibid.
16. Ibid.
17. Ibid.
18. Ibid.
19. *Daily Mail*, 22 July 1997
20. Ibid.
21. *Sunday Times*, 18 October 1998
22. *The Sun*, 2 December 1998
23. *The Trouble at the LSE 1966–67* by Harry Kidd
24. Ibid.
25. Ibid.

26. Ibid.
27. *Sunday Times*, 18 October 1998
28. *Hendon Times*, 12 June 1970
29. Ibid.
30. Ibid.
31. *Daily Mail*, 22 July 1997
32. Ibid.
33. *Tony Blair: The Moderniser* by Jon Sopel
34. *Tony Blair* by John Rentoul
35. Ibid.
36. *Legal Business*, April 1997
37. *Tony Blair* by John Rentoul
38. *Tony Blair: The Moderniser* by Jon Sopel
39. Ibid.
40. Ibid.
41. *Sunday Times*, 18 October 1998
42. The author's own interview, March 1997
43. *Legal Business*, April 1997
44. Ibid.
45. *Sunday Times*, 18 October 1998
46. *The Observer*, 5 April 1998
47. *Legal Business*, April 1997
48. Ibid.
49. Ibid.
50. *The Observer*, 11 May 1997
51. *Harpers & Queen*, January 1991
52. *Legal Business*, April 1997
53. Ibid.
54. Ibid.
55. Ibid.
56. Ibid.
57. Ibid.
58. *The Observer*, 5 April 1998
59. *Daily Mail*, 22 July 1997
60. *Tony Blair* by John Rentoul

61. *The Times*, 28 November 1985
62. *The Guardian*, 21 May 1994
63. *The Times*, 21 May 1994
64. *Sunday Times*, 22 May 1994
65. *Tony Blair: The Moderniser* by Jon Sopel
66. *Tony Blair* by John Rentoul
67. *Blair's Way*, Channel 4, 2 May 1999
68. Ibid.
69. Ibid.
70. *The Observer*, 27 July 1997
71. *The Guardian*, 4 November 1997
72. *The Observer*, 16 November 1997
73. *Daily Mail*, 2 February 1996
74. *The Times*, 7 June 1997
75. *The Times*, 1 December 1997
76. Ibid.
77. Ibid.
78. *The Sun*, 2 December 1997
79. Ibid.
80. Ibid.
81. *The Times*, 2 December 1997
82. Ibid.
83. Ibid.
84. *Daily Mail*, 8 December 1997
85. Ibid.
86. *Daily Mail*, 22 June 1997
87. *Daily Mail*, 29 June 1997
88. *New Statesman*, 6 February 1998
89. Ibid.
90. *The Independent*, 6 February 1998
91. *The Guardian*, 6 February 1998
92. *Independent on Sunday*, 11 October 1999
93. *The Times*, 9 February 1998
94. *Sunday Times*, 8 February 1998
95. Ibid.

96. Ibid.
97. Ibid.
98. *Daily Mail*, 9 March 1998
99. *Daily Mail*, 9 February 1998
100. *The Times*, 25 February 1998
101. Ibid.
102. Select Committee on Public Administration Third Report, Volume 1
103. Ibid.
104. Ibid.
105. Ibid.
106. Ibid.
107. Ibid.
108. Ibid.
109. Ibid.
110. *The Sun*, 4 March 1998
111. Ibid.
112. Ibid.
113. *The Mirror*, 4 March 1998
114. *Daily Mail*, 4 March 1998
115. Ibid.
116. Ibid.
117. *The Times*, 28 May 1998
118. Ibid.
119. Ibid.
120. *The Times*, 25 February 1988
121. *Independent on Sunday*, 11 October 1998
122. *Blair's Way*, Channel 4, 2 May 1999
123. Ibid.
124. *The Independent*, 17 December 1997
125. *The Observer*, 5 April 1998
126. *The Lawyer*, 1 March 1999
127. Ibid.
128. *Sunday Telegraph*, 30 May 1999
129. *The Lawyer*, 1 March 1999

130. *The Guardian*, 2 March 1999
131. *Sunday Times*, 18 October 1998
132. *The Guardian*, 15 July 1997
133. Ibid.
134. *The Guardian*, 29 April 1998
135. *The Observer*, 19 October 1997
136. *The Guardian*, 18 October 1997
137. *The Times*, 17 July 1998
138. *The Times*, 3 December 1998
139. Ibid.
140. Ibid.
141. *The Times*, 15 December 1998
142. Ibid.
143. Ibid.
144. *The Times*, 29 April 1999
145. *The Times*, 26 April 1999
146. *The Times*, 28 April 1999
147. *Independent on Sunday*, 11 October 1998
148. Ibid.
149. *Sunday Times*, 18 October 1998
150. Ibid.
151. *The Times*, 26 June 1998
152. Ibid.
153. Ibid.
154. *The Times*, 15 December 1998
155. Ibid.
156. Copy of speech provided by Lord Steyn's office
157. Ibid.
158. *The Times*, 15 January 1999
159. *The Guardian*, 4 March 1992
160. *The Guardian*, 10 October 1997
161. *New Statesman*, 6 February 1998
162. Ibid.
163. *The Times*, 28 May 1999
164. Ibid.

165. *The Times*, 18 December 1998
166. *The Independent*, 12 March 1998
167. *The Independent*, 22 March 1995
168. Ibid.
169. *Sunday Times*, 18 October 1998
170. *The Times*, 27 March 1999
171. *Sunday Telegraph*, 30 May 1999
172. Ibid.
173. *Daily Mail*, 27 February 1998
174. *The Spectator*, 28 February 1998
175. Ibid.
176. *Independent on Sunday*, 11 October 1998

Bibliography

Crick, Michael, *The March of Militant*, Faber and Faber Ltd, 1986

Hughes, Colin and Patrick Wintour, *Labour Rebuilt*, Fourth Estate Ltd, 1990

Kidd, Harry, *The Trouble at the LSE 1966–67*, Oxford University Press, 1969

McSmith, Andy, *John Smith: Playing the Long Game*, Verso, 1993

Rentoul, John, *Tony Blair*, Little, Brown and Company, 1995

Sopel, Jon, *Tony Blair: The Moderniser*, Michael Joseph Ltd, 1995

Underhill, Nicholas, *The Lord Chancellor*, Terence Dalton Ltd, 1978

Wilding, Norman and Philip Laundy, *An Encyclopaedia of Parliament*, Cassell & Company Ltd, 1971

Index